THE MUSIC OF BEN JOHNSTON

by
Heidi Von Gunden

The Scarecrow Press, Inc.
Metuchen, N.J., & London
1986

Photo credits: Frontispiece photo by Denise Rhode Tipei; used by permission.
Photo on page 166 by David Liptak; used by permission.

Library of Congress Cataloging-in-Publication Data

Von Gunden, Heidi, 1940-
   The music of Ben Johnston.

   Bibliography: p.
   Discography: p.
   Includes index.
   1. Johnston, Ben. 2. Johnston, Ben--Criticism and
interpretation. 3. Composers--United States--Biography.
I. Title.
ML410.J67V6 1986   780'.92'4   86-13954
ISBN 0-8108-1907-4

• CONTENTS •

• FOREWORD •

This book is a history without an ending. Ben Johnston is alive, well, retired from many years of teaching, and he is writing music. The following pages give the impression that his music could have gone in any of other directions than it has. I mean he is greatly gifted and has written many different kinds of music. He is now very accomplished.

His principal concerns have been and continue to be just intonation microtonally extended, and the expressive communication of what he believes to be true both in music and life.

Heidi Von Gunden's highly detailed and informed account of this musical history would not have been possible without her close association with the Johnstons. I know how much pleasure it must have given her to write this book, for, in the two very pleasant years I spent in Champaign-Urbana (1967-69), more and more I knew that being there was being with Ben and Betty Johnston. No day passed without my sharing the evening meal with the family (Betty did all the cooking-- "When it comes to dessert I throw caution to the winds"), and few evenings passed without several rubbers of bridge. Apparently if I were there now I would be the fourth with the author of this book, its subject and his wife. The Johnston children I knew in the sixties are now living in their own homes in other cities.

A very special event while I was in Champaign-Urbana was the publication by Nonesuch of a record with HPSCHD which I made with Lejaren Hiller on one side and on the other side the String Quartet Number 2 of Ben Johnston. I myself don't listen to records but I was glad that his music and mine were somehow brought together.

John Cage

• PREFACE •

The music of Ben Johnston is the story of a struggle to realize a potential. Johnston knew at an early age that he wanted to write acoustically correct music because equal-tempered tuning was a falsehood. It took Johnston many years first to learn how to compose and then slowly to discover how to formulate his understanding of just intonation and its related notation.

For a long time Johnston worked in isolation; few people understood why someone would want to change the standard pitch system. But gradually, as his music began to be heard, especially his string quartets, performers and audiences experienced for themselves the kind of clarity and beauty that is possible with just intonation. As a result Johnston continues to receive commissions for new string quartets, and several recordings of his most recent music are available.

Johnston's credentials are impressive. He studied with Harry Partch, Darius Milhaud, John Cage, and Burrill Phillips, and although some of these teachers influenced Johnston's early music, he has remained an individualist and followed his own creative path. Yet he has written in many different styles: jazz resulting from his Naval service, neoclassicism, and serialism (which he has adapted to serve a functional purpose in just intonation). Much of his work has intuitively predated important trends in contemporary music. He used combinatoriality in the late 1950's, quotations in the 1960's, and returned to tonality in the early 1970's. He even tried indeterminacy and electronic music but has been less successful in these areas.

Johnston's music is complex. He makes pitch and rhythmic demands that at first seem impossible but then become a reality when performers begin to hear the organic relationships that the composer is using. For Johnston, just intonation is not simply a theory--he hears it, and his music shows others how to discover purity of pitch.

Nor is this music just an intellectual exercise. It is an expressive statement originating from Johnston's own sensitivity and awareness. His talent has brought him both joys and sufferings. He has had several bouts with mental illness and has used the images of "building a bridge over the chasm," "cooking an albatross," and "art and survival" to describe his concern about life and contemporary music.

Johnston's development as a composer is associated with the University of

Illinois, where he taught from 1951 to his retirement in 1983. The story of his music is also the story of this institution's commitment to creativity and its sponsorship of Festivals of Contemporary Art. Much of his music was written for faculty artists and premièred at the University.

As a teacher Johnston has applied the same attention and precision that he has in his music. He has been careful to allow each composition student to pursue his or her own style, and in 1983 he was given the "Campus Award for Excellence in Undergraduate Teaching." He has taught an immense number of graduate students and assisted in the beginnings of their professional careers.

The story of Johnston's music is also the story of many friendships. Wilford Leach, the playwright and director, is a friend from college days with whom Johnston has collaborated on several occasions; Ward Swingle has been a friend of the Johnston family since 1949 and has commissioned two pieces for the Swingle Singers; Partch was another friend, and Johnston arranged for several performances of Partch's compositions at various Festivals of Contemporary Art; and John Cage has understood and supported Johnston's talent since the early 1950's. There are many more names that could be mentioned. More appear in the forthcoming chapters.

I am a friend of the Johnston family and a colleague at the University of Illinois. It has been fascinating to explore and analyze his compositions and theories in order to realize and follow the discoveries that Johnston has made about just intonation. His decision to abandon the "acoustical lie" of equal temperament has been far-reaching and, in my opinion, is just the beginning of a future direction that many composers will take, especially in the area of computer music.

The aim of this book is to help the listener hear and understand Johnston's music. The judgments about the music and the analyses are mine, unless otherwise stated. I hope this work will induce more musicians to perform his difficult but rewarding compositions.

Cage is correct--writing this book was a pleasure. I wish to thank Ben and Betty Johnston for their thoughtful replies to my questions. I am grateful to John Cage for reading the manuscript and writing the foreword. William Brooks also read the manuscript, and I appreciate his careful editing and suggestions. I also wish to thank Reverend Richard Kongo Langlois, Roshi, for his help with the jazz material, and Dean Jack McKenzie for reading the chapter "The University of Illinois."

• THE MUSIC OF BEN JOHNSTON •

1 • BEGINNINGS

Ben Johnston's childhood resembles that of an ordinary youngster except that at the age of six years he showed signs of liking the piano. He could play melodies and harmonies by ear.

The Johnston family was not especially musical. His father, Benjamin Burwell Johnston, Senior, was born in Meridian, Mississippi in 1894. He attended the University of Alabama, was interested in journalism, and later became the managing editor of the Macon Telegraph. In 1921 he married Janet Ross. Eventually they had two children, Benjamin, Jr., born on March 15, 1926 in Macon, Georgia, and Janet, born in 1932, who is now Mrs. Ronald Parsons, a mathematics teacher at Visitation High School in St. Louis, Missouri.

The young Benjamin was closer to his mother than his father. As managing editor of a newspaper, Mr. Johnston worked at night and was gone by the time his son returned home from school, so there were not many opportunities to develop a strong father-son relationship. But the family did play games together, especially rummy and anagrams, and game-playing has continued to be a source of entertainment for Ben Johnston and his family.[1]

Mrs. Johnston liked to read, and she was interested in the arts, but her enjoyment of music was somewhat handicapped because she suffered a hearing impairment when giving birth to her son.

Mrs. Fanny Prescott Ross, the young Benjamin's maternal grandmother, lived with the family in Macon, Georgia. She had a piano, and when Benjamin was six years old the family decided it was time for him to begin piano lessons since he seemed to have a sensitive ear for music. He studied with Mrs. A. E. Reese. She was a thorough teacher, providing instruction in notation and theory along with the regular piano lessons, but her young student did not learn to read music well because he depended upon his keen ear to help him learn his weekly lessons.

During this time Johnston attended Vineville Grammar School in Macon, but when he was eleven years old the family moved to Richmond, Virginia, because his father was to become city editor and later managing editor for the Richmond Times Dispatch. Apparently he and the owners of the Macon Telegraph were in conflict over a race issue; Mr. Johnston was considered to be too liberal.

Once the family was settled in Richmond, Ben attended Albert Hill Junior High School. He was a good student, liking literature and even writing poetry. There were no piano lessons that first year in Richmond; nevertheless, Ben used a neighbor's piano to practice and play by ear. Then he started lessons with Miss Eleanor K. Greenawalt, who, assessing her student's weak point, stressed the acquisition of good reading skills.

In 1938, after the Johnstons moved to Virginia, Ben's grandmother died in Macon, and the family returned there for a short time. An event happened which impressed the young musician and influenced his later musical directions. Mrs. Donald Mitchell, his mother's friend who taught at the Conservatory of Music in Macon, took the young piano student (Johnston was eleven years old at that time) to a lecture that was about Hermann Helmholtz's influence on Claude Debussy. Johnston credits this lecture as whetting his curiosity for acoustics which would eventually lead to his interest in just intonation.

The family did not stay long in Macon, returning to Richmond where Johnston continued his piano lessons with Miss Greenawalt. At age thirteen he began to write pieces, often imitating what he found on the back of sheet music where the publisher advertised the beginning staves of new songs and piano pieces. His early manuscript books contain carefully notated pieces, some of which are complete, and others are beginning ideas for a composition.[2]

Miss Greenawalt was a wise piano teacher, because the time came when she told young Johnston that she had taught him as much as she could. The occasion which prompted this decision was when he played the slow movement of Beethoven's Sonata Pathetique, op. 13 for the Women's Club in Richmond. The audience liked his performance, and his teacher recognized signs of promising talent that needed further development.

By now Johnston was attending Thomas Jefferson High School. His new piano teacher was Florence Robertson, the person recommended by Miss Greenawalt. Miss Robertson was a student of John Powell, a prominent pianist, composer, and teacher in Richmond. Powell frequently gave lectures about music which Johnston attended. On several occasions he participated in Powell's master class, and Powell's advice to him was to go to college and major in fine arts. He did not think Johnston had a future as a concert pianist but sensed that the young musician would be a late-bloomer and then could choose a career in music. Meanwhile, Johnston practiced regularly, participated in piano class competitions, where he received outstanding ratings, performed several times for the Musicians Club of Richmond, and was working on such piano repertoire as the Nocturne in E minor by Chopin and the Prelude and Fugue in Eb major from Bach's Well-Tempered Clavier, Book II.

But he was also learning about music from several friends. One was Donald Pippin, a young keyboard prodigy who was a concert pianist with the Richmond Orchestra. Pippin studied with Quincy Cole, the society pianist and music teacher

in Richmond, Virginia. Pippin and Johnston became good friends and shared their
interest in music.[3] At this time Johnston didn't especially like classical music, pre-
ferring the flamboyant style of some nineteenth-century music. Johnston also lis-
tened to contemporary music by Igor Stravinsky and John Cage; the clerk at the
local record store even tried to persuade Johnston to buy a recording of Cage's
music, but at that time Johnston wasn't particularly interested. Later he would
study with Cage.

Besides playing the piano and dabbling in composition, Johnston also played
trombone in the high school orchestra. He began studying this instrument in
Georgia when the public schools were trying to promote musical interests. Later
he played trombone in the Navy band.

Like his father, Johnston had literary talents. During his senior year he
was editor-in-chief of the school newspaper, The Jeffersonian, and during the year
of his editorship the paper won top honors from the Columbia Scholastic Press Association.

Johnston also won the first and second 1943 scholastic awards sponsored by
the Scholastic Magazine for his song "Homeward" and piano piece Fugue in D minor.
The Richmond community was impressed by this honor, and Johnston was able to
play his award-winning compositions at the Musicians Club of Richmond. Several
of the city's prominent businessmen wrote congratulatory letters. Even more en-
couraging was a letter from Paul Thornton, representing the Educational Department of the Radio Corporation of America, which stated: "You have competed
with many hundreds of other students throughout the Nation, and the fact that
you have received distinguished recognition in such competition, is evidence of
your intelligence and ability."[4]

These were signs that Johnston could pursue a musical future, but French
was his scholastic achievement in high school, and in 1943 he won a state scholarship to study French at the College of William and Mary. Johnston accepted the
scholarship even though he wanted to study music, and since there was no music
department at William and Mary, he majored in liberal arts. However, a fortunate
event occurred during his Freshman year. Some of the faculty who taught music
produced a program of his compositions on January 30, 1944, as part of the Student Music Club's Sunday Afternoon Concert series. Johnston was seventeen
years old. The titles of his pieces were: Fugue in D minor, Scherzo in B minor,
and Rondo in D major (all for piano), Sonata for clarinet and piano, "Homeward"
and "The Voice of Autumn" for soprano and piano, Theme and Variations and
Ballade in E major for violin and piano, and Concerto in E for two pianos. The
day of the concert the Sunday edition of the Richmond Times Dispatch published
a feature article about the young composer, stating that he was especially interested in the scientific aspect of composition and that "Ben believes with many
young composers that music is on the eve of a great revolution; that with the
clarification of the scale which physics has given to music there will be new instruments with new tones and overtones. 'And I shall write for them.... People

will not like this new music--not at first. It will be so different--but it will be more nearly perfect.'"[5] It is remarkable that at this young age Johnston knew what he wanted to do, and at this time he was unfamiliar with Harry Partch's or anyone's work in just intonation.

As exciting as this concert and interview must have been for the young composer, Johnston realized that with the escalating events of World War II he should enlist in the armed forces. He chose the Navy, hoping to attend the Navy School of Music because he desperately needed more musical training. By this time he was serious about having a musical career, and the Navy could use his skills for the Navy bands.

But before Johnston entered the Navy, he applied to the Curtis Institute of Music in Philadelphia and had an interview with Rosario Scalero, a well-known composition teacher who had taught Samuel Barber and Gian-Carlo Menotti. Scalero looked at some pieces that Johnston had written (Scalero wanted to make certain that Johnston was not writing popular music) and agreed to accept him after the war was over. But circumstances changed and Johnston never attended Curtis.

Meanwhile, as a trainee, Johnston went to the Chicago Great Lakes Naval Training Center and then to the Navy School of Music in Washington D.C. The aim of the school was to establish professional bands for the Navy, but Johnston did get a chance to study symphonic analysis, counterpoint, harmony, orchestration (mainly writing for bands), basic instrumentation, trombone, and piano. All Navy music students were required to play in the dance band. Since this was a new experience for Johnston, it took a while before he became interested in dance music, but eventually he even decided he wanted to be a dance arranger. One piece he orchestrated was "All the King's Horses," a folk tune that he set as variations for flute, oboe, two clarinets in Bb, bassoon, horn in F, trumpet in Bb, optional trombone, and full strings. Johnston describes the piece as "a la Percy Grainger." In 1946 this piece won the National Federation of Music Clubs' second prize in the class III division for composition for small orchestras.

Johnston was assigned to the flag ship Augusta, which sailed in the Atlantic. It was intended that the ship's band be first class in the style of Glenn Miller's band. The captain, however, often had the band doing other tasks, such as chipping paint, so there was never sufficient time for the band to develop the polish and style that was originally expected. As a result of this and other events, the captain lost his rank. Part of the ship's duty was to transport President Truman to Potsdam, and the band was to be on display. On the return trip Truman was eating with the enlisted men and announced that the war would be over shortly because an atomic bomb had been dropped on Hiroshima. The news about the bombing shocked Johnston. In 1946 he was discharged from the Navy for medical reasons. Not long afterwards Johnston discovered he had a collapsed lung from using improper breathing techniques while playing the trombone.

The time in the Navy had been an adjustment period. Johnston had entered with a limited view of the world but soon learned that life could be quite different from his experiences in Macon and Richmond. He didn't like living under bureaucracy, but the Navy had given him training as a dance band musician. So after leaving, Johnston played piano at the National Theater, a vaudeville house in Richmond, and worked with dance bands. Next he got a job in Norfolk, Virginia, at a supper club, and then he went to Mason City, Iowa, and played with the Carl Bean Touring Dance Band. During this time Johnston was married to a vocalist whom he had met in Virginia. The marriage only lasted six months. For a while he was headed toward a career in popular music, but the elder Johnston sensed that all was not going well; he went to Mason City and convinced his son to leave the dance band and return to college.

Notes

1. This interest is apparent in some of Johnston's later compositions such as the "Game" section of Sonata for Two (1961) and "Knocking Piece II" of Four Do-It-Yourself Pieces (1969).

2. Johnston's mother saved all of her son's manuscript books, programs, and newspaper articles about his concerts.

3. Later Pippin joined the Johnstons while they were staying with Harry Partch in Gualala. See Chapter 2.

4. The letter is dated May 7, 1943 and is included in the scrapbook that Mrs. Johnston kept for her son.

5. This article is also in the scrapbook. Later Johnston spoke about his concern for acoustics after his first year in music school. See "The Corporealism of Harry Partch," Perspectives of New Music, xiii/2 (1975), p. 91.

In 1947 Johnston returned to the College of William and Mary and by 1949 completed his bachelor's degree in fine arts.[1] He laughs at the fact that his minor was in sculpture, an artistic talent that he claims not to possess.

Although Johnston was disappointed with the level of music training he received at William and Mary, he did meet Wilford Leach, someone who would influence his future. Leach was studying to become a theatrical director and asked Johnston to compose the music for Carry Me Back, a musical Leach was writing for a student production at William and Mary. Since Johnston had previously written the score for a student ballet, he agreed to compose the music, and later the musical won the Broadcast Music Incorporated prize for student musicals. The songs were published. As a result Johnston went to New York City and was interviewed by Carl Haverlin,[2] head of the popular music division of Broadcast Music Incorporated. Apparently Haverlin felt that Johnston had a good chance at being a popular composer and was disappointed when Johnston stressed that he wanted to write serious music.

After graduation Johnston returned to Richmond and was persuaded by some friends to teach a class in jazz arranging. The class was held surreptitiously at the Richmond Professional Institute (now the Virginia Commonwealth University). One of the students arranged a meeting between his friend Betty Ruth Hall and Johnston, thinking they might have some common interests. The friend's intuition was correct. The two talked for forty-eight hours; Johnston shared tales about his experiences with jazz bands, and Betty discovered that they were both interested in palmistry. Betty was an art education major at the Richmond Professional Institute. She later taught art at Sullins Girls School in Bristol, Virginia. Betty was in Richmond to complete her degree during the 1949 summer school session. By April of 1950 the two of them would marry.[3]

Johnston knew he needed more musical training if he was going to be a serious composer, but he had difficulty finding a graduate school that would accept him because his degree was in fine arts and not in music. Finally he was admitted to the Cincinnati Conservatory because Luther Richmond, the head of the Conservatory, had been the Superintendent of Music at Richmond and knew Johnston. The composition study at Cincinnati was inadequate. Musically Johnston didn't get along with one teacher, and all he learned from another was how to copy music. The really helpful class was atonal counterpoint taught by Mary Leighton. Johnston credits her as being one of his composition teachers.

While studying with Leighton Johnston experimented with his first 12-tone piece, Etude-Toccata (1949) for piano. He admired Alexander Scriabin's Etude in Thirds, and this influence can be seen and heard in Johnston's Etude which is a study of quickly moving major thirds and minor sixths in the right hand accompanied by a linear presentation of the row (which happened to be an all-combinatorial row) in the left hand. At this time Johnston did not understand the complementary properties of an all-combinatorial row, but chose the transpositions, inversions, and retrogrades that were related to the original row by a major third (O-4; O-8; I-4; I-8) in order to produce the patterns of thirds and sixths. The Etude is divided into five sections, with sections one, three, and five presenting the prime and retrograde forms of the row, and sections two and four featuring the inversions and retrograde inversions. At all times the thirds and sixths are used as invertible counterpoint, as can be seen in Example 1.

Example 1. Beginning measures of Etude showing invertible counterpoint. Used by permission of the composer.

Johnston considered this piece an academic study, and the Etude was not performed on his Master of Music recital. However, he does include it in his professional catalog because the Etude represents his first use of serialism, which would fascinate him for many years.

While at Cincinnati Johnston acquired some teaching experience. The

Conservatory had an unusual policy of requiring everyone to study composition. As a teacher's assistant Johnston was assigned the composition class for instrumental majors. It was at this time that he met Ward Swingle (who later founded the Swingle Singers). Swingle was a student in Johnston's class, and they have been friends ever since. In fact, Ward and his wife, Françoise, hosted the Johnston's wedding dinner, and later the Swingle Singers would commission Johnston to write two compositions for them: "Ci-Gît Satie" (1967) and Sonnets of Desolation (1980).

Swingle also played the piano for several pieces on Johnston's Master's Recital. On the program was a woodwind quintet, a piece for piano, and "somewhere i have never traveled" (1949), a song for tenor and piano using a text by e.e. cummings. Having heard a monophonic recording of this recital, I judged the song as his most successful piece. Johnston has always been concerned about setting a text so it can be heard, and he successfully achieved this clarity in "somewhere i have never traveled." The melody, primarily conjunct, is a singable line in which the pitches and rhythms naturally intone the text. The vocal line is conservative and even resembles a crooning style, but the piano accompaniment outlines a five-octave space with the vocal line being supported by the piano's upper and lower registers. (See Example 2.) At times the widely spaced chords sound bi-tonal (as the circled chords in measure 7), but the spacing, slow tempo, and pedaling suggest that an A fundamental with its supporting lower partials is

Example 2. Beginning measures of "somewhere i have never traveled." Used by permission of the composer.

being sustained while the higher upper partials are changing. Thus in measure 4 the C naturals in the right hand are pitted against the C sharps in the left hand and the E#4 combined with E2 in the left hand[4]; similarly, in measure 3 the pedaling carefully specifies that the contrapuntal movement is a mixing of these changing intervals over the sustained A-E-A drone. The piece is so well crafted with the use of repeated and varied textures and changing harmonic areas that it is successful for both listener and performer.

Thor Johnson, the orchestral conductor at the Conservatory, was present at Johnston's Master's Recital and liked the song so much that he wanted to do a reading of Johnston's orchestral piece, Korybas (which is not included in his catalog). Johnston worked hard preparing the parts but discovered that the conductor had forgotten about his offer. The reading was rescheduled, but it was a disaster. Johnston's Navy School of Music training had been oriented towards band music, and he needed to learn more about traditional orchestration.

A significant event happened in Cincinnati, however, that shaped the future of the young composer's career. Johnston was interested in acoustics and the microtones that are created by the upper partials of the overtone series. No one else shared this interest, but a musicologist at the Conservatory, who was a friend of fellow composer Jim Marks, had a book that he thought Johnston might like. It was Genesis of a Music, by Harry Partch, which had just been published in 1949.[5] Since the musicologist had no use for the book, he gave it to Johnston.

As a result of this gift Johnston wrote to Partch to inquire if it would be possible to study with him, sending the letter in care of the University of Wisconsin Press. His letter was forwarded to Partch, who was then living at Gualala, California. Partch replied that he would accept an apprentice, but warned that Johnston should not become biologically trapped; Partch meant Johnston shouldn't get married. However, Johnston ignored this advice and he and Betty were married in April 1950, while Johnston was completing his work at Cincinnati.

The Johnstons did not know exactly what to expect when they arrived at Gualala in August 1950, but one thing was apparent--they would have to expend a lot of physical labor in preparing an old herdsman cottage as their living quarters.[6] Among other repairs, the roof needed mending, and the Johnstons had to learn how to care for the outdoor privy. All of these jobs were new challenges for Ben and Betty. Neither of them had previous experiences with camping or primitive living.

It was soon evident to Partch that Johnston was not handy with tools and carpentry, but the apprentice did possess a fine ear for tuning. In later years Johnston stated:

> He [Partch] could have wished for a carpenter or for a percussionist.... But he had one thing he had not counted on: someone who understood his theory almost without explanation, and who could hear and reproduce

the pitch relations accurately. He began to grasp that there might be some sort of real convergence between us.[7]

Every day Johnston helped tune Partch's string instruments, such as the Kithara and Harmonic Canon, by tuning them to the Chromelodeon. Johnston was interested in how the instruments were designed to exhibit principles of extended just intonation, Partch's tuning system (see chapter 4 for more details), and the tuning was a practical course in ear training. But Partch was not always patient with theoretical questions and frequently responded with the comment of "Haven't you read the book?," meaning his Genesis of a Music. Worse yet, Partch didn't like being called a teacher and wouldn't discuss compositional questions.

But the Johnstons were helpful in rehearsing and playing some of Partch's compositions. Both Ben and Betty performed on the 78 r.p.m. recordings made of The Intrusions and Dark Brother. Betty is not a trained musician, but Partch showed her how to play the Diamond Marimba and the Bass Marimba. Ben performed on the marimbas and the Kithara. Some of these performances are available on the New World Records release titled "Harry Partch; John Cage" (NW214) where Ben Johnston plays The Rose, The Wind, The Street, and three pieces from Eleven Intrusions.[8] Both Johnstons, plus their friend Donald Pippin (who also came to work with Partch at Gualala), perform in Partch's The Letter (1943) and Cloud-Chamber Music (1950) on a Composers Recording Incorporated (CRI-193). By the early 1950's, when the original tapes of these performances were made, Partch had built his marimbas, Chromelodeon, and Cloud-Chamber Bowls, and was working on the Spoils of War.[9]

One of Johnston's projects was to tune a Kithara so that he could play a minuet by Johann Froberger that would be used as a demonstration of just intonation on the 78 r.p.m. record that Partch was preparing. The minuet would show how Partch's tuning was part of the evolutionary progress of the history of music. Johnston immediately had difficulties. After tuning several triads, he encountered the problem where the supertonic does not work both after the subdominant and before the dominant. It was 22 cents sharp, a tuning error that is called a syntonic comma. Partch silently observed how his apprentice worked with this problem. Johnston's solution was to use extra notes that would accommodate the comma when he retuned the Kithara.

There was another project. Leach, Johnston's friend who wrote Carry Me Back, was writing another play, The Wooden Bird, and he wanted Johnston to compose the music for it. Feeling inadequate because he had just begun working with just intonation and did not have any of his own instruments, Johnston talked to Partch about not wanting to disappoint his friend Wilford Leach. Partch suggested that he and Johnston collaborate. They made a tape of background music which used the Kithara, Adapted Viola, Chromelodeon, Diamond Marimba, Cloud-Chamber Bowls, and Spoils of War and composed some solo pieces which Partch called modern art songs.[10] The tape was sent to Leach, who was in Virginia, and for the performance he had the playback system and speakers hidden on stage so that the sources of the music for The Wooden Bird were not visible to the audience. Later Leach wrote an article about Partch's instruments and theatrical works for Theatre Arts.[11]

While Johnston was at Gualala he had an opportunity to enroll in the University of California at Berkeley. Lauriston C. Marshall, who was the head of the Microwave Radiation Laboratory there, was sharing a Guggenheim Fellowship with Partch in which they were trying to develop an electronic organ that would demonstrate extended just intonation. (Twenty years later the Motorola Company produced such an instrument, called the Scalatron.) Marshall helped Johnston, who was using his G.I. bill, to be admitted to the musicology department at Berkeley. At this time the Doctor of Musical Arts in composition was a new degree that was only offered at a few institutions, such as the Eastman School of Music and the University of Southern California, so Johnston's only choice was to study musicology. His project was to do research about Partch and his music. Roger Sessions, who was chairman of the music department at the University of California at Berkeley, thought the project was interesting, but there were some musicologists who questioned the merit of such a study. Johnston proposed to do the research first before completing course work, which is an unusual procedure, and, again, some faculty members disapproved. However, Johnston took the graduate entrance examinations, doing well in analysis and ear training, and, although he did have deficiencies in music history, he was admitted into the program. He enrolled in a course about the Baroque concerto, took books back to Gualala and tried to study, but having little spare time, he barely passed the course and his standing at Berkeley was tenuous.

About three months after the Johnstons came to Gualala Partch suddenly became ill as a result of an allergic reaction to tick bites. (Partch tended to be a hypochondriac; the Johnstons remember him taking a series of pills before meals that was timed at five minutes before eating, two minutes before, and one minute after meals, and Partch would become extremely upset if meals were not ready at the exact moment.) Partch decided to leave Gualala because he feared for his health. By this time Johnston had been with Partch for six months. But Partch thought that Johnston should study composition with Darius Milhaud, who was teaching at Mills College in Oakland. Partch arranged for the Johnstons to attend a dinner party given by Agnes Albert, a prominent San Franciscan who was Partch's patron and also on the Board of Directors at Mills College. The Milhauds were at the party and arrangements were made for Johnston to begin study with Milhaud in February 1951.

This was fortunate because Johnston still needed to study composition. In an interview with Cole Gagne and Tracy Caras, Johnston remarked:

> I think [studying with Milhaud] did me a great deal of good. If you
> know how to mine the gold that's there, a teacher like that is very good.
> If you don't, you can find it absolutely blank, because he was not a

systematic teacher.   Milhaud was a sort of intuitive, systemless improviser as a teacher.[12]

Johnston showed Milhaud his "Le Gout de Néant" (1950), a piece he had composed at Cincinnati, which Milhaud liked and called a substantial work. He complimented Johnston on his sensitive setting of French. The song's text is a poem from Charles Baudelaire's Les Fleurs du Mal (1857), which is a self-analysis of the poet's depressed state in which he says he is lacking a taste for love.

Johnston organized his musical setting of "Le Gout de Néant" into four sections (mm. 1-20; 21-39; 40-46; and 47-56). The song's low register, triplets, and duplets are reminiscent of "somewhere i have never traveled" (compare Examples 2 and 3), but "Le Gout de Néant" shows signs of a developing compositional craft that includes a more emotional expression. No longer does the vocal line sound like something Bing Crosby might sing, but rather its patterns of major and minor thirds portray the poem's gloominess. Especially expressive is the descending line in mm. 12-14 (see Example 3--the composer made the penciled correction), which Johnston used as a cadential pattern in other parts of the song. The homophonic accompaniment is in the piano's lower registers, using blocks of bi-tonal harmonies which become more dissonant, frequently by means of diminished fifteenths (see the E2 and Eb4 in measure 1 of Example 3 and the G1 and Gb3 in measure 2 of the same example). It is almost as if Johnston were trying to create the mistuned octaves that would be possible in just intonation while using the piano's equal temperament. Later in the song he abandoned this harmonic exploration and used a series of fourths and fifths as a jazz-like walking bass (see Example 4, page 16). (The composer made the pencil corrections for the words "Resigne" and "coeur.")

Johnston wisely maintained these two textures (the homophonic material of Example 3 and the walking bass of Example 4) throughout the composition, so that the text was the focus of attention. The language of Baudelaire's poem is so musical that Johnston deliberately tried not to obscure the natural inflections of the words.

While working with Milhaud, Johnston composed three significant works: "A Nocturnall Upon Saint Lucie's Day Being the Shortest Day" (1951) for baritone or contralto and piano, Concerto for Brass (1951), and Concerto for Percussion (1952), which was completed in absentia from Mills during Johnston's first year of teaching at the University of Illinois.

The text for "A Nocturnall Upon Saint Lucie's Day Being the Shortest Day" is by John Donne (1572-1631), and its depressed and gloomy message resembles "Le Gout de Néant." Donne's images are based upon the theme of annihilation, presented in such phrases as "For I am every dead thing.... He [Alchemie] ruin'd mee, and I am re-begot / of Absence, darkness, death; things which are not" and "But I am none; nor will by Sunne renew." The poet was expressing his despair and unhappiness about his wife's death. Saint Lucie's Day, December

Example 3.   Opening measures of "Le Gout de Néant."   Used by permission of the composer.

21, is the shortest day of the year and augments the theme of darkness and despair.

Johnston's setting of the poem reflects this gloomy message in a style like that of the previous song. Again he used descending passages of duplets and triplets, a conjunct vocal line with some skips, and similar chordal construction. However, there are two hints in "A Nocturnall Upon Saint Lucie's Day" that

Example 4. Jazz-like walking bass in "Le Gout de Néant." Used by permission of the composer.

reveal his latent interest in microtones. One indication is his use of a vocal slide or glissando; the other sign is the enharmonic notation, such as the Fb and Ebb circled in Example 5.

Johnston's Concerto for Brass is more conservative and exhibits a neo-Baroque style. The Concerto's three movements are titled "Prelude," "Fugue," and "Passacaglia." The "Prelude" is short and articulate, using dissonant, descending chromatic lines and a bass ostinato pattern. This short movement seems out of proportion to the rest of the composition. I find the "Fugue" to be more interesting. It is a four-voice double fugue with each subject presented in stretto and with its own countersubject. The articulation and dynamics ensure that the lines are distinct and easy to follow. The "Passacaglia" is not as successful as the "Fugue" because the Passacaglia theme doesn't have the direction it needs--too many C naturals frustrate the sense of a D tonality which Johnston tried to establish. The theme is stated ten times and is heard in augmentation and in canons at the octave and fifth. The movement ends with a chorale clearly in D.

The Concerto is an example of Johnston's developing compositional craft,

Example 5. Enharmonic pitches used in "A Nocturnall Upon Saint Lucie's Day."
Used by permission of the composer.

and Milhaud's interest in counterpoint is evident.[13] The rhythms in this piece
are similar to those used in "somewhere i have never traveled," written a year
earlier, but musically the Concerto is not as interesting or creative as the song.
Although Johnston says he learned a lot from Milhaud, the young composer
seemed to be caught in an academic neo-Baroque style that inhibited freedom of
expression. Johnston was more successful when using texts and writing inde-
pendently of a teacher. His future musical career using extended just intonation
necessitated that he work in isolation.

Notes

1. Johnston graduated with honors. He was a member of Omicron Delta
Kappa and Phi Beta Kappa for which he gave the initiates' graduation speech.

2. Later Carl Haverlin arranged for Harry Partch to receive advance
royalties for his music.

3. Betty Johnston was an active artist until 1979 when her eyesight was
weakened by a nervous infection; she has recently resumed painting. Several of
her paintings are owned by the composer Salvatore Martirano and his family. An

especially striking one is a portrait of Sal that is done in shades of purple and black with sprinklings of sand and gravel to add textural interest.

4. The register numbering is standardized international acoustical terminology. Middle C is C4 and the numbers increase as the registers are higher. Each successive C begins a new register.

5. In 1974 the second edition of Partch's book was issued by Da Capo Press.

6. Johnston related some of his experiences with Partch in "The Corporealism of Harry Partch," Perspectives of New Music, xiii/2 (1975), p. 93.

7. Ibid., p. 95.

8. Johnston also wrote the detailed program liner notes for this album and described the recording of Eleven Intrusions and Dark Brother. For more information about and photographs of Partch's instruments see Harry Partch, Genesis of a Music, second edition (New York: Da Capo Press, 1974). There is also a Columbia stereo recording, "The World of Harry Partch" (MS 7207), where Partch described and demonstrated some of his instruments.

9. Cloud-Chamber Music was also recorded on "Gate 5 Records--Issue A," a recording that Partch issued himself. The Johnstons also performed Waterfall for this record.

10. Johnston has an acetate copy of this tape that I was able to review. The first segment on the tape sounded jazz-like--there was a string walking-bass pattern and cymbals were struck with wire brushes (the kinds of sounds Johnston had been using in jazz bands)--however, as the tape progressed the music became more and more Partch-like, resembling Partch's Barstow and The Letter, especially when Partch was singing by himself. Like all of Partch's music, the texts were clear; there were repeated passages and motives that unified short musical segments within an act, and particular instruments, such as the Kithara and Spoils of War, were used for sound effects.

11. See Wilford Leach, "Music for Words Perhaps," Theatre Arts, January 1953, pp. 65-68.

12. Cole Gagne and Tracy Caras, Soundpieces: Interviews With American Composers (Metuchen, NJ: Scarecrow Press, 1982), p. 251.

13. Johnston made an arrangement of the Concerto for two pianos and four hands so that his piece could be performed at a student composition recital at Mills College. Thirteen years later the Concerto was performed by the University of Illinois Wind Ensemble with Robert Gray conducting.

While completing his Master of Fine Arts degree at Mills College, Johnston applied for several teaching positions. One was at a Baptist College in Blue Mountain, Mississippi, where both he and Betty were offered faculty positions in the music and art departments respectively. Although this offer was attractive, there were two restrictions--no smoking was allowed, and all faculty must be members of the Baptist Church. The Johnstons declined the offers. Neither wanted to make a strong religious commitment, and Betty smoked.

It was fortunate that the Johnstons did not take the positions because Laura Huelster, chairperson of the Dance Department at the University of Illinois at Champaign-Urbana, wanted to hire him. The position was half-time in the Dance Department and half-time in the School of Music. Johnston would be dance accompanist/composer and teach undergraduate theory.

During the 1950's the University of Illinois experienced a period of rapid reorganization and expansion because Governor Adlai Stevenson established a generous budget for education. He wanted the University to become a major educational institution. In 1949 Charles Stoddard became President and was able to bring about an effective transformation. New departmental heads were appointed; faculty size was increased; and outstanding programs were introduced, such as the Festivals of Contemporary Arts, a series of concerts and lectures from 1948 to 1967 that created an international reputation because of the School of Music's dedication to the latest in contemporary music. The early Festivals featured such guest composers as Igor Stravinsky, Paul Hindemith, Aaron Copland, and Virgil Thomson. Later, important works were premièred, like Lejaren Hiller's Illiac Suite for String Quartet (1957).

In addition to the reputation that the Festivals brought to the University, several of the School of Music's directors helped to shape its future. John Kuyppers, a bold and imaginative administrator, championed the idea of the Festival and expanded all areas of the faculty. Soulima Stravinsky joined the piano faculty; Paul Rolland was added to the string division; Ludwig Zirner, who had conducted the Vienna Opera, became opera conductor; Paul Price established an outstanding percussion department; and the Walden String Quartet, which had been at Cornell, was in residence.

Johnston joined the faculty in the fall of 1951, the beginning of this expansion. Several important events happened during his first year. He completed his Master of Fine Arts thesis piece, <u>Concerto for Percussion</u> (1952), in absentia from Mills. Milhaud did not like the composition, but approved it, and Johnston received his degree. Perhaps, one reason for Milhaud's diffidence was that the <u>Concerto</u> seemed closer to Partch's influence than Milhaud's. The percussion instrumentation and the titles of the three movements--"Orgy," "Dirge," and "Ritual"--suggest Partch's influence. An even more daring aspect is that Johnston used some indeterminacy in composing "Ritual," the last movement (see Example 1). The bongo drums (stave 3) and the tam-tam, timpani, and cymbals (stave 7) establish separate ostinati while the claves (stave 2) and the Indian and congo drums (stave 4) have rhythms that do not follow a set pattern. Johnston drew numbers from a hat to determine their durations. The piece is dedicated to Paul Price, who was head of the percussion department and a strong supporter of Johnston's music. Price left the University of Illinois to establish a performance and teaching career in New York City.

Example 1. Use of indeterminacy in "Ritual" from <u>Concerto for Percussion</u>. Used by permission of the composer.

The <u>Concerto for Percussion</u> had other professional benefits. During Johnston's first year as a faculty member, Charles Shattuck, a director in the Theater Department, was looking for someone to write the music for his production of Arthur Gregor's play, <u>Fire</u>. Johnston's name was mentioned. Not knowing Johnston, Shattuck suggested that one of the composer's scores be sent to Gregor in New York City for evaluation. The <u>Concerto</u> was sent to Gregor, who then forwarded it to John Cage, and Cage's reply was favorable. Although

Plate 1. John Cage and Ben Johnston at the Art Institute of Chicago in October 1983. Courtesy of a friend.

Johnston doesn't remember much about his incidental music for Fire, saying the music was not that good, he does associate the score with his introduction to John Cage, who later would become Johnston's teacher and friend.

Johnston first met Cage during the Contemporary Arts Festival of 1952. Cage gave a lecture titled "To Describe the Process of Composition Used in Music for Piano 21-52," later published in his book Silence.[1] The lecture evoked a controversial reaction from the audience. Some considered his musical statements blasphemous. Johnston introduced himself to Cage after the lecture and discovered that Cage already knew him because of the Concerto for Percussion. Cage invited Johnston to come to New York City during the summer to study with him and suggested some preliminary work, such as hearing and analyzing Anton Webern's music. Unfortunately Johnston did not have access to Webern scores or recordings and found his first year of teaching so demanding that he did not complete the preparation, so he felt he could not study with Cage. However, Johnston did go to New York City for several weeks during the summer and, together with Earle Brown, spent some time helping Cage prepare Williams Mix (1952), an 8-track tape piece that required many hours of splicing and joining tape. Later in 1957 and 1959 Johnston would have an opportunity to study with Cage, and during 1967, when Cage was a Visiting Associate in the Center for Advanced Studies at the University of Illinois, Johnston and Cage became good friends.

Like the School of Music, the Dance Department was also expanding under the guidance of Margaret Erlanger, a new chairperson. It was important to her that the dance students be trained in the main currents of American dance repertoire. She had Sybil Shearer from the Doris Humphrey School of Dance as a guest teacher; Merce Cunningham was in residence for a year; and Alwyn Nikolais choreographed and participated in the 1957 production of Harry Partch's Bewitched (1955). Erlanger encouraged the dance students to attend the American Dance Festival held during the summer at New Haven, Connecticut. For several summers Johnston went to the Dance Festival as a dance accompanist; he played for Martha Graham and Doris Humphrey. Erlanger also hired Margret Dietz, a European trained in the Wigman School of Dance. Dietz and Johnston collaborated on several projects.

The majority of Johnston's compositions were for the Theater and Dance Departments. However, during 1953 he wrote three pieces for piano--Satires, Celebration, and Portrait. He does not consider these significant, although Celebration, originally an accompaniment for a dance, was published. It was written for Virginia Freeman, who taught in the Dance Department, and she choreographed the piece for her students. The music is modal, and Celebration's main interest lies in its rhythmic aspects. Asymmetrical meters constantly change, as in Example 2, giving the music a percussive and dance-like quality. The pitch material shows no indication of Johnston's later microtonal music, although Celebration has a definite emotion marked "Joyous and unrestrained." Johnston has always been concerned about expressiveness. Later he would be able to use strict serialism, demanding microtonal tuning, and proportional rhythms to express rapidly changing emotional qualities.

Piano Solo

BEN JOHNSTON

Example 2. Opening measures of Celebration showing rhythmic variety. Published by Orchesis Publications. Copyright 1960.

Some of Celebration's rhythms were influenced by Burrill Phillips, a senior member of the theory/composition division of the School of Music with whom Johnston was studying. Phillips had written music for dance, theater, and films and was especially interested in Stravinsky's music. It was not difficult for Phillips to encourage Johnston to explore rhythmic intricacies since he had already had experience with composing for dance bands.

Originally Johnston intended to work on a doctorate, which explains why he was studying with Phillips, but the Doctor of Musical Arts in composition was not offered at the University of Illinois, and it did not seem feasible to Johnston to get a degree in Musicology, which would have been the only other possibility. Later, Otto Luening, one of the pioneers in electronic music, convinced Johnston that the merit of his compositional career surpassed the need for further degree work, and Luening wrote a letter in support of this judgment to the faculty of the School of Music.

In 1954 Johnston was able to collaborate with his friend Wilford Leach on a play The Zodiac of Memphis Street, also known as "Trapdoors of the Moon." (Leach came to the University of Illinois in 1953 at Johnston's suggestion, completing his Master of Arts degree in speech in 1954 and his Doctor of Philosophy degree in theater in the Department of Speech in 1956.)[2] The play is about a grandmother and her grandson. The old woman is thought to be a witch, and there are scenes where she is visited by imaginary witches. Leach's play was designed to allow Johnston to compose dance music for Margret Dietz, the dancer from the Wigman School, who was featured in a lead role.

Altogether there are fourteen musical numbers in the play; several are dances with titles like "Game," "Pas de Trois," "The Imaginary Marriage,"

"Children's Hallowe'en," and "Guadalupe's Hallucination." Each of the two acts begins with a prelude; the first has an obvious samba tempo which introduces the play's dance-like character. Johnston chose to use a small chamber ensemble of two violins, viola, cello, double bass, harpsichord, piano, and two percussion-ists, so that he could imitate the sound of a string orchestra while adding percus-sive color. He used solo percussion for two musical numbers, the "Epilogue" and "Children's Hallowe'en." This last piece is for timpani and bongo drums and is fast and showy. Although Johnston's music for Zodiac of Memphis Street is tonally and formally conventional, its rhythmic aspects are progressive. There are so many meter changes (even several metric modulations), unequal subdivisions, and superimposed rhythmic patterns that the listener is aware of the dance tempi and patterns, such as the samba and tango, while being fascinated by the inter-ruptions and elaborations of these familiar figures.

Johnston's next composition, Night (1955), was a commission for the 1955 Festival of Contemporary Arts. Night is a cantata for women's chorus, solo bari-tone, and a chamber ensemble consisting of Bb clarinet, French horn, Bb trumpet, trombone, four timpani, tam-tams, cello, and string bass. The text is a poem by Robinson Jeffers (1887-1962). Johnston chose Night as a tribute to his father, who liked Jeffers' poetry and identified with the poet's ideas about atheism. Al-though young Johnston did not share his father's spiritual views, Jeffers' poetry, especially Night, appealed to him because of the poet's many references to the coastal area around Monterey, California. Such lines as "The deep dark-shining Pacific leans on the land / Feeling his cold strength / To the outmost margins" reminded Johnston of the time he spent at Gualala, which is in the northern part of the state.

The cantata format of Night is appropriate since the text is long. Although the music is continuous, it divides into ten sections with the chorus singing four of them. The solo baritone presents the majority of the text while the frequent instrumental interludes provide color and texture. The listener immediately hears some references to Milhaud's instrumentation and harmonic idiom in the opening measures of the cantata, especially the bassoon melody set within a context of ninth and eleventh chords (see Example 3).

The choral parts are either a cappella or set against an Eb drone. Johnston achieved a thick harmonic blend by using parallel second inversion chords or quintal harmonies. A vocal fugue in the middle creates a contrasting texture to this homophonic context.

Night is neoclassic, and the vocal lines (both solo and choral) are conserva-tive. The text is set so that one hears the ebb and flow of the ocean's tide. In-strumental drones and ostinati patterns help suggest the ocean's stability, while frequent meter changes suggest a state of constant change. The vocal lines are also wave-like with small rising and falling patterns (see Example 3).

At this point Johnston was not exploring new compositional ground. Night

Example 3. Opening measures of <u>Night</u>. Used by permission of the composer.

resembles his earlier song, "Le Gout de Néant," but <u>Night</u> is a much longer piece and an instrumental ensemble replaces the piano. Having studied this music I think that length and color were two areas that he needed to expand in his music.

One reason Johnston was entrenched in neoclassicism was that since 1953 he had been writing for either dance or theater, often titled dance-theater. These were collaborative situations, and in many instances the music was secondary to the dance or drama, with the composer subject to the dictates of another's ideas. Therefore, it is not surprising that Johnston had not discovered his own sense of style and musical expression. Another reason was that he was not ready to risk writing in just intonation. He needed to develop a valid theory that would be acceptable to his colleagues.

He tried to break out of this neoclassic mold with his next composition, <u>St. Joan</u> (1955), which originally was a ballet for Sybil Shearer, a member of the Doris Humphrey studio in New York City who came to the University of Illinois as a guest teacher for a year. Shearer planned that her dance of <u>St. Joan</u> would be a full-length solo performance. The first part would portray the developing character of Joan, while the second would feature the rising opposition, trial, and martyrdom of the saint.

Although Johnston composed music for the entire dance, it was never performed. This was frustrating because he had written over an hour's worth of music that seemed useless. But by 1958 he had arranged parts of the dance into a piano suite which Claire Richards, a member of the piano faculty, performed.[3] The suite was twenty-seven minutes--the longest single work Johnston had created up to this time.

Compositionally the listener recognizes that St. Joan has several problems. There is no overall formal plan. One hears an introduction, an extended through-composed melodic section, and then a cadence. A free "murmurando" section follows, and suddenly a rhythmically interesting fugue appears. The fugal texture gradually dissolves into a meandering part which seems meaningless. Afterwards, there is a complete break, and a long passacaglia begins. This, plus a short epilogue, completes St. Joan.

Part of Johnston's problem was that originally action would complete the meaning of the music. If the music were entirely programmatic (at times it is, especially during the "murmurando" and a funeral march section) then it might support its twenty-seven minutes, but much of the piece is intended to express Joan's character and emotional state, which is difficult to follow abstractly. Also, the piano is a limiting instrument, and at times Johnston succumbed to writing clichés that resembled the reiterated chords in the beginning of Richard Addinsell's Warsaw Concerto. I think that the first half of St. Joan, especially the through-composed melody and the fugue, are the most successful. The "Passacaglia and Epilogue" are less interesting.

However, in 1960 Johnston did orchestrate these sections, and the material was well-suited for orchestral color even though the orchestration is conservative. There are no extended instrumental techniques, no mixing of registers or fusing of orchestral colors. Instead, Johnston used a textbook approach to writing for orchestra. Some of the better moments occur when a muted trumpet plays off-stage, and a flute melody is accompanied by celesta and non-vibrato divisi violas playing fifths.

One significant detail in the orchestration concerns Johnston's use of enharmonic notation. In the original piano score the funeral march begins with a melody in the third register using the pitches G# G A Ab Eb D while in the orchestral version the trombone is given the same material, but the pitches are Ab G Bbb Ab Eb D, which shows Johnston's growing sensitivity to tuning.

But St. Joan was an important piece for Johnston. Even though it was begun as a collaboration, eventually he was forced to make purely musical decisions about its composition.

It was at this time that Johnston composed an unusual piece, Three Chinese Lyrics (1955) for soprano and two violins. He abandoned the security of neo-classicism, with its contrapuntal techniques and dance forms, and began to experiment with pitch and timbre. Burrill Phillips criticized St. Joan for having too many notes and suggested that Johnston try to be more economical. This observation, plus the austerity that the Chinese poems imply, drastically affected his compositional style. The string writing in these songs is entirely different from the standard dance band string parts of Zodiac. Actually, until this time, Johnston had done very little string writing, and the Three Chinese Lyrics become prophetic of his future string quartets. The violins are used both coloristically and as equal participants with the vocal line. Although he experimented with such techniques as mutes, non-vibrato, sustained harmonics, double stops, drones, and registral changes, the writing sounds unaffected and perfectly suited for the text.

The lyrics are three poems by Rihaku, a Chinese poet better known as Li Po, who lived from 701-762. Ezra Pound translated many of Li Po's poems, including the three that Johnston used: "The Jewel Stairs' Grievance," "Taking Leave of a Friend," and "Lament of the Frontier Guard."[4] Johnston had been familiar with the poems for some time because while they were at Gualala Betty had set "The Jewel Stairs' Grievance" for voice and guitar, and Partch had used some of Li Po's poems.

When Johnston set the text he had the violins provide an emotional and spatial frame for the words. For example, the first song, "The Jewel Stairs' Grievance," begins with the muted violins playing dissonant counterpoint. The listener is introduced to a vocabulary of intervals that features seconds and thirds. There is no apparent linear order, such as a serial row or canonic action, so the listener is free to enjoy the expression of the music for its own sake. Johnston's setting of "The Jewel Stairs' Grievance" resembles a Chinese scroll--the lines are sparse yet suggestive of meaning that the listener must supply. The syllabic vocal line is mostly stepwise, often outlining major or minor thirds, much like the violins did in the opening measures (see Example 4). Frequently the vocal line is unaccompanied, and if the violins are used, they provide drones, ostinati, and other pitch supports for the vocal line.

Example 4. Opening measures of "The Jewel Stairs' Grievance" from Three Chinese Lyrics. Used by permission of the composer.

The second song, "Taking Leave of a Friend," alternates between passages for the violin and solo voice. The introduction, which Johnston specified should sound as if it were "In Stillness and Space," is the second violin playing an ascending melody outlining thirds, while the first violin plays harmonics that are so high that they sound like white noise. The angular vocal line seems disturbing because wide leaps of fourths, fifths, and sevenths are prominent and tend to obscure the text; however, frequent repeated notes make the text more audible.

Example 5. Opening measures of "Taking Leave of a Friend" from Three Chinese Lyrics. Used by permission of the composer.

The main impression of the song is the hopelessness that these departing friends are experiencing. Johnston achieved this feeling by avoiding obvious symbolic gestures (such as imitating the poem's sonic imagery of neighing horses as the two people depart in opposite directions) and emphasizing a spatial distance, as in the closing measure where the soprano sings in her low register while the violins play high harmonics.

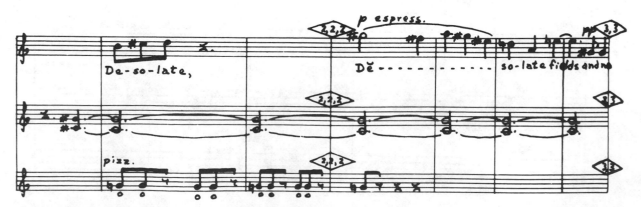

Example 6. Vocal melisma in "Lament of the Frontier Guard" from Three Chinese Lyrics. Used by permission of the composer.

As a contrast, "Lament of the Frontier Guard," the last song, is dramatic, with the violins actively portraying the intense sorrow of viewing the ruins of a besieged village at the North Gate. The vocal line contains many octave leaps and several melismas, as in Example 6.

The violins have two basic textures that maintain the intensity of the scene's horror. One texture is an ostinato-like pattern that Johnston used in several different ways. First it is heard as a pizzicato introduction that is shared between the two instruments (see Example 7). The precariousness of this passage, in which one violinist might easily lose concentration and miss a note, adds to the dramatic tension.

Example 7. Introduction to "Lament of the Frontier Guard" from Three Chinese Lyrics. Used by permission of the composer.

Later the texture changes to a simpler ostinato of repeated notes, but this time Johnston used a proportional tempo with triplet eighth notes in the second violin and triplet quarters in the first violin, while the voice is performing the basic pulse of a quarter note per beat (see Example 8, page 30). He later employed this technique in his string quartets.

There are places where the violins' perpetual motion sustains the intense emotion of the "Lament" to such an extent that Johnston provided relief by using a contrapuntal modal melody for the violins while the voice has a pentatonic melody emphasizing octave leaps. Later the voice sings unaccompanied in several recitative-like passages.

Johnston had proven himself a talented song writer in such solo songs as "somewhere i have never traveled" and "Le Gout de Néant," but the Three Chinese Lyrics are so different from anything he had done before that they sound inspired. Although this type of vocal and string writing was experimental, the songs are so well made that the listener would expect that the composer

Example 8. Proportional tempi in "Lament of the Frontier Guard" from Three Chinese Lyrics. Used by permission of the composer.

had been writing in this style for quite some time. Part of the songs' success lies in their sensitivity to the texts. The music is not a translation of the poem, as happens with word-painting, but rather an expressive statement of the text's meaning.

Meanwhile Johnston turned his attention to a large theatrical project, another collaboration with Wilford Leach. The occasion was a script that Leach wrote titled Gertrude, or Would She be Pleased to Receive It?[5] The characters are: Gertrude and her friend Isadora, Ernest the dog, an angel, and the announcer. Since the characters are required to sing and dance, Leach used Bertolt Brecht's technique of having the substitute singers and dancers visible on stage with the actors. The play is divided into the following five scenes:

scene 1 - "Gertrude defies the elements"
scene 2 - "The Temptation of Gertrude"
scene 3 - "Gertrude arranges a picnic" (a scene that is announced but not performed and is replaced with a Scarf Dance)
scene 4 - "The Mad Scene from 'Gertrude'"
scene 5 - "Gertrude entertains in the arboretum"

The play is a delightful spoof to which the audience continually reacts with peals of laughter. The announcer titles each scene, explaining the action and situation to the audience, but Gertrude and Isadora are unaware of the information, especially the presence of an angel and the supernatural aspect of the events that are taking place (such as a thunderstorm and later the death of Ernest the dog). In the end Gertrude never recognizes the angel (she has not been pleased to receive it--the angel), and in the future she is doomed to live alone in a house with a thousand windows. The announcer tells the audience that he is disappointed that the mystery play had no detective and no solution, but instead presented temptation and despair. Gertrude succumbed to both.

Johnston has a sparkling sense of humor and enjoys puns, often injecting them during unexpected moments of a conversation. Gertrude gave him an opportunity to display his musical humor, and he did so with style. Part of the reason he was able to do this so successfully was that since the Three Chinese Lyrics he had acquired a mastery over his materials. His music had a confidence that in Gertrude is heard as the ability to imitate different musical styles so convincingly that it is humorous, and his choice of style was perfect for the occasion and adds a further dimension to the script's character portrayal.

The instrumentation is for three flutes (one doubling on piccolo), two Bb clarinets, bassoon, percussion, guitar (this part may be performed by a harpsichord), cello, double bass, three solo voices (soprano: Isadora; contralto: Gertrude; and tenor: the Angel), and a four-part chorus.

The opera begins with an instrumental "Prelude" in F major that exaggerates the doubly dotted rhythmic gestures of the old French Overture while using several passages of secundal harmony that sound dissonant and disturbing in the tonal context of the surrounding music. The audience suspects from the sound of the "Prelude" that Gertrude will probably be a spoof but there will also be some unusual dimension to the play's events.

Musically Johnston was able to create an opera out of Leach's play. There are arias, choruses, duets, recitatives, a monologue, and a dance. (Ernest the dog performs a Scarf Dance as a spoof on the name Isadora, since the dancer Isadora Duncan was choked to death by a scarf caught in the wheels of a car. Not long after his dance Isadora has poor Ernest put to sleep because she thinks he is foaming at the mouth.) But Johnston also associated specific musical styles with each character. The Angel's aria is melismatic and in a Baroque style, as seen in Example 9, pages 32-33. Later in the last scene the Angel's musical portrayal changes, and he sings in a slow blues style while describing what he foresees as Gertrude's future, which is temptation and despair.

Since Gertrude is unaware of the nature of the events taking place, her musical style changes. A harpsichord accompanies her recitative in the first scene, making the music sound like a portion of a Baroque opera, yet the words that Gertrude sings have no relationship to the music being heard. The text is "I'm reminded of a little incident that happened to a lady I knew once who was wife to a man who worked for the plant where they take nitrogen out of the atmosphere instead of mining it in Peru where they have a good many seagulls." The situation is humorous because it is so incongruous. Earlier in the scene, when Gertrude is first introduced to the audience, she sings an aria that sounds like something Stravinsky might have written. The clear tonality of the neoclassic writing presents Gertrude as a neutral character, which, of course, she isn't.

Later Gertrude sings a duet with the Angel, and the music resembles an Elizabethan lute song. As her madness becomes more apparent Johnston has

Example 9. "The Angel's Aria" from Gertrude. Used by permission of the composer.

Gertrude sing in different styles so that towards the end of the opera she sings the blues with the chorus. This is a dramatic change from her previous Stravinsky-like and quasi-Elizabethan musical portrayals. In Example 10 the chorus is relating Gertrude's thoughts. The blues style is manifested in the vamping guitar chords, the double bass line, and the improvisatory bassoon gesture.

As a contrast to the melancholic Gertrude, Isadora is portrayed as a shallow and flamboyant person; she enjoys watching her scarves blowing in the wind and is especially fond of Gertrude's dog Ernest. However, she arranges to have Ernest killed. The irony of the situation is that her main operatic aria occurs after she destroyed the creature she loved. She sings about her memories of Ernest, saying what a good dog he was and how he preferred her to Gertrude. Johnston set this song as a simple modal da capo aria and has Isadora accompanied by a counterpoint of three flutes. The music's starkness is a damaging statement about Isadora's character and how ruthlessly she had had Ernest killed.

Isadora has another song--a "Monologue" in scene five--in which she expresses her wish to go for a ride in the country. By this time the audience realizes Gertrude's pathetic mental state, and Isadora seems unaware of what is taking place. She sings a simple little song with a melody that has shifting tonal centers and a sparse chordal accompaniment that at times is bi-tonal. The music shows that Isadora and Gertrude are living in two different worlds.

Johnston and Leach made certain that each character would have several solos. Of course, Ernest, the dog, never sings, but he dances with Isadora's scarves. Johnston's musical parody is in an exaggerated Renaissance dance style. The constantly changing meters and unequal phrase lengths match the awkward dog-like movements of the dance. The tempo marking is "Politely frantic."

The chorus has several important numbers and always sings in four-part harmony, and, like the music for the other characters, its selections change style. In Scene I they perform a Renaissance madrigal. The text is a weather report. Johnston's modal harmonies, textures, and rhythms are an imitation of Monteverdi's style, as can be seen in Example 11, page 36.

The chorus' second madrigal introduces Scene V which takes place in the arboretum. The mood is melancholic because it is a hot summer day, but there is a most unusual aspect which is explained in the text: "... it is sunset just at daybreak, just at daybreak it is sunset." Johnston used the same kind of texture as in Madrigal I, but this time the harmonies are more contemporary, such as chords of the ninth, eleventh, and thirteenth in a highly chromatic context. These dissonant sounds are meant to portray the scene's mood with its strange superimposition of daybreak and sunset. A third madrigal, which is similar to the second one, ends the opera.

Example 10. The chorus in blues style from Gertrude. Used by permission of the composer.

Example 11.   Renaissance madrigal sung by the chorus from <u>Gertrude</u>.   Used by permission of the composer.

Leach left Urbana before the opera was performed, and for a while it appeared that the performance would be cancelled, but it was finally produced. It was fortunate for Johnston that the opera was performed where his colleagues and friends could hear it, because in Gertrude he demonstrated how well he could write tunes that people remember even years later. But, more important- ly, Johnston was using the kind of stylistic borrowing and juxtaposition in Ger- trude that George Rochberg and Peter Maxwell Davies, among others, were to feature in their music of the sixties and later.[6] Gertrude has been performed in the states and Europe by La Mama, a theater company founded by Leach.

After completing Gertrude, Johnston was involved in providing incidental music for Ring 'Round the Moon, a play by Jean Anouilh which was first pre- sented in New York City in 1950. The University of Illinois production was in 1954. The script required that Johnston only compose one piece, a "Mexican Tango," which is scored for piano, violin, and cello, but he used the "Tango" to experiment with a new idea. Before writing the music he did a character analysis of the leading roles in the play, judging the main character, Lady In- dia, to be a purposeful and bullying woman while Patrice, the opposing charac- ter, was a weak, cowardly, and effeminate man. Then, Johnston decided what the expressive quality should be for each measure of the dance and devised the precompositional plan shown in Figure 1.

(A) Vamp
(B) Minor theme
    A and B represent false aggressiveness
[C] 1/2 cadence; dominant pedal; posed, artificial
(D) Stop time (dipping)
(D) Variation of (D) (crossover); the (D) sections are ritualized melodrama
(E) Major theme; false sentiment

Figure 1. Precompositional plan of expressive qualities for "Tango." Used by permission of the composer.

Johnston spent the summer of 1956 at the American Dance Festival held at Hartford, Connecticut. While there he wrote Two Dances: I of Burden and II of Mercy for Margret Dietz. These were solo piano pieces that are still in sketch form. Johnston does not consider them representative of his best work, explaining that he wrote them when there was friction among the faculty mem- bers of the dance department, and this affected his work.

While at the Dance Festival he tried to select a choreographer for Harry Partch's The Bewitched--A Dance Satire (1955), which was to be performed at the next year's Festival of Contemporary Arts. Johnston approached Martha

Graham and Doris Humphrey, but both declined the offer because Partch had a reputation of being difficult to work with. However, Humphrey recommended Alwyn Nikolais as a possible choreographer.

A busy year for Johnston was 1957.[7] Although most of the Festival Committee had never heard Partch's music, they were acquainted with Partch's book, Genesis of a Music, and were curious about his work. But there were several financial problems connected with producing The Bewitched, although the Fromm Foundation was helping to support the festival and commissioned the new pieces, including Partch's. As a solution Johnston took a personal loan with a local bank to help fund the production, hoping that the return from the ticket sales would repay the amount. Luckily it did. Johnston also helped to make all the necessary arrangements for the production. John Garvey, a member of the Walden String Quartet and the School of Music faculty, conducted the performance. There were several tense incidents during the preparation of The Bewitched when Partch threatened to cancel the performance because of his objections to Nikolais' choreography. Partch felt that Nikolais' movements were not realistic enough. He was much more pleased when the work was performed again on April 21, 1959, at the University of Illinois, and Joyce Trisler did the choreography.

During the preparations for the Partch première and after completing Gertrude, Johnston spent several years perfecting his Septet (1956-58), a piece he considers to be the summation of his neoclassic works. While creating the Septet he was able to solve some compositional problems, but at the same time he was forced to face some serious questions about the future direction of his work.

The Septet is divided into three movements and lasts thirteen minutes, a fairly long piece for Johnston. Previously he had been writing shorter compositions that depended upon movement, text, or theater for their form, so the Septet was a bold step at creating absolute music. Johnston had also been experimenting with economy of materials, and this piece was a successful attempt to make the best possible use of thematic ideas. He used a quasi-rondo form for all three movements so that sections could be repeated and extended while still maintaining cohesiveness, something that was lacking in St. Joan.

The Septet shows Johnston's mastery of traditional craftsmanship. The listener is not aware of stops or hesitations because sectional seams are hidden with elongations and elisions, often making the graceful melodic lines seem even longer than they are. Some of the music sounds like parts from Gertrude, although none of the Septet is an exact adaptation of the opera; Johnston was not ready to abandon stylistic material that had proven to be so successful.

Several characteristic melodic gestures unify the three movements. Fourths are a predominate interval--the listener often hears descending and ascending leaps outlining fourths as is shown in Example 12. The fourths are frequently filled-in and become thematic material.

Example 12. Opening measures of Septet. Used by permission of the composer.

Example 13. Baroque characteristics of melodic material in the second movement of Septet. Used by permission of the composer.

Johnston also used some neobaroque qualities, such as hammer-head figures of repeated notes and written-out ornamentation, to project the long spun-out melodies. This is especially obvious in the slower second movement (see Example 13, page 39).

Although the melodies are lyrical and well-suited to the Septet's instrumentation, again the rhythms are the piece's most interesting aspect. Many of the phrases have anacrusis gestures that produce a forward motion. The numerous ostinati create a texture that could become boring, but Johnston wrote constantly changing meters so that the ostinati were asymmetric and unpredictable (see the cello and double bass lines of Example 13). Several sections are even polymetric, as in Example 14, in which the bassoon and French horn are playing in thirds with changing meters of 4/4, 5/8, and 7/8 against the cello's and double bass's irregular ostinato notated in a 4/4 meter.

Example 14. Polymetric section from the third movement of Septet. Used by permission of the composer.

Johnston considers his Septet to be a piece that Milhaud would have liked, probably because of its modal melodies and contrapuntal textures, such as the canon at the octave in the first movement and the inverted canon in the second movement (see Example 15). This example is also bi-tonal--the flute and oboe are in F minor while the bassoon is playing in F# minor, another compositional trait of Johnston's former teacher.

The Three Chinese Lyrics, Gertrude, and the Septet were Johnston's most outstanding compositions from his beginning years at the University of Illinois.

Example 15. Canonic inversion and bi-tonality in the second movement of Septet. Used by permission of the composer.

Each piece is interesting in itself; yet all of this music was so diverse that it would have been difficult to predict at this time the future direction of his work.

Notes

1. See Silence (Middletown, CT: Wesleyan University Press, 1961), pp. 60-62.

2. For more information about Leach's work at the University of Illinois see Wilford Leach, "The Function of the Director Under the Stanislavsky System," unpublished master's thesis, University of Illinois, 1954 and "Gertrude Stein and the Modern Theatre," unpublished doctoral dissertation, University of Illinois, 1956.

3. A tape recording of this performance is available in the library archives. The score for St. Joan is xeroxed pages from Johnston's manuscript book in which the composer edited his material. No new music was written in 1958; instead, entire sections of the original manuscript are missing (for instance page one is followed by page nineteen).

4. For more information about Pound's English translations of these poems see Wai-lim Yip, Ezra Pound's Cathay (Princeton, NJ: Princeton University Press, 1969). Also Johnston was not able to hear his songs performed until

November 1957 when they were programmed as part of a Composers Forum at the Donnell Library in New York City.

5. It is possible that Leach intended his Gertrude to be some kind of portrayal of Gertrude Stein since he was studying Stein's theatrical work at that time.

6. For an excellent study of musical quotation see Michael Hicks, "On Quoting Quotations," unpublished doctoral dissertation, University of Illinois, 1984.

7. Johnston described The Bewitched in Walter Zimmermann, Desert Plants: Conversations with 23 American Musicians (Vancouver, BC: Aesthetic Research Centre of Canada, 1976), pp. 350-365.

The Septet exposed some serious problems. Johnston needed to change styles
and create an original approach. His colleague Lejaren Hiller in collaboration
with Leonard Isaacson was making history with the première of Illiac Suite for
String Quartet (1957), music composed by a computer program. There was such
a furor when Hiller's music was performed at the University of Illinois that one
of the audience members threw chairs as a rebellious statement against such music. Johnston has never been a member of the avant garde, but his dated style
of composition began to be obvious. Cage had already shocked the music world
in 1952 with 4'33", his famous silent piece, and Edgard Varèse was preparing
Poème électronique, an electronic tape piece that was premièred at the Brussels
World Fair in 1958. Johnston needed to experiment with new compositional techniques and ways to develop and extend his ideas.

These changes began to occur with Gambit (1959), a piece for dance that
was commissioned by Merce Cunningham, who was a visiting faculty member in the
Dance Department during the 1956-57 academic year. Margaret Erlanger approached Cunningham about commissioning the music for several dances. He
agreed that it was a good idea and suggested that she select two local composers. Erlanger chose Chou Wen-chung, who was a visiting faculty member in the
School of Music, and Johnston. Cunningham selected the dance's title, Gambit,
meaning a calculated move, such as a beginning strategy in chess. Johnston
was concerned that Cunningham, who often collaborated with Cage, would expect
Johnston's music to be like Cage's, and Johnston felt he could not write using
Cage's indeterminate method. Cunningham understood the concern, and all he
requested was that Johnston give him a detailed rhythmic analysis of the piece--
it was not necessary that the dancers hear the music ahead of time.

Johnston composed the score during his summer fellowship at Yaddo in
Saratoga Springs, New York. His original idea was to write three Preludes,
three Interludes, and three Postludes whose titles could be shuffled together to
determine the order of performance. Later Johnston abandoned this plan because
the dance would be too long and decided to write two Preludes, Interludes, and
Postludes that would follow the order of Prelude 1, Interlude 1, Postlude 1, and
so on. Johnston chose to use an orchestral ensemble of oboe, Bb clarinet
(doubling on Eb alto saxophone), bassoon, Bb trumpet, trombone, percussion,
guitar, piano, violin, viola, cello, and double bass. He needed to write for
larger ensembles, but this instrumentation hindered Cunningham from programming Gambit at other places. Johnston felt that the music could also be independent

from the dance, and he titled the concert version of his score Ludes for twelve instruments.

The listener notices, however, that Johnston used the ensemble awkwardly. He was still under the influence of his dance band experience, writing a Tango section in "Postlude 1" and extended passages for alto saxophone and solos for snare drum and percussion in other parts of the score. There are even several passages for guitar, but the instrumental balance is wrong and the guitar writing is too thin. Some of the movements are quite short (for instance "Interlude 1" lasts one minute and five seconds); other movements have short sections.

But Gambit marks a turning point in Johnston's musical style. Part of the piece is neoclassic (the music of "Prelude 1" sounds like an imitation of Stravinsky), while other movements are serial, such as "Interlude 1," the beginning of which resembles Anton Webern's textures and gestures. Johnston was still trying to face some compositional problems that had become apparent with the Septet.

Johnston tried using serialism with some movements of Gambit, especially "Interlude 1" (see Example 1). The alto saxophone at [A] has the first linear statement of the row, which is E D C# Eb F G F# Ab A B C Bb. It divides into four trichords having set types 013 and 024. Johnston, however, did not use the row so that these properties were audible. Instead, he used portions of it to form ostinati, such as those at three measures before [A] and two measures before [B] in Example 1. In addition, Johnston did not always follow the serial order strictly, and an extended solo drum passage interrupts the continuity, causing the listener to forget the previous serial organization.

"Prelude 2" is also serial. Its row is different--F# G# D E G F B Bb A C# C Eb--and divides into a tetrachordal pattern. There is no interruption to the serial ordering, but Johnston chose to use some notes out of order and continued to form ostinati as material for accompaniment.

The row for "Interlude 2" is similar to that used for "Prelude 2," except that the ordering of the first and last tetrachords is slightly different.

"Postlude 2," the last movement of Gambit, has some Stravinsky-like gestures, as in the beginning of "Prelude 1," but there are passages using the row from "Interlude 2." At this time Johnston was not technically proficient with serialism; he probably should have used only one row for the entire piece, and he could have made its trichordal or tetrachordal structure apparent to the listener. But this kind of organization was not a concern of his during the late 1950's.

Gambit was premièred at the 1959 Contemporary Arts Festival at the University of Illinois. Johnston remembers that Cunningham found the music difficult because it was so tight and had too specific a time scale. He claimed that dance needed to have a more rapid time scale than the music. Johnston's energetic tempi forced the dancers to move at an extremely fast speed.

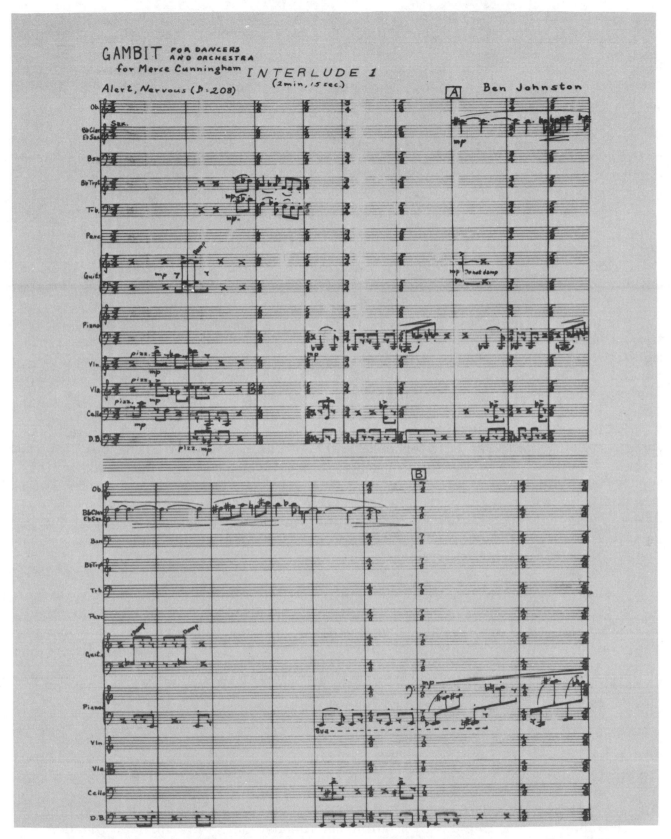

Example 1. First page of "Interlude 1" from <u>Gambit</u> showing use of serialism. Used by permission of the composer.

During this same year Johnston wrote Nine Variations for string quartet (1959), his first work for this medium, and an ensemble that he would later use for extensive experimentation with just intonation. This piece, however, was composed before Johnston felt confident about writing new tunings, so the quartet is in equal-tempered tuning, with the exception of microtonal changes produced during a cello drone.

Although the Variations and Gambit are serial, the string quartet is a much better composition. It has a focus and sense of progression because Johnston designed the piece so the listener really hears variations. The movements are short, and the ideas are so concise and economical that one must pay attention to every detail. Pitch and rhythmic motives are developed, and frequent repetitions and recapitulations clarify material. And, unlike the other works Johnston wrote in the late 1950's, there is very little stylistic borrowing, with the exception of an obvious Stravinsky-like passage in the sixth variation and other ostinato figures. Johnston quoted himself in several sections that sound like the Three Chinese Lyrics. There are extended silences that could be considered an imitation of Cage's music, but Cage, with whom Johnston was studying at that time, remarked that Johnston's use of silence differed from Cage's. Cage recommended that Johnston make several changes in the Variations. The melodies needed to be more pointillistic, and the middle variation was too short. Johnston incorporated these suggestions which improved the piece significantly.[1]

There is no theme in the Variations, but a rhythmic figure, two pitch motives, and an oscillation between calm and nervous activity form the basis of the piece's evolution. The two pitch motives are derived from the head and tail of the 12-tone row: G# A G E D# A# D B C F F# C#. The head motive (G# A G) is a half and whole step while the tail motive (C F F# C#) suggests fourths and fifths. The rhythmic figure introduced in "Variation 1" becomes prominent in variations 5, 7, and 9, and the shift between calm and nervous activity is an emotional theme that is always present.

The 12-tone row for the Variations is not combinatorial and has no particular features other than the head and tail motives discussed earlier. Johnston used all four forms but without transpositions because the head motive is consistently associated with the original pitches of G# A G. He did reorder the row several times so as to stress the tail's intervals of fourths and fifths. The Variations proceed in a systematic presentation of the rows, a reordering, and a final recapitulation of all rows as shown in Figure 1.

The opening measures of "Variation 1" clearly present the row's head motive, as heard in the first violin's prolonged G#6, the viola's A4, and finally the first violin's G6 in Example 2. The reiteration, dynamic envelop, bow changes, and silence inform the listener that the piece is highly structured, and every detail is important. Each phrase begins with a varied statement of these pitches, and the silences are filled with meaning as the listener waits to hear the next note.

Variation 1 - prime
Variation 2 - inversion
Variation 3 - retrograde-inversion
Variation 4 - retrograde
Variation 5 - inversion and retrograde-inversion
Variation 6 - reordering of row stressing fifths
Variation 7 - reordering of row stressing fourths
Variation 8 - prime
Variation 9 - all the above forms of the row

Figure 1.   Row forms used in <u>Nine Variations</u>.

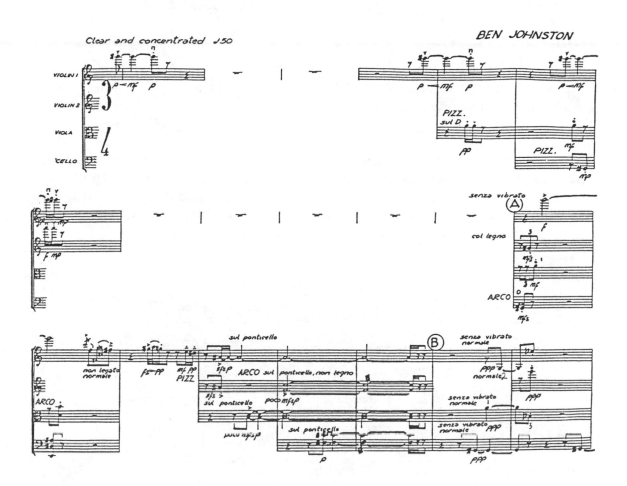

Example 2.   Beginning measures of "Variation 1" showing head motive.   Copyright 1985 by Smith Publications.   Used with permission.

"Variation 3" presents the retrograde-inversion form of the row which introduces the tail motive of fourths and fifths.   The beginning phrase states these intervals which are then repeated as a fused staccato chord (see

Example 3). Johnston was careful to ensure that the listener has an opportunity to hear and understand how the piece is working.

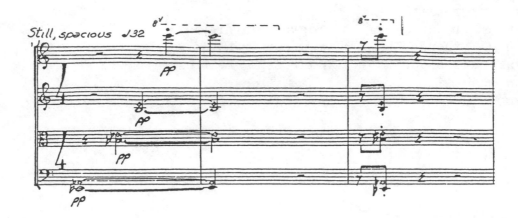

Example 3. Beginning measures of "Variation 3" showing tail motive. Copyright 1985 by Smith Publications. Used with permission.

Later, in "Variation 4," both the head and tail motive are emphasized in an "Appassionata" passage using repeated ostinati in which the first violin and cello are in canon with each other, the first violin having the head and tail motive of the retrograde form of the row while the cello performs the tail and head of the retrograde inversion (see Example 4).

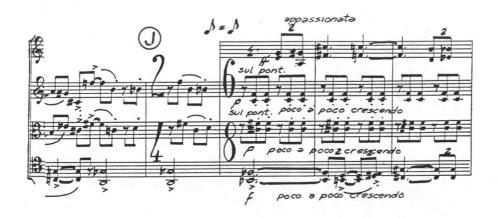

Example 4. Head and tail motives used canonically in "Variation 4." Copyright 1985 by Smith Publications. Used with permission.

The rhythmic motive introduced in "Variation 1" as three grace notes formed from the tail motive (see Example 2, page 47) becomes a five-note group in "Variation 4." This grouping is noticeable due to the pattern of loudly articulated eighth notes at the beginning of "Variation 4," and the fiveness becomes even more apparent in "Variation 5," where five is set as polyrhythms in the proportions of 5:1, 5:2, 5:3, and 5:4 (see Example 5). The rhythmic motive is changed to a seven-note arpeggio figure that highlights the quartal qualities of "Variation 7," and the arpeggio is elongated to include seven and sometimes nine notes in "Variation 9," in which the figure consistently reiterates the head motive of G♯ A G.

Example 5. Uses of the rhythmic motive in <u>Variations</u>. Copyright 1985 by Smith Publications. Used with permission.

There is also an emotional motive of opposing calmness and nervousness that groups the odd-numbered and even-numbered variations together. This can be seen and heard in the expressive markings that head each variation. Also, the odd-numbered "calm" variations are consistently longer than their more active neighbors (see Figure 2, page 50).

Since the <u>Variations</u> were written in 1959, the tempi and durations were not proportional (Johnston began to experiment with temporal proportionality in 1962 with <u>Knocking Piece</u>), but the expressive and emotional contrasts represent

Variation 1 - Clear and concentrated ♩ = 50 (2'36")

Variation 2 - Sharp ♩ = 160 (32")

Variation 3 - Still, spacious ♩ = 32 (3'8")

Variation 4 - Impetuous ♩ = 192 (45")

Variation 5 - Fluid, pulsating ♩ = 64 (2'17")

Variation 6 - Assertive ♪ = 228 (1'10")

Variation 7 - Rather ominous ♩ = 56 (1'36")

Variation 8 - Nervous, driving ♪ = 288 (48")

Variation 9 - Minute, atmospheric ♩ = 44 (2'36")

Figure 2. Expressive markings, tempo, and duration in Nine Variations.

aspects that had been developing since his early songs and music for theater and dance. It is almost as if each variation were a character or personality that Johnston was trying to portray, much like the pre-compositional plan that he made for the "Mexican Tango," the incidental music for Ring 'Round the Moon. This emotional contrast is even more apparent in Sonata for Microtonal Piano/ Grindlemusic. Johnston's music is sparse but concentrated; and because of this and the motivic use of serialism and rhythmic figures, the Nine Variations are the most Webernesque of all his early works.

Johnston resisted the temptation to pursue totally this style of writing. If he was going to use serialism, then he wanted to relate this system to various aspects of his musical interests. He had an opportunity to do so when John Garvey, director of the jazz bands at the University of Illinois, requested that Johnston compose some music for the band's yearly tour. Johnston wrote two pieces, Ivesberg Revisited (1960) and Newcastle Troppo (1960). Both use serialism but in the context of various scale forms, improvisation, and quotation.

Ivesberg Revisited is a passacaglia on the theme "Yesterdays" by Jerome Kern. Its five variations feature Kern's melody but surrounded with a mixture of chromatic and whole-tone scales, two-tone rows (one of them a serialized bass line that Johnston derived from the famous row that begins Alban Berg's Violinkonzert), klangfarben passages, and sections recalling Charles Ives' Fourth Symphony in which Ives quotes well-known material. The Ives and Berg quotations explain the significance of Johnston's title--Ivesberg Revisited. Musically I do not find this piece successful because there are too many diverse elements,

but Ivesberg Revisited is an experiment with the possibility of combining serialism with other material within a jazz style. Several aspects of the piece are pre-
cursors of future directions that Johnston would use. Quotations are important
in Sonata for Microtonal Piano/Grindlemusic (1965) and "Ci-Gît Satie" (1967).
Serialism becomes an organizational procedure in his early use of just intonation,
especially String Quartets Numbers 2 and 3.

Newcastle Troppo is a set of variations on Cole Porter's tune, "What is this
thing called love?" This composition sounds more like a piece for jazz band because Johnston provided opportunities for improvisation. The title is a pun re-
ferring to "carrying coals to Newcastle," a coal-mining area (thus a pun on Cole
Porter's name) and troppo means "too much." Some of the lines are serial in the
sense that a collection of twelve notes is used with no note out of order, but the
collections themselves are not used serially. Johnston intended that both pieces
would convey a message to the audience. In program notes he stated:

> The surface of these pieces is double-exposed. Both are "big band
> arrangements" of standard pop tunes in a style reminiscent of the last
> great heyday of big jazz bands in the U.S., the period of World War II
> and just after. At the same time these pieces comment critically upon
> what they seem to be, insisting, for instance, upon a tension between
> "40's" jazz harmonies and serially derived pitch structures. Ivesberg
> evokes the ghosts of Ives and Berg, not only in its ambivalent tonal
> language, but also in its obsession with musical quotations. The tune
> is Jerome Kern's Yesterdays. Newcastle is so called because it is based
> upon Cole Porter's What Is This Thing Called Love? Its musical com-
> ment should be hard to miss.

After composing Ivesberg Revisited and Newcastle Troppo Johnston was
still searching for his musical identity. Later, in Sonata for Microtonal Piano/
Grindlemusic he would use quotations to a greater extent, but in 1961 he was
continuing to experiment with serialism.

During this year he wrote the incidental music for Mary Arbenz's production of The Taming of the Shrew at the University of Illinois. Only one piece
was needed, and Johnston was not given much advance notice, so the music is
not serial. Instead, he wrote in a neoclassic style similar to that used in the
Septet. He knew the piece would work. It was scored for oboe, trumpet, guitar, string bass, and percussion.

During the same year he composed Sonata for Two (1961) for violin and
cello, a strange piece that combines serialism, tonality, and improvisation. It is
in four movements; the second and fourth movements are serial but use different
rows. The first movement is motivic and tonal. Melodic gestures are repeated
and then expanded in a textural setting similar to the string writing in the
Three Chinese Lyrics. The listener hears an exposition, development, and recapitulation. The varied rhythmic groupings of 2, 3, and 4 resemble Johnston's
other neoclassic writing (see Example 6, page 52).

Example 6. Beginning measures of first movement of <u>Sonata for Two</u>. Copyright 1984 by Smith Publications. Used with permission.

The second movement is marked "Slow, Concentrated" and its row of B D C# A# C E G D# F# A F G# features minor thirds much like the row of the <u>Etude</u> for piano (1949). This movement gave Johnston an opportunity to further experiment with expressive string writing using timbral nuances to create sections of fused timbres as the beginning measures in Example 7, and then contrapuntal melodic lines. At no time did Johnston feel bound by the traditions of serialism or by a pre-existing plan that had to be rigidly followed. The row was an initial idea that needed shaping and could be modified when necessary, as happens during the middle section of this movement.

Example 7. Beginning measures of the second movement of <u>Sonata</u>. Copyright 1984 by Smith Publications. Used with permission.

The <u>Sonata</u>'s third movement is titled "Game" and is an improvisation. The performers are given scale patterns, meters, and suggested rhythmic figures, some of which are designed to result in metric modulation. Detailed instructions explain how to prepare for the improvisation, but all of this information suppresses spontaneity. This was Johnston's first attempt to include improvisation, and he agrees with me that it was a mistake. The previous music was so carefully written that the improvisation sounds out of place. Johnston's idea was that the improvisation would be the scherzo, which suggested to him a sense of play or a game. Other composers were trying this idea of incorporating improvisation in a section of a structured piece, as in Pauline Oliveros's Outline for Flute, Percussion, and String Bass (1963) and Robert Erickson's Chamber Concerto (1960). The Oliveros piece was not too successful, however, and only exceptional performers can make the improvisation work in Erickson's Concerto.

The last movement of Johnston's Sonata returns to serialism and uses a different row of Bb A C B D C# E Eb Gb F Ab G, an all-combinatorial row. It is easy to follow since Johnston primarily used the original version and its retrograde in various kinds of canons. The movement ends with a recapitulation of its beginning, a frequent trait in Johnston's serial music.

Johnston's Duo for Flute and String Bass (1963) was written after he had begun to use just intonation; however, this piece is in equal temperament and serialism is its main interest. Microtones serve only as decorative inflections and are notated graphically (as shown in the flute part of measures 1 and 2 of Example 8). The piece was commissioned by Bert Turetzky, double bass player, and his wife, Nancy, who plays flute.

Turetzky is well known for his interest in extended playing techniques and

Prelude (I)

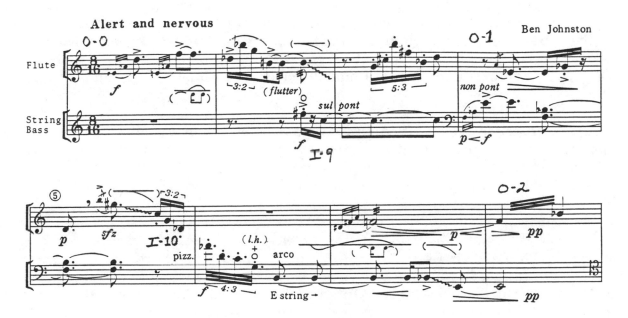

Example 8. Beginning measures of "Prelude" from Duo for Flute and String Bass. Copyright © 1976 by McGinnis & Marx. Reprinted by permission.

unusual timbres for the double bass, which many composers have featured in works commissioned by him,[2] but Johnston used this commission to experiment further with serialism, having combinatoriality unify Duo's three short movements--"Prelude (I)," "Interim (II)," and "Flight (III)." These neoclassic titles suggest a traditional use of serialism. Unlike earlier serial pieces, all of the pitch material in Duo is serial. In the liner notes to the Advance recording of Duo Johnston states: "The pitch organization ... [is] based on twelve-tone rows made up of combinatorial hexachords. The two rows used in the outer movements are both shown, during the second movement, to be derived from a simpler row composed of symmetrically arranged segments."[3]

The basic row is Db C A G# B Bb Eb D E F G F#, an all-combinatorial row. However, this is not the true row for the piece. The rows for the three movements and their derivations from the basic row are shown in Figure 3.

"Prelude" consists of six phrases that are clearly perceived because each phrase begins with the grace note figure which appears in measure one of Example 8, page 53). However, the phrases do not coincide with the beginnings of row statements, although the listener is definitely aware that there is a systematic control of pitch.

The row for "Prelude" (Eb Ab D E A F Db Bb G B F# C) is a semi-combinatorial row that produces its complement at I-9. Johnston divided the row into trichords and used ten versions of the row (O-0; O-1; O-2; O-10; O-11; I-7; I-8; I-9; I-10; I-11) in this short piece of thirty-six measures. The transpositions were chosen because together they constitute a chromatic series (0-1-2-3-4-5-6-7-8) whose hexachord (0-1-2-3-4-5) is the structure of the basic row. The rows of "Prelude" are presented so that there are varying conjunctions between their beginnings and endings, thus suggesting a network of commonly shared trichords, but this is only the case with two transpositions, 1-6-0 of O-1 equaling the ending trichord of I-9 and 2-7-1 of O-2 equaling the ending trichord of I-10.

Although the piece is titled Duo, which suggests an equality between the two instruments, the flute part is more prominent, especially in the two outer movements. Johnston probably gave the majority of the pitch material to the flute so that his serial plan could be more clearly distinguished.

This, however, is not the case with the second movement, "Interim," since the basic row is created by equal action between the two instruments. The functional row is Db C D Eb F# G A G# B E Bb F. Two tetrachords are chromatic, and the third suggests fourths and fifths, important harmonic intervals in both the second and third movements. "Interim" is especially interesting because the row ordering is not obvious. There are several possible interpretations, such as canonic action between the two instruments, simultaneous hexachords performed as a duo which produces the basic row, or a linear and timbral presentation of tetrachords, but only the above row sufficiently explains the piece's pitch action.

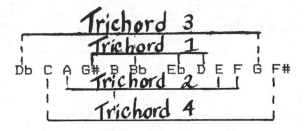

Row for the First Movement

Eb Ab D E A F Db Bb G B F# C

Relationship to the Basic Row

Trichord 3
Trichord 1
Db C A G# B Bb Eb D E F G F#
Trichord 2
Trichord 4

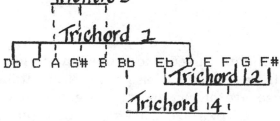

Row for the Second Movement

Db C D Eb F# G A G# B E Bb F

Relationship to the Basic Row

Trichord 3
Trichord 1
Db C A G# B Bb Eb D E F G F#
Trichord 2
Trichord 4

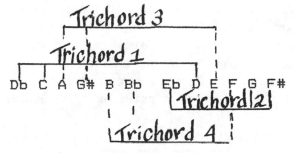

Row for the Third Movement

Db D C Eb F# G A G# E B Bb F

Relationship to the Basic Row

Trichord 3
Trichord 1
Db C A G# B Bb Eb D E F G F#
Trichord 2
Trichord 4

Figure 3. Row relationships in Duo.

Interim (II)

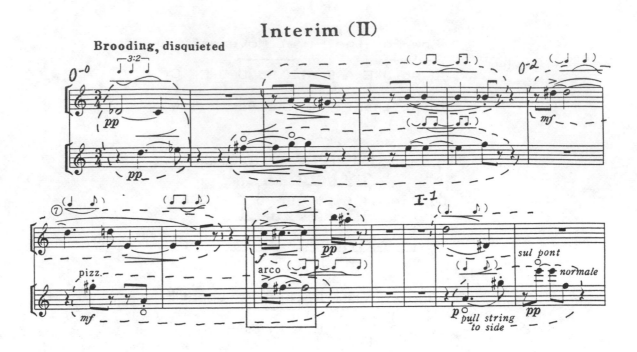

Example 9. "Interim" from Duo. Copyright© 1976 by McGinnis & Marx. Reprinted by permission.

Example 9 shows how Johnston used microtonal inflections as nuances which define the row. Also, there are four times when the pitches C G C# F# are heard as simultaneities. These are an important feature that occurs in four of the seven versions used. The rows are marked in Example 9, and the simultaneity is boxed.

"Interim" also has a durational scheme. The individual gestures are dyads that contain an obvious long-short or short-long figure. Various durations are used, such as four to one (♩♪), three to one (♩.♪), three to two (♩.♩), and so on, with only a few durations repeated, but there is no specific pattern. Even the period form (there are three periods with each separated by two measure rests) observes the long-short, short-long plan with the first period dividing into two phrases of five and four measures respectively; the second period has four measures and six measure phrases; and the last period has two phrases of two and three measures each. Periods one and two form a ratio of 5/4 and 2/3 while periods two and three form the ratio of 2/1, familiar ratios in just intonation.

"Flight" is fast and virtuosic with a tempo marking of "headlong," a frequent movement in many of Johnston's previous works, such as Three Chinese Lyrics. The row, Db D C Eb F# G A G# E B Bb F, is derived from a reading of the combined flute and double bass lines of "Interim." There are several examples where the tempo increases by a ratio of 3/2, but these changes are elementary. "Flight" divides into two sections with an interlude between them

Flight (III)

Example 10. Beginning measures of "Flight." Copyright © 1976 by McGinnis & Marx. Reprinted by permission.

*) Play exactly as if beginning a typical Da Capo

Example 11. Ending measures of "Flight." Copyright © 1976 by McGinnis & Marx. Reprinted by permission.

and an ending cadenza shared by both instruments. The cadenza recalls previous material, elaborating upon the fifths that were used in "Interim," stating the beginning measures of "Prelude," and recapitulating the first three measures of "Flight." The piece has an unfinished feeling because the recapitulation suggests a Da Capo that does not take place. These repeated gestures are easily recognized, and it is almost as if the piece ends with a deceptive cadence (see Examples 10 and 11, page 57).

For Johnston serialism was not a strong compositional aesthetic. He used the system because it was a technique that he needed to study, and composing was the best learning method for him. Serialism was an interim interest while he was preparing to write in just intonation.

Notes

1. Johnston remembers that most of Cage's suggestions concerned the use of time. This was especially true of a jazz piece, Diversions for Four, that Johnston was writing for Gunther Schuller at that time. Cage said the piece needed to be longer, and since Johnston did not have time to complete the composition, Schuller never premièred it. Diversions for Four was premièred at Northwestern University on November 19, 1983, and Johnston agreed with my comment that the piece was too short, remarking that this was the same criticism that Cage had made. Johnston does not include this piece in his catalog.

2. For more information about new techniques for the double bass see Bertram Turetzky, The Contemporary Contrabass (Berkeley, CA: University of California Press, 1974). Turetzky discusses many of the pieces that he commissioned; however, he does not mention Johnston's Duo.

3. Advance Recordings, FGR-1.

5 • EXPERIMENTS IN JUST INTONATION

In 1959 Johnston received tenure in the School of Music at the University of Illinois, and his sabbatical year, which followed the tenure decision, marked an important development in his career--it was time for him to begin composing in just intonation, the tuning system that Partch used.

Since he was eleven years old Johnston had been concerned about pitch integrity, and his own good sense of hearing told him that equal temperament's consonants were not accurate. The tuning adjustments which make all half steps equal create beating dissonances (a grayness associated with all consonants other than the octave, the only true consonant in the 12-tone temperament). Perfect fifths are flat, and major thirds are too wide. Johnston's work with Partch showed what it was like to use acoustically pure intervals.

Tuning has been a historical problem, and various tuning systems which produce microtones have appealed to some twentieth-century theorists and composers. One solution is the multiple division of the octave into 24, 36, or 48 pitches through equal temperament of some interval, such as dividing a semi-tone into two, three, or four parts. The result preserves equal temperament's scales and adds microtonal pitches that can be decorative or expressive, as in some compositions by Charles Ives and Alois Hába.[1] Ferruccio Busoni advocated dividing the whole tone into six equal parts producing a 36-tone temperament,[2] and Julián Carrillo experimented with dividing the whole tone into as many as sixteen equal parts. During the early 1930's Joseph Yasser studied the structural changes of scales in many musical cultures and concluded that equal temperament should be extended to include 19 tones per octave (12 + 7) using a tuning system based upon a tempered fifth which is 7 cents flatter than a pure fifth.[3] Adriaan Fokker, a Dutch physicist, worked to establish a 31-tone temperament,[4] and there is a group of musicians in the Netherlands which promotes music for this temperament.

The theorists David Krachenbuehl and Christopher Schmidt have studied the history of consonance and dissonance, and their research resulted in speculations about the evolutionary development of chromatic (12-degree), hyperchromatic (22-degree), ultrachromatic (41-degree), and microchromatic (78-degree) pitch systems using the prime numbers of 3, 5, 7, 11, 13.[4A]

Kraehenbuehl and Schmidt first examined Pythagoreanism (a 2, 3 system because the tuning is based upon octaves and fifths) which is presumed to be the tuning used during the Middle Ages. Its pure fifth (3/2) produces a major third (81/64) that is too large for triadic music's harmonious interval of 5/4. Lower numbered proportions indicate simpler relations heard as a greater degree of consonance. The 81/64 ratio explains why at one time this large third was considered a dissonance. Kraehenbuehl and Schmidt suggest that gradually, as thirds were used melodically, they were retuned as acceptable consonances (5/4), and accompanying this change was a new tuning system using the prime numbers 2, 3, 5. Just intonation, the 2, 3, 5 system, includes the major third (5/4) as a consonant interval and a harmonic ingredient of triadic music.

Historically, there have been serious problems with just intonation which caused the system to be generally abandoned. One difficulty is that the fifth from D to A (using a C major scale in just intonation) is not a 3/2 ratio but 40/27, a fifth that is 22 cents flat and unacceptable as the fifth of a supertonic triad. Johnston's solution is to enlarge the scale to at least 53 tones per octave (see Figure 2 in Chapter 6) to accommodate multiple diatonic pitches for tuning purposes by using a + to raise a pitch 22 cents. This inflection is a comma. Thus, there are two A's--A for the third of a sub-dominant triad and A+ for the fifth of a supertonic triad--and other inflected pitches, so that correct fifths are maintained. The scale includes C+ C#+ Cx+ D+ E+ F+ F#+ Fx+ G+ A+ A#+ Ax+ B+ and can be enlarged to contain an infinite number of pitches, such as D#+ and G#+. These relationships invert for fifths that are tuned below, such as the sub-dominant triad of F, and are represented by a minus (Bb-) that, again, maintains triadic purity. The - lowers a pitch by 22 cents. Johnston's 53-tone scale also includes Dbb- Db- D- Eb- E- F- Gbb- Gb- G- Ab- A- Bbb- Bb- B- C-. Twenty-eight of the 53 tones are commas.

This procedure may be clarified by an explanation of the pitch and ratio lattices that Johnston uses when he composes (see Figure 1).

The lattices show how pitches are related by fifths (columns) and thirds (rows). Notice that a fifth above D requires the addition of a + (the syntonic comma), making the correct pitch A+. Similarly, the fifth below F is Bb- and would be used for the triad Bb- D- F. Bb- is lower than Bb (which is one block west of D on the lattice), and Bb D F would not be the pure beatless consonance that is the basis for just intonation because not all members of the triad are adjacent to each other on the lattice.[4B] (Adjacency is either a 3/2 or a 5/4 ratio.) Thus, the performer must think and hear harmonically in a manner which is somewhat analogous to the skills that jazz musicians develop for realizing chord symbols. Problems arise when instruments of fixed pitch, such as woodwinds, try to play in just intonation. In this case they must find alternate fingerings that produce the necessary pitch adjustments. It is much easier for singers, string players, and some brass players to achieve the correct tunings by ear.

Another criticism of just intonation is that modulation is not possible because no interval can be divided equally. Enharmonic pitches do not exist; B# does not equal C. Deriving the chromatic scale involves a history of controversy that Partch has documented.[4C] Johnston's solution is included in his 53-tone scale,

Ab+	C+	E+	G#+	B#+	$\frac{81}{50}$	$\frac{81}{80}$	$\frac{81}{64}$	$\frac{405}{256}$	$\frac{2025}{1024}$
Db	F+	A+	C#+	E#+	$\frac{27}{25}$	$\frac{27}{20}$	$\frac{27}{16}$	$\frac{135}{128}$	$\frac{675}{512}$
Gb	Bb	D	F#+	A#+	$\frac{36}{25}$	$\frac{9}{5}$	$\frac{9}{8}$	$\frac{45}{32}$	$\frac{225}{128}$
Cb	Eb	G	B	D#	$\frac{48}{25}$	$\frac{6}{5}$	$\frac{3}{2}$	$\frac{15}{8}$	$\frac{75}{64}$
Fb	Ab	C	E	G#	$\frac{32}{25}$	$\frac{8}{5}$	$\frac{1}{1}$	$\frac{5}{4}$	$\frac{25}{16}$
Bbb-	Db-	F	A	C#	$\frac{128}{75}$	$\frac{16}{15}$	$\frac{4}{3}$	$\frac{5}{3}$	$\frac{25}{24}$
Ebb-	Gb-	Bb-	D-	F#	$\frac{256}{225}$	$\frac{64}{45}$	$\frac{16}{9}$	$\frac{10}{9}$	$\frac{25}{18}$
Abb-	Cb-	Eb-	G-	B-	$\frac{1024}{675}$	$\frac{256}{135}$	$\frac{32}{27}$	$\frac{40}{27}$	$\frac{50}{27}$
Dbb--	Fb-	Ab-	C-	E-	$\frac{2048}{2025}$	$\frac{512}{405}$	$\frac{128}{81}$	$\frac{160}{81}$	$\frac{100}{81}$

Figure 1. Pitch and ratio lattices for a 2, 3, 5 system in just intonation.

which contains twenty-five chromatic pitches (the standard twelve plus thirteen other pitches replacing the enharmonicity of equal temperament). The accidentals, # and b raise or lower a pitch by 25/24 or 70 cents, and x and bb raise or lower a pitch by 140 cents. These accidentals plus the syntonic comma of + or − make it possible to tune any fifth (3/2), just major third (5/4), just minor third (5/3), and their inversions. The lattice in Figure 1 can be extended infinitely in either direction using the notation described above.

These exact pitches placed in specific harmonic contexts make any modulation possible theoretically. Modulations that are located within adjacent areas of the lattice, however, are easier to perform because fifths and thirds are available as tuning aids. These modulations are apparent to the listener (see the discussion about Sonnets of Desolation in Chapter 9), whereas modulations in equal temperament are frequently difficult to recognize and identify, an experience that is all too familiar to aural skills teachers. Johnston often writes passages that travel up and down a lattice through a series of fifths, and to someone familiar with just intonation, these passages in tonal music indicate modulations, or, in the case of serial music, they indicate a transposition or change in a tone row.

Partch worked with this system, and he solved the obvious problems of retuning instruments and instructing performers by creating his own instruments, replacing traditional notation with a system of ratios, and training a small group of musicians to perform his music. He extended consonance to include proportions using 7 and 11. The septimal minor third of 7/6 is smaller than the 6/5 just minor third but still a consonance, and 11/9 is a small-number proportion producing a major third that is smaller than the just major third of 5/4. These intervals are not available in equal temperament, and extended just intonation using systems including the 7th, 11th, and 13th partials will be explained in more detail in later chapters. One of the advantages of just intonation is that any interval is possible because tuning is based upon a continuum of ratios.

It was the correctness of just intonation that appealed to Partch and Johnston.[5] Both knew that a composer using a different tuning system must work in isolation and have a courage of conviction that would be a support through many difficulties. For Johnston, correcting the acoustical lie of equal temperament was almost a religious issue. His solution would be to use just intonation within the context of western European musical heritage. Johnston needed to develop his own theories about just intonation and to design a notational system that expressed exact pitch ratios.

He decided that electronic music would be the best way for him to work with just intonation's scales and microtones, since, unlike Partch, Johnston felt no inclination to build instruments. Also, the University of Illinois had just established its own Electronic Music Studio, and he wanted to acquire the necessary skills for working in that medium.

Johnston was particularly interested in using a synthesizer that Milton

Babbitt was having installed at the Columbia-Princeton Electronic Music Center. Theoretically, precise pitch control could be obtained with oscillators, and Johnston hoped to produce various scales tuned in just intonation. He needed an instrument so he could test the accuracy of his ear with respect to pitch relations based upon the overtone series.[5A] It had been almost ten years since he had worked with Partch's instruments, and even that had only been for a period of six months.

Therefore, Johnston applied for and received a Guggenheim Fellowship to work at the Columbia-Princeton Music Center where he would be able to study with theorist Edward Cone and with Vladimir Ussachevsky and Otto Luening, pioneers in the field of electronic music. Getting the grant was not an easy task. Some of the faculty at the University of Illinois who should have been supportive of Johnston and his microtonal project were not and refused to write letters of recommendation.

Previously, after first meeting Cage in 1952, Johnston had considered applying for a Fulbright Fellowship to study at Pierre Schaeffer's Studio des Recherches de la Musique Concrète in Paris. This was the studio in which Schaeffer and his associates were working with the taped environmental sounds of musique concrète. Johnston had a similar plan for trying to realize microtones electronically. However, the Fulbright would probably have meant giving up his job at the University of Illinois (he did not have tenure at that time), and since he and Betty wanted to raise a family, it did not seem wise to leave the Champaign-Urbana area.

But when the Guggenheim Fellowship became available, the entire Johnston family moved to New York City for a year even though a third child was expected.

There was another reason why the Johnstons wanted to be in the New York area. Both Ben and Betty were interested in Gurdjieff's teachings (Gurdjieff claimed to possess spiritual wisdom from the East that was unknown in the West), and there was a Gurdjieff Foundation in New York City where they could study. Working with the proper teacher was considered essential if one were to progress spiritually. The Johnstons studied with Christopher Freemantle and Mrs. Louise Welch. Part of the attraction of the previously considered Fulbright study in Paris had been the opportunity to attend the Gurdjieff Institute at Château Prieure in Avon near Fontainebleau. Johnston had been attracted to the writings of Gurdjieff and P. D. Ouspensky (one of Gurdjieff's famous followers) about time.

However, the plans for the Guggenheim Fellowship did not work out exactly as Johnston had hoped. First, the Columbia-Princeton Electronic Music Center was not completed, and Babbitt, who was coordinator, did not like the idea of having visitors using the synthesizer. This was disappointing for Johnston, and when he spoke to Cage about the situation, Cage mentioned that it was unfortunate that Johnston hadn't proposed to work at Richard Maxfield's electronic music studio at The New School in New York City. Apparently Cage felt Maxfield would be more sympathetic to Johnston's project. As an alternative solution Cage recommended that Johnston study with him. This was agreeable, and Johnston described their working sessions in the following interview with Cole Gagne and Tracy Caras, "I would drive up there [Stony Point] once a month. It was really very valuable. He [Cage] didn't stop me from doing what I was doing; he simply criticized--and very perceptively--what I was doing.... He didn't try to push me in the direction of his work."[6]

One thing Johnston did learn as a result of his Fellowship was that his aptitudes were not suited to electronic music. Later, in 1972, he and Ed Kobrin, a specialist in computer music, tried to establish a computer program to determine various scales tuned in just intonation. This research is documented in an article "Phase 1A" published in Source[7]; however, Johnston never used the computer compositionally.

Having returned from his year in New York City, Johnston was faced with an artistic dilemma--electronics would not be his medium for microtonality, so the only solution was to use conventional instruments and to devise a notational system which would require musicians to produce the kind of tunings he heard.

Eventually the string quartet would be his most successful medium, but meanwhile Johnston was also working with serial techniques and found that it was possible to combine serialism with microtonality. Five Fragments (1960) for alto singer, oboe, cello, and bassoon with texts from Henry Thoreau's Walden was the first composition Johnston wrote combining microtones and serialism. However, the piece sounds more serial than microtonal with its pointillistic vocal line and repeating interval patterns. As in the Septet, the row is all-combinatorial (D B D# F# Fx+ A#+ C# A+ C+ E+ Ab+ F+), but the piece does not make use of these properties. Instead, the trichords feature tunings of just major and minor thirds (convenient intervals for just intonation), and Johnston inverted, permuted, and repeated the trichords as he wished. See Example 1 where the trichords are circled. Notice the notation of double sharps, pluses, and minuses.

Unfortunately the choice of oboe and bassoon added performance difficulties to an already challenging piece because these reed instruments must make fine tuning adjustments in order to maintain the ratios required of just intonation. However, Johnston's colleagues Sanford Berry (bassoonist) and Blaine Edlefsen (oboist) were willing to experiment with locating the required tunings, and the score includes their fingering charts showing how to produce the necessary pitches. The following preface is also included to provide the musicians with some explanation of the pitch notation.

PITCH NOTATION AND USAGE

This music is to be played in just intonation, which means that perfect

FIVE FRAGMENTS

text from Thoreau's WALDEN

by BEN JOHNSTON

Example 1. Trichords used in the beginning lines of Five Fragments. Copyright 1975 by Smith Publications. Used with permission.

unisons, octaves, fifths and fourths, and major and minor thirds and sixths are to be played as free from beats as possible. The term "just intonation," which has been used to designate keyboard tunings necessitating a fixed scale is here used to designate a mutable tuning reflected in the notation (see below). The type of just intonation here used presumes the consonant intervals to be those of triadic music (perfect primes, octaves, fifths and fourths, major and minor thirds and sixths). All other intervals, traditionally considered dissonances, result from the adding and subtracting of consonant intervals. For each note in this piece a triadic reference is present either in melodic or harmonic context, with few exceptions. The exceptions are scalar passages, where segments of just-tuned major scales are the basis.

The notation shows which intervals are consonant, in the following manner: A, B, C, D, E, F, G (uninflected) refer to tuning of Just Intonation C-Major Scale (F, A, C; C, E, G; G, B, D are just triads, in ratios 4:5:6). The accidentals # and b, which raise and lower, respectively, by 70 cents, are joined by the additional accidentals + and -, which raise and lower, respectively, by 22 cents. The latter are used primarily to keep just consonances (octaves, unisons, perfect fifths, perfect fourths, major thirds, minor thirds, major sixths and minor sixths) in tune (without acoustical beats). In all but a few cases, simultaneous intervals notated as consonances (not their enharmonic "equivalents") and inflected similarly by accidentals, should be acoustically consonant. The exceptions are: F's or A's tuned to D's are notated F+ or A+; Bb's or D's tuned to F's are notated Bb- or D-; F's or A's tuned to D+'s are notated F++ or A++, etc; Bb's or D's tuned to F-'s are notated B-- or D--, etc; these procedures are not different when sharps or flats are present.

The second of the Five Fragments is for voice and oboe. The voice uses the same row as the "first fragment" but the tuning is different. The F#+ is higher than F#; Fx becomes G; A# is replaced by Bb; C# is Db; and the last trichord remains the same. Although these changes in notation cause pitch differences, they do not affect Johnston's use of serial technique. Serially the two rows are identical because the same pitch classes are represented. The oboe accompanies the voice with an instrumental line that uses a freer and quasi-12-tone row that frequently outlines triads to help maintain tuning stability.

The "third fragment" is not serial, but five trichords (023; 013; 012; 034; 024) are used as cells that are frequently transposed. These cells have the same structure as the row so that the movement maintains a similar interval patterning.

The "fourth fragment," for voice and bassoon, freely combines both trichords and tetrachords. The voice has collections 0235, 025, 0245 during this short movement while the bassoon creates a slow palindrome using the trichord 012. Its pattern in tempered notation is B B# C# D Db C B C Db D Db C B but the sound is much more interesting in just intonation (B B# C# D- Db-- C- B- C Db- D Db C B) in which the only identical pitches are the beginning and endings B's.

Johnston returned to serialism for the last fragment, which is for the entire ensemble. The row uses the same trichordal structure of 034 and 014 as the first movement, but more than four trichords are often heard before the row is completed because each phrase of the text uses one row.

Johnston's row technique in Five Fragments was more sophisticated than in such earlier pieces as Gambit, in which he only used a row for selected movements and even confused the serialism more by employing different rows in the same piece. Gambit's stylistic changes and neoclassic setting tended to aurally disguise the serialism, whereas the Five Fragments sound ordered. This is particularly noticeable in the beginning solo vocal line's jagged contours (see Example 1, page 65), which suggest serialism.

The consistent trichordal patterning emphasizing major and minor thirds is a unifying factor that is present in all the movements of the Five Fragments. Later Johnston would direct more conscious efforts towards integrating different elements of a composition by means of the same controlling factor. However, the most significant feature of Five Fragments is the just intonation.

Johnston could accurately hear this lattice because the tuning in thirds and fifths was the same system Partch had used; however Johnston was inexperienced with composing in just intonation at the time of Five Fragments. (Most of his writing since then has been for singers and stringed instruments.) The

beginning vocal solo (see Example 1) is demanding since the singer has no accompanying instrument from which to hear and tune pitches. Instead, tuning
must be done linearly. Now he would hesitate to begin a composition with long
solo passages.

During the early 1960's Johnston assumed more responsibilities in the
School of Music. In 1961 he was asked to chair the Festival of Contemporary
Arts planning committee. This meant that he would be responsible for the 1963
and 1965 Festivals. He agreed to serve for five years. This was an exciting
and influential position. There were sufficient funds to plan and execute a 1963
Festival that included lectures by Pierre Boulez and Edward Cone, a concert performed by the Hartt Chamber Players, a session about improvisation and indeterminacy, a jazz program performed by the Eric Dolphy Quartet and the University
of Illinois Jazz Band conducted by John Garvey, a recital of contemporary organ
music performed by Marilyn Mason, and various concerts given by School of Music
ensembles.

Although these responsibilities were demanding, Johnston continued to experiment with just intonation. In 1962 he wrote A Sea Dirge for mezzo-soprano,
flute, violin, and oboe. The text, from Shakespeare's Tempest, is the song sung
by Ariel, the spirit who attends Prospero during his exile on an enchanted island.
Johnston chose the text because he liked it, and he is always careful to only
select literature or poetry that he considers to be strong and proven works.

A Sea Dirge is easier to perform than Five Fragments because there are
several improvements for the singer.[8] She is always accompanied by an instrument that provides a tuning pitch, and although the song is serial, the vocal
line is usually independent of the serial process (see Example 2, page 68).

The row is all combinatorial (F E D# G# G F#+ A#+ B A C D C#+), but
because of the just intonation the ratios between the half steps are not all the
same size--they are either 15/16 or 24/25. Johnston used the row trichordally,
as shown in Example 2, in which the trichords are circled. Notice that the
singer has the first eight pitches of a freely varied row which is completed in
the violin line in measures three and four while the oboe, violin, and flute begin the piece with motivic gestures provided by the row.

Although the construction of the row produces chromatic lines, the tunings
are based on intervals of the perfect fifth (3/2), just major third (5/4), and just
minor third (5/3), thus providing an opportunity to use chromaticism with microtonal inflections while at the same time emphasizing consonant intervals. For example, the vocal line has three different C's (C, C+, and C++) and two C#'s
(C#+ and C#++) which are the result of maintaining beatless consonances. The
reason there is such pitch variety is because Johnston used the row nine times
during this short song's forty-seven measures. Four statements begin on F+,
and the rest are transpositions starting on F, Gbb, Gbb+, E#+, and F++, all
microtonally related to the original F+. Johnston described how he derived these

Example 2. Beginning measures of A Sea Dirge. Copyright 1974 by Smith Publications. Used with permission.

pitches in his article, "The Genesis of Knocking Piece."[9] The tuning is a series of just thirds stacked as thirteenth chords that are connected to each other by common tones forming perfect fifths. These relationships are easier to understand if they are plotted on the lattice. Figure 2 shows how the first statement of the row is a network of adjacent relationships.

```
                        C #+

                D   F#+   A#+

                G   B     D#

                C   E     G#

                F   A
```

Figure 2. 12-tone row used in A Sea Dirge.

By itself A Sea Dirge is not an important work except that Knocking Piece (1963), Johnston's famous composition for two percussionists, was derived from A Sea Dirge's pitch ratios.[10] Originally Knocking Piece was to be part of a collaborative theatrical production with Wilfred Leach for a play In Three Zones. Johnston had elaborate ideas for a continuum of pitched to non-pitched instruments including a sound system, an orchestra, and a piano tuned in just intonation. Leach, however, felt that these plans were too complicated, and the play was produced without Johnston's music.

But Johnston did realize a part of his original plan. The beginning of In Three Zones is a modernization of the Faust legend that was adapted for Stravinsky's L'Histoire du Soldat. This gave Johnston the idea to design a composition in which two percussionists would perform knocking sounds inside the piano to portray a soldier who has sold his soul to the devil and returned to his home only to find he can not enter the locked house. Johnston described his plan for Knocking Piece as follows:

> My idea was to have two percussionists cross the stage to the piano just as the soldier goes to sleep. They would then play on the inside of the piano. For this spot I composed Knocking Piece. The idea of a negative transformation pervaded the conception, suggested by the Faust theme, the film in negative [Leach was going to use a film as part of the play's action], and the bitter homecoming. The image of the most elaborate of instruments, and in this context the most perfectly in tune [it would be tuned in just intonation], seemingly violated by two percussionists with sticks and mallets, concentratedly focussing like surgeons, bore out this theme of destruction.[11]

The piece is difficult, and at first it was considered impossible. However, Jack McKenzie (who taught percussion in the School of Music at the University of Illinois and who is now Dean of the College of Fine and Applied Arts) and Tom Siwe (who was a percussion student in the early 1960's and is now Director of Percussion Studies and Chairman of the Percussion Division) premièred the piece, although some sections were edited in order to make the performance easier.[12]

Like A Sea Dirge, Knocking Piece is based upon the ratios 3/2, 5/4, 4/3, 6/5, 8/5 and 5/3, which create tempi analogous to interval relationships of a perfect fifth, a just major third, a perfect fourth, a just minor third, and a just minor and major sixth. Johnston used these ratios to create a work based entirely on metric modulation. The listener hears a counterpoint of continually changing tempi which overlap and evolve from previous rates of speed. Knocking Piece starts simply with percussionist A (the person performing the top stave) setting a tempo that is kept for eight beats. Meanwhile, percussionist B (the person performing the bottom stave) establishes a tempo that is 5/4 the rate of the beginning tempo because this part's five beats is in the space of the other part's four beats. The bottom tempo is a major third (4/5) faster. (See measures three and four of Example 3, page 70.) By measure four percussionist A is beginning a new tempo which is slower, being 3/4 (a perfect fourth) slower than B's rate of speed. Thus, supposing that the initial tempo was eighth note equals 60, B's tempo in measure three would be 75 and A's tempo in measure five would be 56.25.[13]

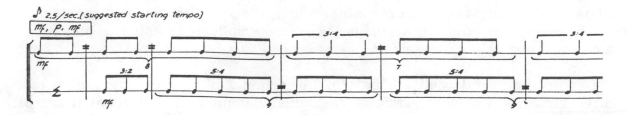

Example 3. Beginning measures of Knocking Piece. Copyright 1978 by Smith Publications. Used with permission.

The performers are free to determine several aspects, such as what part of the piano should be struck and beginning speed. This note is included with the score:

> The sustaining pedal can and should be used, ad lib. Pitch should be used only as color, if at all. Typical piano sounds should be avoided. The same sound should be used for successive notes which have the same speed, but contrasting sounds (to varying degrees) should enter with each change of note speed. The equal marks across bar lines mean that the same note speed should be maintained in spite of a change in notation. In general, specific kinds of sounds should predominate within a given phrase. All sounds should relate to knocking. A general dynamic level is given for each phrase (within boxes, at phrase beginnings). Changes of dynamic level are also indicated. The tempo of the opening is at the performers' discretion; it is strict thereafter. Not all the notes must be played. Rests are permitted if rhythmic patterns are clear. If the unity and simplicity of the knocking sounds are over emphasized, the realization will be monotonous. If the rationally controlled shifting of tempi are not mastered, the realization will deteriorate into feigned vandalism. If the marathon ensemble cooperation and concentration required fail, the performance will be impossible to execute. A spirit of competitiveness between the performers will destroy the piece. The players must be friends; in quick alternation each must support the other.

Knocking Piece is an intense study of concentration. Some of the most difficult parts are unison tempi where any flaw is apparent. It is obvious to the audience that the performers must be constantly aware of what they are doing, and any hesitation in one part will immediately affect the outcome of the piece. The contrapuntal relationship between the musicians resembles the dux comes situation in a Bach Invention; at one point percussionist A (who has had the slower tempo) shifts and has the faster tempo, much like an invention's motive or subject changing from the right to the left hand. This is not heard by the audience, but is an important structural point for the performers.

The idea of using rhythm as a structural foundation replacing a pitch scheme is a concept that several composers experimented with during the 1950's. Elliott Carter is famous for his work with metric modulation, and at the 1953 Festival of Contemporary Arts Johnston heard a performance of Carter's String Quartet number one (1951) which is an early use of metric modulation. Later, Johnston read Stockhausen's article "....how time passes...." in die Reihe[14] in which Stockhausen suggested the possibility of substituting tempo relationships for those of pitch, but Johnston found the presentation shallow.

During the late 1950's he was studying P. D. Ouspensky's ideas about the dimensionality of time as stated in A New Model of the Universe.[15] Ouspensky described time as having the three dimensions of duration, velocity, and direction. Duration and velocity are familiar temporal qualities but, according to Ouspensky, direction is something that cannot be measured because it is not a quantity but an absolute condition. For him, time is best represented by a spiral which is a three-dimensional curve. In another book, The Psychology of Man's Possible Evolution,[16] Ouspensky described man as having three centers (the intellectual, the moving and instinctive center, and the emotional). Each of these centers has its own rate of speed with the intellectual being the slowest, the moving and instinctive centers faster, and the emotional center the fastest.

These ideas fascinated Johnston, and he even wrote a paper titled "A Semantic Examination of Music" for a philosophy course that he was taking at the University of Illinois. In this paper Johnston discussed the meaning of music from a philosophical and psychological background and then focused upon the topic of music and time. He wrote: "The truth would appear to be to view any event as an organic whole without slicing up duration arbitrarily into chronological units which have no structural significance."[17]

Having begun to experiment with just intonation and serialism, it seemed natural for Johnston to try to apply some kind of ordering to rhythm. But Johnston confesses that the technique required to play Knocking Piece went beyond his own musicianship. The piece was an abstract idea that worked. Later he added expressive elements, such as changes in dynamics. This is a working procedure that Johnston frequently uses so that the nuances highlight the music's expressiveness but also contribute to clarifying its structure.

It was fortunate for Johnston that there was an occasion to première this work. He needed to hear his recent music and to discover how much the audience understood his experiments. In 1963 the composer Salvatore Martirano joined the faculty and initiated a special concert series at his home, a round house that he was renting in Urbana. The building's shape, especially the living room's, was ideal for concerts. Martirano, Johnston, and others were involved in a series of performances scheduled throughout the year. The concerts were invitational (this was due to some zoning restrictions), and a social hour followed. Because these concerts were not associated with the University, scheduling and programming were flexible. The Festival of Contemporary Arts had to be planned a year in advance, so the Round House Concerts, as they were called, made an excellent showcase for resident and visiting composers. The guests included a variety of people from the University community, and the concerts were well received.

Knocking Piece and Sea Dirge were premiered on December 14, 1963, at the first Round House concert. At that time Knocking Piece was performed as an abstract work; McKenzie and Siwe did not use any theatrical implications, although some performers have tried to emphasize the piece's destructive message. Jocy de Oliveira and Rich O'Donnell wore surgical garb when they performed it at the MUSICIRCUS, a concert Cage arranged at the University of Illinois' Stock Pavillion.[18] During the 1960's and 70's Knocking Piece was a disturbing work assaulting the piano, a symbol of Western musical culture. This certainly was the reaction when in 1966 the University of Illinois' Contemporary Chamber Players performed the piece at Darmstadt, Warsaw, Paris, and London. Johnston has stated: "People do indeed get very upset. It is a work that implies violence, even vandalism. As such, it is a disturbing work."[19] Since then Knocking Piece has lost some of its threatening qualities and is becoming a classic of percussion literature.

Notes

1. For a survey of microtonal music see William Duckworth and Edward Brown, Theoretical Foundations of Music (Belmont, California: Wadsworth, 1978), pp. 293-302. Also, Joel Mandelbaum did a comprehensive study of tuning systems in his "Multiple Division of the Octave and the Tonal Resources of 19-tone Temperament," unpublished Ph.D. dissertation, Indiana University, 1961.

2. Ferruccio Busoni, Sketch of a New Esthetic of Music, translated by T. Baker (New York: Schirmer, 1911).

3. Joseph Yasser, A Theory of Evolving Tonality (New York: American Library of Musicology, 1932).

4. Adriaan D. Fokker, New Music with 31 Notes, translated by Leigh Gerdine (Bonn-Bad Godesberg: Verlag für systematische Musikwissenschaft, 1973).

4A. David Kraehenbuehl and Christopher Schmidt, "On the Development of Musical Systems," The Journal of Music Theory, Spring 1962, pp. 32-65.

4B. For more information about Johnston's use of ratio lattices see his articles "Tonality Regained," American Society of University Composers Proceedings, 1967, pp. 89-98 and "Rational Structure in Music," American Society of University Composers Proceedings, I/II, (1976-77), 102-118. Other composers have used tuning lattices. See Fokker, New Music with 31 Notes, notes 13 and 14 in chapter 6, and Mandelbaum, "Multiple Division of the Octave and the Tonal Resources of 19-tone Temperament."

4C. Harry Partch, Genesis of a Music, second edition (New York: Da Capo Press, 1974).

5. Other composers who are using just intonation are James Tenney, Larry Polanski, La Monte Young, Lou Harrison, and Chris Forster. Ear Magazine East, volume 7, number 3 is devoted to microtonal music. Interestingly, Johnston's music is not mentioned, with the exception of a short review of his String Quartets Numbers 3 and 4 which were performed at the "New Music America 1982" held in Chicago.

5A. During the 1950's Partch and L. C. Marshall tried to design an electronic organ that could be tuned in just intonation. Their efforts were unsuccessful. Later Johnston would have access to an instrument that Motorola built called the "Scalatron" that can be tuned in different intonations.

6. Cole Gagne and Tracy Caras, Soundpieces: Interviews With American Composers (Metuchen, NJ: Scarecrow Press, 1982), p. 253. Johnston had an opportunity to criticize Cage's work, Theater Piece (1960) for one to eight performers. Johnston thought that Merce Cunningham and his dancers who participated in the piece were not totally sensitive to Cage's aesthetic of just letting the events happen naturally and that the dancers' movements were too studied.

7. "Phase 1a," Source, VII (Summer 1970), 27-42.

8. A Sea Dirge is dedicated to Jantina Noorman, a soprano who was in the Champaign-Urbana area but then moved to England. The première was performed by Grace Wilson, a faculty member of the University of Illinois.

9. "The Genesis of Knocking Piece," Percussive Notes, March 1983, pp. 25-30. There is an error in the chart on page 27. The F in the top stave of system two should be F+ and not F as is printed.

10. He described his compositional procedure of determining the metrical ratios in "The Genesis of Knocking Piece."

11. "The Genesis of Knocking Piece," p. 27.

12. Thomas Siwe, "Performing Ben Johnston's 'Knocking Piece,' Then and Now," Percussive Notes, March 1983, pp. 32-35. Note Siwe's descriptions of some of the early difficulties with the piece and how students have now developed the rhythmic skills so that the piece is frequently performed on percussion recitals.

13.   The suggested starting tempo on the published score is eighth note equals 2.5 seconds. The publisher, Sylvia Smith, states that this is only a suggested practice tempo and an actual performance should begin with a faster speed.

14.   Karlheinz Stockhausen, ".....how time passes....," die Reihe, volume 3, 10-40.

15.   P. D. Ouspensky, A New Model of the Universe (New York: Knopf, 1948). For information about the dimensionality of time see pp. 372-379. Johnston was also influenced by Elliott Carter's lecture "The Time Dimension in Music" which was presented as part of the Festival of Contemporary Arts at the University of Illinois on March 6, 1965 and Robert Erickson's "Time Relations," Journal of Music Theory, Winter 1963, pp. 174-194.

16.   P. D. Ouspensky, The Psychology of Man's Possible Evolution (New York City: Hedgehog Press, 1965).

17.   This passage is from Johnston's unpublished paper.

18.   For more information about Cage see Stephen Husarik, "John Cage and LeJaren Hiller: HPSCHD, 1969," (American Music, volume 1, number 2, Summer 1983) 1-21.

19.   From "Notes of General Interest" which preface Knocking Piece.

By 1964 Johnston was feeling more confident with just intonation and serialism. This may be due partly to the fact that during this year his first important theoretical article, "Scalar Order as a Compositional Resource," was published in Perspectives of New Music.[1] Here he explained his use of just intonation, showing how this tuning produces scales that he considers to be perceivable organic relationships that can be applied to pitch schemes, serial techniques, and durational plans.

Some of his ideas were derived from S. S. Stevens' work in psychology in which Stevens established four kinds of scalar measurements--nominal, ordinal, interval, and ratio.[2] Johnston applied these measurements to music. Nominal scales are used in traditional musical analysis, such as assigning letter names to sections (AABA); ordinal scales are used in dynamic markings (pp, p, mp); interval scales are the basis of metrical beats and the melodic use of pitch; and ratio scales structure the harmonic use of pitch.

Johnston also described the tuning process for a 53-tone scale in just intonation and included a chart of the scale. In several places he proposed the organic properties of proportional (ratio) organization, saying that it has "much more mnemonic power" than linear ordering (he cited intervallic contour, motif, and serial patterning as examples of linear ordering) and even suggested some possible durational proportionality.

"Scalar Order as a Compositional Resource" represents an important step in Johnston's creative development. It forecast the future direction of his music where all elements of a composition would be related to each other through some type of scalar ordering. This article was also the beginning of Johnston's contribution to the continuation of Partch's work. Later Johnston summarized his position thus:

> Rather soon I felt that my eventual task would be to alter attitudes, especially theoretic currents within the mainstream, from the mainstream, to the mainstream. It would be my role to bring his [Partch's] work into relation with accepted traditions and recognized challenges to tradition, and to whatever extent necessary and possible to bring these enormous trends into relation to some of his most important achievements.[3]

This scalar research made it possible for Johnston to establish an intellectual integrity using the rigors of serialism, if he so desired, while still exploring just intonation and its related benefits, such as a continuum of consonance and dissonance that could give new meaning to tonality and permit a wide range of expressive qualities. This freedom, which resulted from adopting ratio scale ordering, suggested many compositional opportunities. Johnston considered interval-scale thinking limiting because it emphasizes symmetry of design while "Ratio-scale thinking, on the contrary, emphasizes a hierarchical subordination of details to the whole or to common reference points. The harmonic and tonal meaning of proportional pitch structures is clarity and a sense of direction."[4]

Some of the ideas contained in this article are apparent in Knocking Piece (1962) and String Quartet Number 2 (1964). The quartet was Johnston's first piece written in just intonation to gain public attention. Herbert Brün, a colleague at the University of Illinois, arranged for the La Salle Quartet to perform Johnston's first string quartet, Nine Variations. As a result, the Quartet asked Johnston to compose a piece especially for them. The La Salle Quartet is such a fine ensemble that Johnston felt this was his opportunity to write a piece in just intonation for a professional group; however, the Quartet never performed the piece and, instead, the Composers Quartet premièred String Quartet Number 2 on July 14, 1966. A performance by this quartet is available on the Nonesuch recording H-71224.[5] This recording helped to establish Johnston's reputation as a composer of microtonal music. Even though there was some delay in the première of this work, the commission headed Johnston in the direction of composing experimental works for string quartet, a medium that he continues to use.

Johnston was working on his String Quartet Number 2 during the time that he was studying the teachings of Gurdjieff, and this influence is significant in the Quartet's second movement. Also, this piece exhibits a degree of sophistication with serialism that is similar to that heard in Duo for flute and string bass.

The Quartet is in three movements, all of which are in just intonation using the ratios of 3/2 and 5/4. (The lattice for these relationships is illustrated in Figure 1 of Chapter 5.) Movements I and III use serialism, although only the middle portion of the third movement is serial. The second movement uses a special formula for deriving pitch which will be explained later. The Quartet is extremely difficult to perform, and it is even a challenge to follow the score while listening to a performance.

The first movement uses the row shown in Figure 1. Notice that the trichords feature major and minor thirds (favorable intervals for just intonation), and that the last three trichords are structurally related to the first one.[6]

Each measure of the Quartet has twelve pitches, one from each pitch class. There is no particular ordering for which form of the row is used because there is another pitch pattern working. The movement is fifty-four measures long to match Johnston's 53-tone scale in just intonation that he described in his article

C Eb E B G# G Bb Bbb Gb Db D F+
   O   I   R   RI

Figure 1. Row used for Movement I of <u>String Quartet Number 2</u>.

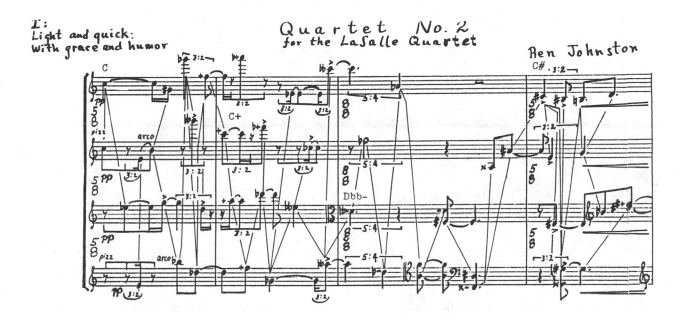

Example 1. Beginning measures of the first movement of <u>String Quartet Number 2</u>. Copyright 1985 by Smith Publications. Used with permission.

"Scalar Order as Compositional Resource." Each measure's tuning relationships are based upon ascending degrees of that scale. The scale begins on C. The first note of violin I in measure one is C; violin II in measure two has C+; the viola sounds Dbb- in measure three; and violin I has C# in measure four. These notes are circled in Example 1, and the entire movement follows the exact order of the scale which is reproduced in Figure 2, page 78. The movement returns to C for the final measure which explains why the fifty-fourth measure is extra. The lines in Example 2 indicate the tuning relationships. They show the performers how to listen, and which tunings are their responsibility. There are no parts.

The effect of this process is that the serial order is always ascending as in a spiral while the intervals are staying the same size--just major and minor thirds and perfect fifths. The listener has the sensation of having heard many different pitches within the normal range of a string quartet. The analyst discovers a major difference between Johnston's use of serialism and that of other serialists--

C	C+	Dbb−	C♯	C♯+	Db−	Db	Cx+	D−	D	D+	Ebb	D♯	Eb−	Eb	Dx	E−
1/1	81/80	128/125	25/24	135/128	16/15	27/25	1125/1024	10/9	9/8	729/640	144/125	75/64	32/27	6/5	625/512	100/81

AB A ABBC AB A AB ABBC A AB AB A ABBC A AB ABBC A

(E−)	E	E+	Fb	E♯	F−	F	F+	Gbb−	F♯	F♯+	Gb−	Gb	Fx+	G−	G	G+	Abb	G♯	Ab−	Ab	Gx	A−
(100/81)	5/4	81/64	32/25	125/96	320/243	4/3	27/20	512/375	25/18	45/32	64/45	36/25	375/256	40/27	3/2	243/160	192/125	25/16	128/81	8/5	625/384	400/243

AB AB A ABBC A AB AB A ABBC AB A AB ABBC A AB AB A ABBC A AB ABBC A

(A−)	A	A+	Bbb−	A♯	A♯+	Bb−	Bb	Ax+	B−	B	B+	Cb	B♯	C−	C
(400/243)	5/3	27/16	128/75	125/72	225/128	16/9	9/5	1875/1024	50/27	15/8	243/128	48/25	125/64	160/81	2/1

AB AB A ABBC AB A AB ABBC A AB AB A ABBC A AB

KEY: A = $\frac{2048}{2025}$ B = $\frac{32805}{32768}$ C = $\frac{1600000}{1594323}$ ∴AB = $\frac{81}{80}$ ∴BC = $\frac{15625}{15552}$ ∴ABBC = $\frac{3125}{3072}$

(A > C > B; A > BC)

♯ = $\times\frac{25}{24}$ x = $\times(\frac{25}{24})^2$ b = $\div\frac{25}{24}$ + = $\times\frac{81}{80}$ − = $\div\frac{81}{80}$

Figure 2. 53-tone scale in just intonation.

for Johnston scalar order is structural and serialism is just a means to exhibit his scale.

The movement contains additional pitch interest. Certain measures are repeated, but transposed. The most obvious is when the pitch G (the dominant) is reached--the music is identical to the first measure with the exception that measure 32 (G, the thirty-second note of the scale) is transposed up a fifth. This correspondence continues for the next five measures and then is abandoned for a short time. There are other repetitions throughout the movement which form a palindrome of ABCACBA (see Figure 3, below). The repetitions are identical transpositions with the exceptions that new material in mm. 38-42 introduces the C section and the last A section is shortened.

A	B	C	A	C	B	A
mm1-15	16-25	26-31	32-37	38-46	47-51	52-54

Figure 3. Palindrome sectional repetitions in the first movement of String Quartet Number 2.

The repetition of transposed material makes this movement more intelligible to the listener, and Johnston indicated ritards, accelerandi, and other nuances which define the repetitions. The first measure almost becomes a theme, and it is especially recognizable as it ends the movement.

This pattern, shown in Figure 3, becomes significant when examining the structure of Johnston's 53-tone scale. The distance between scale degrees is measured by a series of intervals keyed as A, B, C, AB, BC, and ABBC (see Figure 2). The number of elements being repeated in the scale and the formal plan is the same (three marked as A, B, and C), although the formal repetition does not follow the interval pattern. However, Johnston did use this interval pattern to structure the changing meters in this movement. There are two meters used, 5/8 and 8/8, and whenever the 8/8 occurs, the scale degree has been reached that forms the interval of ABBC (3125/3072) which is the interval that delineates the borderline between the twelve pitch regions. The first use of 8/8 is the measure that precedes the appearance of C#. See measure three of Example 1, page 77 and consult Figure 2 for the interval patterning.

The second movement, marked "Intimate, spacious," is slower so it is easier to hear the justly tuned harmonic and melodic intervals. In the record jacket notes to the Nonesuch recording Johnston described this movement:

> I used mostly consonant intervals and "diatonic" dissonance, a harmonic idiom of rapid chromatic changes and microtonal cross relations, far closer in sound to Gesualdo than to Bach. These pitch relations describe a strict spiral pattern, ascending one octave of a 53-tone just intonation scale.

There are chromatic melodic sections expressing intense emotion and a recurring eighth note figure of fifths and thirds (or an inversion of these intervals) that draw attention to the continually rising pitch pattern. The listener hears the spiral; however, the pitch plan is impossible to follow. It is not serial, there are few repetitions, and the tuning does not provide clues as to how pitch is ordered; yet it is apparent that some selection process is operating.

Johnston did use a plan based on the numbers three, six, nine, and seven. These numbers are used in a symbol called the enneagram, a Sufi figure which is a circle containing a triangle and a hexagon that twists back upon itself (see Figure 4, page 80).[7] The symbol dates at least to the fourteenth century or possibly even to the time of the discovery of the number seven. According to Gurdjieff, who used the enneagram to explain how events conform to cosmic laws, the enneagram was a symbol of secret knowledge, and his followers credit him as introducing the enneagram to the West.

Part of Johnston's interest in the symbol was its musical appropriateness. Gurdjieff taught that the enneagram was a representation of the law of sevenfoldness which he compared to a 7-toned scale, using solfège syllables to express transforming action (see Figure 4). Notice that the scale steps skip numbers 3 and 6. Gurdjieff considered the 9, 3, and 6 a triad representing the three sources, crucial developments that add dynamism within transforming action, and new scales can begin at the 3 or 6.

The numbers 3, 6, and 9 are an endless succession because when one is

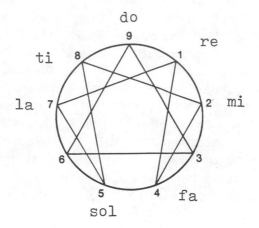

Figure 4. Enneagram.

divided by any of them, the decimal expression is a repetitive series of that particular number, such as 1/3 = .33333 ..., 1/6 = .66666 ..., and 1/9 = .99999.... A different pattern appears when one is divided by seven, such that 1/7 = .142857142857.... It is this succession of 142857 that forms the twisted hexagon of the enneagram (see Figure 4), and according to Gurdjieff this sequence of numbers plus the triad explains the structure of any process that maintains itself by self-renewal.[8]

Johnston told me that he used the enneagram as the basis of the second movement of <u>String Quartet Number 2</u>, but that he forgot the exact plan because he destroyed the sketches for this quartet during the late 1960's as a statement of his rejection of the Gurdjieff movement. He even had some difficulty remembering how to draw the enneagram. Johnston did recall that first he determined that this movement would be built upon an A mode (aeolian) tuned in just intonation, and then used the enneagram to select pitches.[8A]

The intervals for the scale steps are shown in Figure 5. The music progresses in a scalar fashion, as shown by the measure numbers, and the A center is clear to the listener because the movement begins and ends on an A.

The enneagram does structure the movement, and it is possible to plot how Johnston used the number sequences 142857 and 936 (the numbers of the hexagon and triangle) to determine how pitches would be chosen for the scalar intervals of 9/8, that is the distance between A and B, C and D, and F and G. He began with the 9 of the enneagram, calling that number A, and then moved one scale step away from A in his 53-toned scale to A+. The next number in the progression is 4, which is A#+ (the fourth note from A), and the formula follows with 2 (Bbb-), 8 (B-), 5 (Bb-), and 7 (Ax+). This sequence can be checked by

A	B		C	D	E	F	G	A
		intervals						
9/8	16/15		9/8	10/9	16/15	9/8	10/9	
		measure numbers						
1-13	14-24		25-41	42-50	51-59	59-69	70-82	

Figure 5. Ratios and measure numbers for the mode of A tuned in just intonation as used in the second movement of String Quartet Number 2.

consulting Figure 2, page 78, and the enneagram representation as shown in Figure 6. Added to this sequence are articulations of 9 (A), 3 (A#), and 6 (Bb). These pitches and numbers are labeled in Example 2 (page 82), measures 1-18 showing the beginning part of the spiral that rises from A to B.

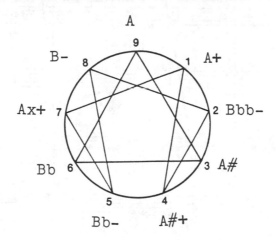

Figure 6. Enneagram representation of the interval 9/8 showing the distance between the pitches A and B.

The other 9/8 intervals in the scale (C to D and F to G) use the same pattern, although sometimes a number is omitted due to error or some musical consideration.

The number sequence for the interval 16/15 (B to C and E to F) is 27548. Since B is "re" of the mode, the B begins at the second position on the enneagram, skipping the triad 936. The same procedure is used for E to F except the E begins on 5 (also skipping the triad) and produces the pattern 518[7]2, a transposition of 27548. The 7 is bracketed because it is missing in the score (see Figure 7, page 83).

The 10/9 interval has nine scale steps between G and A and conforms to the enneagram pattern by having G in the first place and A in the ninth. The

Example 2. Measures 1-18 showing enneagram structure of the second movement of <u>String Quartet Number 2</u>. Copyright 1985 by Smith Publications. Used with permission.

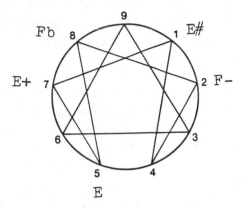

Figure 7. Enneagram representation of 16/15, E to F.

pattern is 1496789, an altered version of the enneagram that emphasizes the last three notes of the scale (Ab, Gx, and A-) so that the return to the original A is clearly heard.

The pitch A is also prominent in the last movement in which Johnston used a melodic motive of ascending and descending microtonal intervals (see Example 3). It is difficult because the performer must tune the intervals by ear since there are not many harmonic references; however, the approximate distances, such as

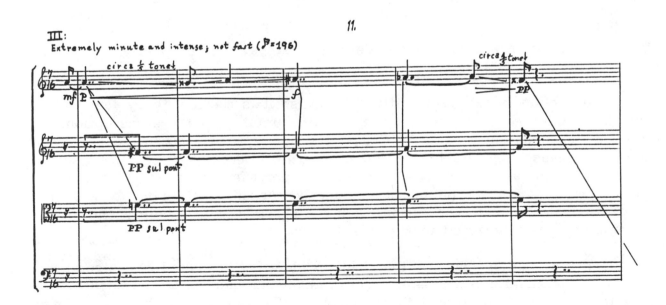

Example 3. Beginning measures of the third movement of String Quartet Number 2. Copyright 1985 by Smith Publications. Used with permission.

"circa 1/5 tone, circa 4/5 tone," are indicated. The motive sounds like a passage that Harry Partch would have written for his adapted viola, and it is easy for the listener to follow the progress of the motive as it changes duration, instrumentation, transposition, and tuning.

The movement is sectional, but there is an element of redundancy that is suspicious. The movement's three sections become a retrograde inversion at the midpoint. Johnston cleverly designed his material so that the motive works equally well forwards or backwards, and the sections increase in tempo and density with the midpoint being almost unbearably active. The B section still features the motive but the tempo is now "Quick, mercurial," and generally the texture includes all four instruments in contrast to the first section which was more sparse.

The C section is serial, and the row is arranged like the beginning motive so that each scale degree is surrounded by microtonal intervals. See Figure 8 where the scale degree steps are circled.

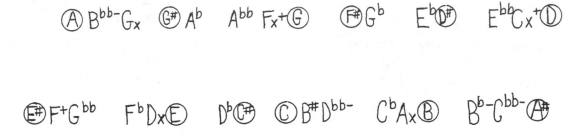

Figure 8. Serial row decorating scale degree steps.

The section is extremely difficult because it is marked "Very fast, with suppressed excitement." The lines are contrapuntal, and there are options for repeated measures; however, the Composers Quartet chose not to do the repeats, probably because it would have been too easy to lose one's place in the score. The music is so fast and intense that the listener might think it is improvised. But, the midpoint of the palindrome is clearly marked with double forte-piano chords that alert one to the turning point. These measures before and after the midpoint are illustrated in Example 4.

There are other features that help to identify the palindrome structure. Section A has several passages of timbral changes, such as legno battuto, legno spiccato, and short microtonal thumb pizzicati that are obvious in the A' retrograde inversion. Section B has descending diatonic lines, non vibrato, and louré sul tasto that are very noticeable in B'. Using a palindrome is not something new to serial writing; in Johnston's case, this kind of structure eliminated some of the problems of making choices amongst the availability of so many

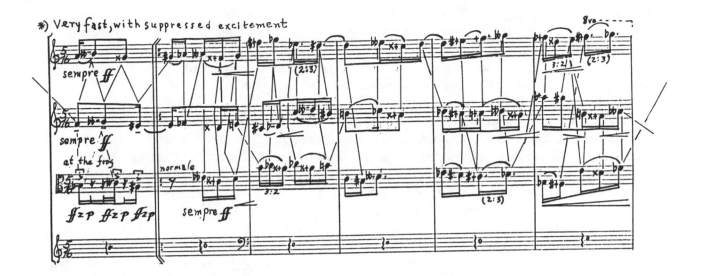

Example 4. Midpoint of the palindrome used in the third movement of String Quartet Number 2. Copyright 1985 by Smith Publications. Used with permission.

different pitches because the retrograde uses the same pitches as the first half of a piece. His creative approach, however, was to do this in a microtonal setting that was both intelligible and expressive.

The next piece in Johnston's catalog is a continuation of some of the ideas he experimented with in String Quartet Number 2. Actually, he had been planning Sonata for Microtonal Piano/Grindlemusic (1964) since his Guggenheim Fellowship in 1959 and even showed Cage some of the sketches at that time. Johnston spent several years trying to learn how to internalize the microtonal scale that he described in "Scalar Order as a Compositional Resource." The Sonata is complex for several reasons. Johnston incorporated many of the compositional ideas that interested him. All four types of scalar order are used; the piano is tuned in just intonation; there are several quotations of serious and popular music; three of the four movements are serial, and there is even a serial rhythmic row in the last movement; ratios control tempi and sectional durations; frequent polymetric figures abound; and the performer has some choice about which of the two versions (Sonata or Grindlemusic) to present.

Johnston designed the work so that it would have differing expressive and emotional qualities. The two versions themselves make a drama. Because of this drama Johnston has called this piece "Janus-faced," and although the intellectual complications are numerous, the emotional content is bewildering--an aspect that the listener immediately notices. Each of the four movements has expressive markings. In the Sonata version they are I. Still but tense, II. Brash, tempestuous, III. With Awe, and IV. ♩ = 90. Then, within each movement there are frequent emotional changes, such as Movement I's "Still but tense," "Violent,"

"Agitated," "With fury," "Threatening," "Quiet," "Fragile, delicate," "Suddenly violent," "With redoubled fury," and "Racing." The second movement is an emotional rondo alternating between moods of "Brash, tempestuous" and "Phlegmatic." These sudden changes mark structural elements, but they also explain content that is not within the intellectual realm.

In a sense this composition is Johnston's "Tristan und Isolde." Sonata/ Grindlemusic is not about human love, but some of the composer's philosophical and spiritual experiences, namely his work with the Gurdjieff Foundation. Grindlemusic (the other face of the Sonata) is a satirical parody of Gurdjieff himself. By the time Johnston was completing this piece he was disillusioned with the Foundation. There have been many uncertainties about Gurdjieff's method of teaching, and Ouspensky and J. G. Bennett, who broke from the Foundation, have written about some of these difficulties. Gurdjieff was even portrayed as the villainous character named Grindle in a pornographic novel, Candy, by Terry Southern and Mason Hoffenberg.[9] Grindle seduces Candy, the young heroine who is trying to follow the spiritual path that the teacher had suggested to her. Johnston had read Candy and addresses her in the last line of his notes about the Sonata. He says: "Sonata, what do you want? Candy?"[10] There is no indication of what these words mean, so readers are confused.

Because Grindlemusic has a different orientation from Sonata, the sequence of movements in Grindlemusic is different. The movement markings are: I. "Premises; ♩ = 90" (Movement IV of the Sonata), II. "Questions; Still but tense" (the other Movement I), III. "Soul Music; With Awe" (also the third movement of the Sonata), and IV. "Mood Music; Brash, tempestuous" (formerly the second movement). Again, there are structural reasons for this ordering, but the two versions are quite different emotionally. The Sonata moves from fast to faster to slow to slower, while Grindlemusic is slow, fast, slow, and fast.

Layered with this musical duality of a sonata or a character portrayal of Grindle is the structural use of two popular jazz tunes, "I'm in the mood for love" and "What is this thing called love?" The tunes are stylized into two 12-tone rows that dominate much of the pitch material. This was possible because these tunes were fairly chromatic, so that when each was arranged in a 12-tone row, its identity could be somewhat maintained if so desired. They are not as clearly recognizable, however, as in Newcastle Troppo and Ivesberg Revisited.

In addition, the tunes' ballad form of AABA is the architectural basis of the entire piece. There are four movements, which Johnston considers to be an AABA design, and this plan works for both the Sonata and Grindlemusic. The B movement is the third movement in both versions, and the A labeling has many references, such as: all A movements are serial (B is not serial), and the order of the A movements is changeable.[11] Each movement itself is a four-part sectional form of AABA and within each of these parts the phrases divide into an AABA sequence. That explains the frequent changes in emotional markings, such as the numerous emotional changes in Movement I mentioned earlier. Many of the markings coincide with the beginning of phrases within the AABA micro-structure of the piece.

The Sonata is a challenge even for the most experienced of pianists. Claire Richards, who premièred St. Joan and a person with whom Johnston studied, requested that he write this piece for her. Richards premièred the Sonata in 1965 at a Round House Concert and later performed the piece on a concert series titled "The Twentieth Century Piano Sonata."[11A]

Not surprisingly, the piece is extremely difficult to perform, and the first problem is having a piano tuned in just intonation. Johnston included a note to the performer saying that it is possible to practice the Sonata on a conventionally tuned piano but that much of the work's conception about irony, parody, and consonance and dissonance would be lost. The score contains a notation and tuning guide, a diagram showing tuning order, and an explanation of how to retune the piano using the Scalatron tuner.

In the early 1970's the Motorola Company was experimenting with designing an electronic organ that could be easily tuned in various intonations. This has been the dream of many people interested in different tuning systems. Fokker had a pipe organ built to realize his tuning system, and Partch and his friend L. C. Marshall were collaborating on a design for an electronic organ during the early 1950's. However, it was not until 1973 that Johnston discovered that Motorola had actually constructed such an organ. After hearing it demonstrated, Johnston requested that the Research Board of the University of Illinois purchase it. By 1973 Johnston had the organ in his studio and then added Scalatron tuning directions to all his former pieces using just intonation.

The Sonata was written before he had the organ, and because of this the tuning took a long time and Johnston needed to be present to help the tuner hear the correct ratios. According to the note on the Scalatron tuning directions Johnston envisioned pianists traveling with the Scalatron (it is a small organ that would not be too difficult to transport); however, Motorola has stopped making the Scalatron and Johnston usually assists in the tuning process.

He described the tuning for the Microtonal Sonata as

> chains of just-tuned (untempered) triadic intervals over the whole piano range in interlocked consonant patterns. Only seven of the eighty-eight white and black keys of the piano have octave equivalents, one pair encompassing the distance of a double octave and the remaining six pairs separated by almost the entire length of the keyboard. Thus there are eighty-one different pitches, providing a piano with almost no consonant octaves.[12]

This was the tuning plan that he had envisioned for the collaboration with Leach on Three Zones.

The score is notated in just intonation, so the pianist must learn a new notational system. For example, middle C happens to be notated as C but C an octave higher on the keyboard is notated and sounds Dbb, a pitch that is 77 cents sharper than the standard C.

While the Sonata was in the planning stages Johnston prepared a detailed series of tuning notes, proportional systems, and other materials that were to be incorporated. This is typical of the way Johnston works. He prepares worksheets that govern pitch and rhythmic structure and then adds expressive details that help to clarify these choices, much as a visual artist adds shading or outlining. He lent these worksheets for the Sonata to Cage, but, unfortunately, they were destroyed in a fire. Johnston does not remember the exact details of his plans; however, it is possible to extract parts to explain how the piece works and to point out subtleties that may not be heard.

The entire Sonata is dominated by the progression I, IV, V, I, which is the basic harmony of the two jazz tunes. Using C as a tonic, this progression can be translated into the ratios of 3/2 (V or G as a fifth above C), 5/4 (IV or A as a 5/3 below C and F as a 4/3 or fifth below C), 2/1 (I or C), and their inversions. The Sonata's tuning system is also based upon the ratios of 3/2 and 5/4 and the lattice that was mentioned earlier.[13]

As in previous works, Johnston used row technique freely. Some passages are serial, and others are not. The 12-tone row derived from "What is this thing called love?" is Bb G A Ab Gb F E Eb Db C D B. Notice that the row divides into two hexachords, the second being a retrograde inversion of the first. The row for "I'm in the mood for love" is E F# F Eb Db D Ab G A B C Bb, and this row also divides hexachordally with the second hexachord being a retrograde and tritone transposition of the first one. The melody of the song's first phrase contains six notes forming the hexachord E F E D C D. Compare these pitches with the first hexachord of Johnston's row and notice the differences between the two.

During the beginning measures of "Still but tense" (the first movement of Sonata) Johnston states the row as dyads that are out of order. Minor thirds form a diminished seventh chord in the right hand as an upward stacking of thirds, while the left hand forms the same chord but in a downward progression. The process is reversed, and the durations are diminished in measures four and five (see Example 5).

It is not until measures fourteen and fifteen that a portion of the row becomes linear, but the listener is not aware of this material due to the speed and unfamiliar tuning. Structurally measure 14 begins the second "a" section of the "aaba" phrase design present within the larger beginning A section of this movement.

"Brash, tempestuous," Movement II of the Sonata, is the most clearly organized in terms of pitch. Johnston used a second row, the one based on "I'm

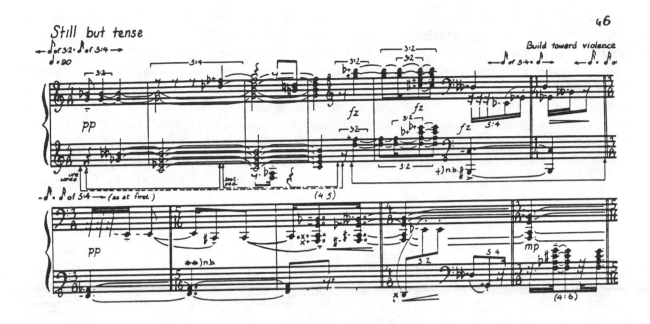

Example 5. Beginning measures of "Still but tense" from Sonata for Microtonal Piano/Grindlemusic. Copyright 1976 by Smith Publications. Used with permission.

Example 6. Beginning measures of "Brash, tempestuous" from Sonata showing row presentation. Copyright 1976 by Smith Publications. Used with permission.

in the mood for love" (shown in Example 6) and several prominent musical quotations. In the first measure the row is stated as two hexachords with the right hand sounding order numbers 0-5 and the left hand having numbers 6-11. But this order is not maintained because in measures three and four the row is rearranged and presented as two trichords and a hexachord. See Example 6 where this presentation is labeled.

In addition to the row which controls almost every measure of this movement, Johnston inserted four quotations. Three are heard in the B section which begins with a jazz walking bass, a familiar texture in Johnston's music. The first quote is the opening three-note motive (down a major third and up a whole step) of Jerome Kern's tune "Yesterdays." The motive is difficult to recognize because of the thick chordal texture, but the pitches are circled in Example 7. Following this is a short quote of "Es ist genug!," the chorale melody that Alban Berg used in the Adagio section of his <u>Violinkonzert</u>, and Johnston used precisely the same pitches for his quote (see Example 7). The third quote is the opening measures of the "Prelude" to Wagner's <u>Tristan und Isolde</u> and of all the quotes, it is the clearest.

Example 7. Quotations used in "Brash, tempestuous" of <u>Sonata</u>. Copyright 1976 by Smith Publications. Used with permission.

Example 8. Bartók quote in <u>Sonata</u>. Copyright 1976 by Smith Publications. Used with permission.

The last quote appears in the final A section of the movement and is unmistakably a motive from Bartók's <u>Fourth String Quartet</u> except Johnston set the motive as augmented sevenths which sound like mistuned octaves (see Example 8).

The last movement, marked ♩ = 90, uses a strict serial pattern which is an adaptation of "What is this thing called love?" For someone who knows the tune it is fairly easy to follow, especially since Johnston takes the opportunity to reinforce the melody with four octave doublings--Fx+, Gx, Dx, and B♯ which represent four of the six possible octaves in this tuning system.

Although the <u>Sonata</u> is a significant piece in terms of its serialism, just intonation, and quotations, the way Johnston used time is even more experimental. Tempo changes between movements, sections of each movement, and even a durational row in the <u>Sonata</u>'s fourth movement (♩ = 90) are determined by the changes (I, IV, V, I) of "I'm in the mood for love" and "What is this thing called love?" The chart in Figure 9 shows the beginning tempo of each movement of both the

Sonata			Grindlemusic		
I	♩ = 90		I	♩ = 90	
II	♪ = 180	90/180 = 1/2	II	♩ = 90	90/90 = 1/1
III	♩ = 60	180/60 = 3/1	III	♩ = 60	90/60 = 3/2
IV	♩ = 90	90/60 = 3/2	IV	♪ = 180	180/60 = 3/1

Figure 9. Chart of tempi between movements of <u>Sonata/Grindlemusic</u>.

Sonata and Grindlemusic and the proportions that are formed between these tempi. From the chart one can see that the tempi are either a fifth (3/2 or 3/1 which equals V) or an octave (1/2 which equals I) relationship.

Figure 10 is a chart of the tempo changes in the Sonata's third movement, "With Awe." The beginning tempo is 60 and the ending tempo is 90, a 2/3 relationship. All other tempo changes involve ratios using the series 2:3:4:5.

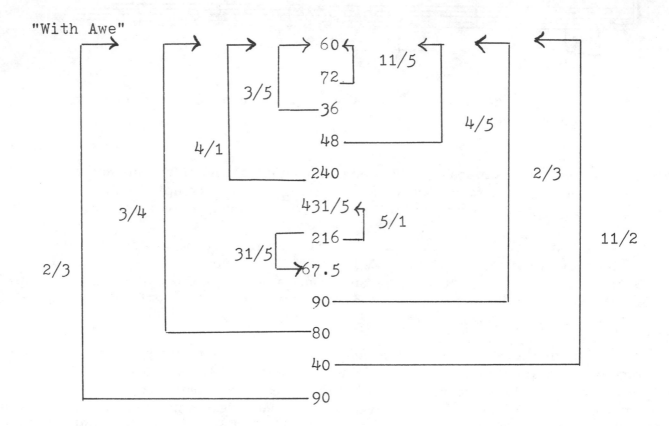

Figure 10. Tempo relationships in "With Awe" from Sonata/Grindlemusic.

The end of each movement provides a metric modulation that establishes the correct tempo for the next one. The last two measures of "Still but tense" and the beginning measure of "Brash, tempestuous" (Movements I and II of the Sonata) are shown in Example 9. Notice that there are two legends, one labeled "S" and the other "G." These represent the Sonata and Grindlemusic. If one is following the Sonata version, then the thirty-second tied to the dotted sixteenth becomes the eighth note of the quintuplet figure in the right hand part of the next movement.[14] Thus the proper metric modulation occurs.

These tempi changes are analogous to the pitch relationships that Johnston used with his lattice of 3/2 and 5/4 ratios. In fact, the tempi form three lattices,

Example 9. Tempo modulations between movements of <u>Sonata</u>. Copyright 1976 by Smith Publications. Used with permission.

one of slower tempi where the half note is the pulse counter, another of faster tempi where the quarter note is the pulse counter, and a last lattice of very fast tempi where the eighth note is the pulse counter. Like the pitch lattice, the columns are read as a 3/2 ratio and rows are read as a 5/4 ratio. These lattices are shown in Figure 11, page 94. For example, using the lattice of the half note as counter and taking a tempo of $\bullet$ = 45, the tempo a fifth faster is 45 × 3/2 = 67.5 (which is the tempo one block north of 45), and a tempo a major third faster is 45 × 5/4 = 56.25 (one block east of 45). The same procedure applies to all of the lattices. Moving from one lattice to another involves either dividing or multiplying by multiples of 2.

All of the tempi in this piece are located on the lattices in Figure 11. This shows that Johnston considered duration in a harmonic order just as pitch forms an overtone series. In fact, it is theoretically easier to do this since duration does not suffer from distortions as pitch does in equal-tempered tunings, although ritards, accelerandi, fermati, and so on could be considered tempering elements for duration. However, as is well-known, complicated and subtle rhythmic distinctions are generally not a part of the Western European musical culture. But the possibilities of using temporal ratios that resemble pitch ratios have fascinated some contemporary composers, especially Karlheinz Stockhausen, Elliott Carter, Olivier Messiaen, and Conlon Nancarrow.[15]

Figure 12, page 94, is a chart of this harmonic ordering of durations. In order to make rarely used durations, such as 5, 10, and 13, easier to read, Johnston created the notational symbol of an open dot for values that are 5/4, such as the durations 5 (an eighth note which equals four thirty-second notes and a fourth of that value totaling 5 thirty-seconds), 10, 13, 20, and 29. This

Half Note as Counter

64.8	81	101.25	126.5625
43.2	54	67.5	84.376
28.8	36	45	56.25
19.2	24	30	37.5
12.6	16	20	25

Quarter Note as Counter

194.4	243	303.75	405
196.6	162	202.5	253.125
86.4	108	135	168.75
57.6	72	90	112.5
38.4	48	60	93.75
25.6	32	40	62.5

Eighth Note as Counter

259.2	324	405	506.25
172.8	216	270	337.5
115.2	144	180	225
76.8	96	120	150
51.2	64	80	100

Figure 11.   Tempo lattices.

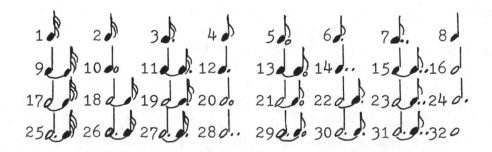

Figure 12.   Durational values in a harmonic series.

notation is frequently necessary when using 5/4 or 4/5 polymetric rhythms.   See Figure 12 for the durational chart which uses the thirty-second note as the basic unit of measurement and Example 10 which illustrates the open dot notation in 5/4

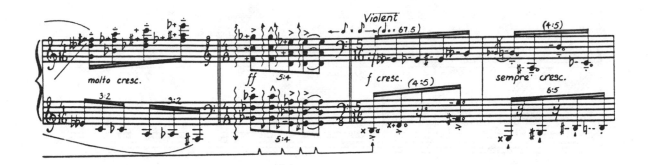

Example 10. Notational symbol of a hollow dot for ratios of 4/5, mm. 23 and 24 of "Still but tense" from Sonata. Copyright 1976 by Smith Publications. Used with permission.

and 4/5 polymetric rhythms. Also, this symbol is an important indicator of metric modulation as in Example 10 where the open-dotted quarter represents the duration of the entire measure written as a 5/16 meter.[15A]

There is one more use of time involving ratios of 2:3:4:5. This is a serialized durational row that Johnston used for the Sonata's last movement, ♩ = 90. The row has eleven durations which are 15, 21.428571, 22.5, 30, 33.75, 36, 38.571428, 45, 67.5, 90, 180. The duration of 30 is used twice. Each one of these durations is related to ♩ = 90 as a ratio of 2, 3, 4, or 5 as shown in Example 11 (page 96), and Figure 13 (page 97). The beginning and ending of the durational row does not coincide with those of the pitch row (which is based on "What is this thing called love?"), but the durational row is repeated in its prime version and transposed by metric modulations involving, again, the ratios of 2,3,4,5, such as ♩ = 90 in Example 11 and ♪ = 270 in Example 12 (page 97). This last tempo is a result of several previous metric modulations.

These similarities between pitch and duration were a result of Johnston's study of Ouspensky's dimensionality of time. The ideas are appealing, especially since they present an organic approach to time and pitch, but the difficulties of realizing these temporal ratios are enormous--they are more difficult than the ratios in Knocking Piece, although the ratios are similar. In his notes to the performer which accompany the Sonata Johnston stated:

> Tempos and durations are strictly proportional and should be inter-related in the manner notated. If the absolute tempo of the piece were slowed or speeded slightly, it would matter less than if tempo proportions (and therefore phrase and sectional proportions) were distorted either for technical or expressive reasons. Small-scale compensated deviations in the nature of rubato are not disruptive, however.

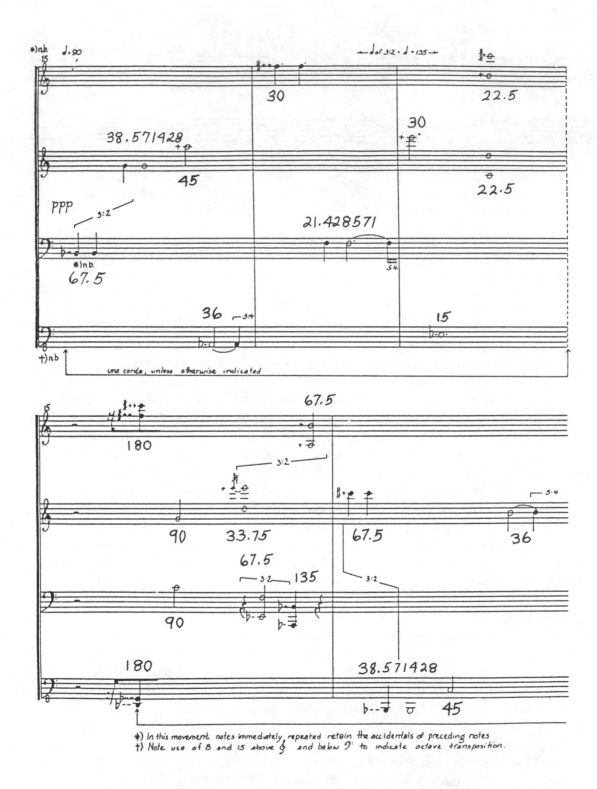

Example 11. Durational row in the fourth movement, "♩ = 90," of _Sonata_. Copyright 1976 by Smith Publications. Used with permission.

$$90/15 = 6 \qquad 90/38.571428 = 21/3$$

$$90/21.428571 = 41/5 \qquad 90/45 = 2$$

$$90/22.5 = 4 \qquad 90/67.5 = 11/3$$

$$90/30 = 3 \qquad 90/90 = 1$$

$$90/33.75 = 22/3 \qquad 90/180 = 2$$

$$90/36 = 21/2$$

Figure 13. Chart of relationships of durational row.

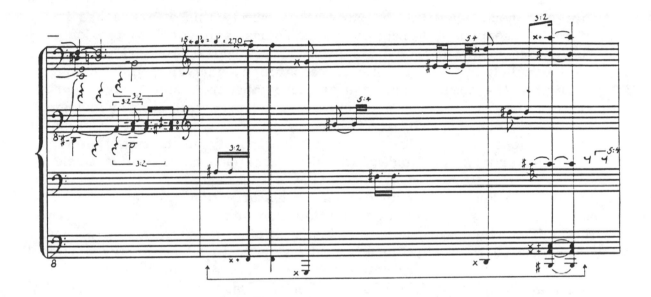

Example 12. Transposed durational row and metric modulation of 270 in the fourth movement, "♩ = 90," of Sonata. Copyright 1976 by Smith Publications. Used with permission.

The Sonata for Microtonal Piano/Grindlemusic was an important experimental work for Johnston. In comparing this piece to St. Joan, his other large-scale piano piece composed nine years earlier, it is amazing to see the technical development that he had achieved by 1964.[16] His tuning system was operative; he was fluent in the various uses of serialism; and he was pushing rhythmic advances to their outermost limits. One aspect, however, remained constant--Johnston was concerned that his music be expressive and communicative. The problem with the Sonata is that its expression is violent and disturbed, and this intensity almost becomes unbearable for both listener and performer. These emotions reflect Johnston's personal state at this time. He was recuperating from a spiritual crisis in which he rejected the teachings of Gurdjieff. This experience was so intense that it affected Johnston's mental health, and he was hospitalized for a period of time.

Part of this pressure was also a result of being chairman for the Festival of Contemporary Arts, which was a time-consuming responsibility, but one which also gave Johnston the opportunity to consider the role of contemporary music seriously. In the 1963 Festival program he wrote the following:

> To most people contemporary music is a problem. It would be equally true to say that to most of us contemporary life is a problem. Many of the reasons are the same. If contemporary music produces images of tension and anxiety (and worse states) we cannot deny it is holding up a mirror. It is often difficult to look. We would prefer something easier and more beautiful, but to demand merely this of art makes it a form of escapism. A habitual psychological state of high tension such as contemporary life tends to produce is a matter for serious concern. Art can help us by bringing to recognition, analyzing and making intelligible the complex patterns of these tensions. Music which evades the issue of complexity and tension is not accepting its psychological responsibility.... To extend musical order further into the jungle of randomness and complexity--and without simply eliminating that jungle-- that is perhaps the fundamental aim of contemporary serious music.[17]

Naturally the Festival occupied much of his attention, but Johnston was able to continue his own studies of just intonation and scalar resources. Other universities and colleges were initiating festivals of contemporary music, and Johnston was invited to Illinois Wesleyan where he lectured about "Proportionality and Expanded Music Pitch Relations."[18] In this lecture he took a bold stand about Schoenberg's claim of "the emancipation of dissonance," stating that consonance and dissonance have a new meaning with the refinement of pitch made available from ratio scales. Johnston also implied that it would be possible to arrange sounds of complex timbre and noise in a rational system of order which could replace randomness and indeterminacy. Serialism, too, benefited from the use of rational scales because, according to Johnston, the grayness of tone resulting from a lack of precise pitch definition could be eliminated by the clarity of harmonic relations inherent in rational scales. Much of the material presented in this lecture was an extension of Johnston's initial ideas about just intonation that were stated in his "Scalar Order as a Compositional Resource." However, he did add a statement about expressive content saying "... I have also felt that twelve-tone method has limited the emotional scope of musical composition rather drastically...."[19] This attention to the emotional aspect, which had concerned Johnston in the Sonata, is apparent in String Quartet Number 2 and has continued to be an important part of his compositions.

The 1965 Festival of Contemporary Arts featured the St. Louis Symphony

Orchestra conducted by Eleazar de Carvalho with Jocy de Oliveira as piano solo-ist, a concert by the Contemporary Chamber Players of the University of Chicago directed by Ralph Shapey, and lectures by George Perle, Jozef Patkowski, Elliott Carter, Peter Yates, Milton Babbitt, and John Cage. Johnston made several im-portant professional contacts during this Festival. Jozef Patkowski (director of the electronic music studio in Warsaw) invited Johnston and the University of Illinois' Contemporary Chamber Players to Poland during the summer of 1966, and Johnston has visited Poland several times since then. Also, Peter Yates, the music critic and initiator of the famous Monday Evening Concerts in Los Angeles, shared Johnston's interest in microtonality and became a supporter of Johnston's music.[20] Another important outcome of the Festival was that Carvalho commis-sioned Johnston to compose a piece for the St. Louis Symphony Orchestra.

The success of the Festivals helped to generate an idea that involved Johnston for several years and gave him opportunities to have some of his pieces performed. In 1965 he applied to the Research Board of the University of Illinois for a grant to support a summer workshop in the analysis and performance of contemporary music. It was at this time that Kenneth Gaburo's New Choral Music Ensemble evolved and that the Contemporary Chamber Players of the University of Illinois were established. The workshops drew attention to the University of Illinois' commitment to contemporary music and attracted many students.

Another outcome of both the Festivals and the workshops was that the faculty composers were beginning to receive international attention. In the sum-mer of 1966 the Contemporary Chamber Players made a European tour where per-formances were scheduled for Darmstadt, Paris, London, Cologne, and Warsaw. Originally Johnston had planned to have his piece Lament performed on the tour. Lament was an instrumental arrangement of the third movement of his String Quartet Number 2 but the piece was never performed because it was too difficult. Instead Knocking Piece was his contribution to the showcase of the creative ac-tivity of mid-western American composers, and the piece generated both interest and controversy.

A sabbatical year for Johnston was 1966, and he was awarded an Associate Membership in the Center for Advanced Study at the University of Illinois and a Sabbatical Leave Grant from the National Council on the Arts and the Humanities. He used this time to compose String Quartet Number 3 and Quintet for Groups, the commission for the St. Louis Symphony Orchestra.

Johnston did not have a lot of experience writing for orchestra. His stu-dent piece Korybas (1950) was a disaster, and Passacaglia and Epilogue from St. Joan (1960) was never performed publicly, although it was read by the Southern Illinois University Symphony. Johnston did not let this inexperience hinder him from making elaborate plans for a daring piece that challenged composer, conduc-tor, performers, and audience.

By this time Johnston's interest in scalar order's precise use of pitch

extended to such areas as duration, timbre, and even emotional content. The
Quintet has all of the complexities of earlier pieces, such as metric modulations,
polyrhythms, superimposed tempi, a combinatorial row, and a scale of thirty-one
pitches. Two pianos and two harps are tuned in just intonation (one piano uses
the same tuning as the Sonata). But the Quintet also has a new aspect involving
the scalar ordering of a gradual transformation from the chaos of noise and randomness present in graphic notation and improvisation to the strict control of
serialized microtonality and temporal proportions. Johnston achieved this progression by using different scalar forms (nominal, linear, interval, and rational)
to control various aspects of the composition. Because the scales provided different degrees of ordering, he decided to incorporate such polar elements as
serialism and indeterminacy, soloistic and ensemble writing, and various levels
of temporal organization in one composition. The fact that he was experimenting
with a symphony orchestra, a group that usually takes a conservative approach
to music, did not constrain him. Carvalho had agreed that the piece could be
microtonal.

The Quintet was premièred in St. Louis on March 24 and 25, 1967 after a
distressing rehearsal where some of the string and percussion players refused to
cooperate.[21] The microtonality was not as great a problem as the sections of
graphic notation. Apparently there was already some unrest between the conductor and the orchestra, so that the fact that Carvalho had commissioned the
piece created even more antagonism. Unfortunately the performance was not
recorded. Tape-recording a portion of the orchestra's program was prohibited
by the musicians' union, and the Quintet has not been performed since then, so
there is no way of actually hearing the piece. The score is not published, but
Johnston does have his original manuscript and several pages of sketch material.

Barney Childs copied the piece and later wrote an analytical article "Ben
Johnston: Quintet for Groups" which appeared in the 1968 issue of Perspectives
of New Music.[22] Childs was unable to attend the performance, but he understood the work as "a kind of manifold, a totality of interworked gamuts and
spectra" that consisted of three levels: the theoretic, the dramatic, and the
symbolic. Transformation was the basic process that controlled these levels.
Childs isolated several parts of the piece, calling the analysis a "cut through
this manifold" and showed how Johnston used two opposite approaches to pitch--
serialism (an all-combinatorial row) and indeterminacy (graphic notation and improvisation), two ratio scales--the Fibonacci series (1, 2, 3, 5, 8, 13 ...) and
the harmonic series (1:2:3:4 ...) that control rhythm and formal durations, and
the four scales (ordinal, nominal, linear, and ratio) to order the piece's theoretical material.

Johnston divided the orchestra into five groups (woodwinds; brass; percussion, including two pianos and two harps; one half of the strings; and the remaining strings) so that each group of this quintet would have its own particular
character and function. Childs briefly described this dramatic level of Quintet
for Groups.

The developmental operation of serial material [revealing the row and permuting the trichords] is carried on within each group.... At the same time, each group has a dynamic function in the piece at all levels, and interaction of groups alters musical developments within groups: that is, instruments of each group are related within the group by analogous behavior, with major changes in this overall behavior stimulated by other groups.... Group III ... acts as a catalyst [because the pianos and harps are tuned in the ratio scale], gradually revealing the order behind what at first appears to be chaos and acting.[23]

Childs did not label the other four groups; however, the idea of transformation and polar differences mentioned at the beginning of his article is also apparent in Johnston's pre-compositional plan, in which certain identities were assigned to each group.[24] He considered the woodwinds to be dominating soloists. At the beginning they were to exhibit individual assertion with no leadership and then gradually join the brass and become leaders at the end of the piece. Durationally the woodwinds would be occupied with tempo proportions.

The brass had an opposite function--they were a choir which at first was stiff, block-like and overwhelming, but then became more fluid, individualistic, and finally soloistic. This group was also dominating and used its assertion in the vertical dimensions. Its temporal scale was durational proportions.

Johnston labeled the percussionists (including pianists and harpists) a nurturing chamber ensemble. At first its position was supportive, then soloistic, gradually becoming more organized. Finally the group becomes instructive, with the piano acting as a leader since it was tuned in just intonation. The other percussion instruments represented the opposite spectrum of irrational pitch. The entire group participated in the tempo proportions, often having difficult polyrhythms to perform.

Both groups of strings were a passive mass representing background and chaos. Their pitch material defined contours and bands, and their rhythmic activity was large durations. At first all the strings were to act as one individual, but at the end their identity would be perceived as two separate and contrasting groups.

Interestingly, the groups actually acted out their parts during rehearsals. The string players were an angry mob refusing to cooperate, and the brass and woodwinds showed their leadership. Some of their members talked to Johnston after the rehearsal expressing interest in microtonality and how much they liked his piece. Later Childs examined the orchestral parts and found that many of the brass and woodwind players penciled in the fingering that produced the appropriate microtones indicated in the score, while the string players crossed out such complexities as Gx and replaced them with diatonic spellings.

This pre-compositional plan shows how Johnston organized the dramatic elements so groups progressed through an ordered sequence of change that enabled the listener to hear the Quintet as a fiveness. Also, the plan is reminiscent of how he worked with Leach and others in analyzing personality traits of various characters in the drama and then writing the music accordingly, such as in the "Tango" in Ring 'Round the Moon. This approach is also similar to Partch's desire that his music be corporeal, that it have a body feeling about it. Although Johnston's Quintet is an example of advanced serial and proportional systems, it also makes an expressive statement.

Peter Yates was present at the première, and Childs quotes Yates as stating

> The audience divided between applause and booing, testifying to the vitality of a composition which didn't leave its hearers indifferent. The enthusiasts kept the applause going until the booers quit.... Occasions like this make possible the existence of a native music.... For me [Yates] at first hearing it wasn't what the music is but what it did that was important. [25]

Part of this reaction may be due to the fact the idea of creating order out of chaos was both an artistic and personal concern for Johnston. During the mid and late 1960's Johnston lectured about crossing the chasm of social and political unrest saying that "If we are to build a bridge over it [the chasm], we will have to anchor its ends far in the past and far in the future." [26] Both tradition and technology would provide these needed anchors, but Johnston was searching for his own artistic anchors. Technology had proven to be a failure for him during his Guggenheim fellowship at the Columbia-Princeton Electronic Music Center, and tradition would have become an albatross in the sense that during his earlier years Johnston ran the risk of recreating neoclassic models of familiar styles and textures. However his discovery of the extended musical usage of scalar order revealed many more creative possibilities. Johnston described these as "My own search is for philosophic, theoretic, and practical means broad enough to include the whole world of sound or any fraction of it I may prefer, cohesive enough to integrate into a single whole, diverse elements of style, technique and acoustics." [27] Scalar order as he used in Quintet made this possible.

Later, in a paper "On Bridge-Building," which Johnston presented to the American Society of University Composers in 1975, he defined the chasm as an abyss and said that this abyss could

> be understood to be atomic holocaust, ecological disaster, world revolution, apocalypse, or simply a private season in hell, it is very much a phenomenon of our lives today. I began to see that I had been writing most of my works in relation to this experience. Today [1975], when things seem at least temporarily less disaster-prone I still feel very much that we are walking the knife-edge and that the best prophetic capabilities artists can muster are very much needed by humanity today. [28]

Johnston had several nervous breakdowns during the mid-1960's and early 1970's and was still searching for a spiritual teacher or system that understood the abyss. For a while that teacher was Idries Shah, a Sufi whom Johnston met and corresponded with, but a true teacher-student relationship never developed.

The Quintet shows signs of the abyss. In a sketch titled "Orchestra piece: sequences and timing" Johnston planned the emotional quality and proportional durations for each of the five groups. During pages 1 to 2 the woodwinds are assertive and become more so during page 3. The strings are brooding during pages 3 to 5 and become violent during pages 5 to 7. The emotional tone for pages 8 to 9 is delicate but finally becoming blurred during pages 10 to 12. The woodwinds and brass interrupt this state and their assertion leads to a climax that builds from pages 14 to 18. Brooding returns when the strings join the entire ensemble and chaos finally becomes order.

This sketch reveals several aspects of how Johnston designed his pieces and his working process. The emotional content was important to him, an aspect that was well defined before he began to consider details of pitch and rhythm. Certain expressive qualities are present in compositions written during the 1960's. Markings of "violent," "brooding," "delicate," "intimate," "still but tense," and "phlegmatic" are heard in the string quartets and the Sonata, although such actual expressive labelings do not appear in the score of the Quintet.

The sketch and the score also indicate that Johnston began by first plotting time. The score is carefully measured out with bar lines dividing measures according to his proportional scheme using the Fibonacci series and harmonic relations. The ratios are even labeled. This preliminary temporal approach to a piece's structure, plus Johnston's meticulous use of charts, is somewhat like John Cage's careful and time-consuming compositional process of letting chance determine content, especially during the 1950's for such works as Landscape Number 4 for Twelve Radios. Both composers spend many hours charting controlling elements. In Cage's case it is the realization of hexagrams from the I Ching while Johnston makes charts of temporal and pitch ratios.

String Quartet Number 3 was composed during the winter of 1966. It was not commissioned but was the result of an especially creative period for Johnston. He wrote the quartet in one month, an unusually short period of time, but it was not premiered until March 15, 1976 when the Concord String Quartet performed it at Alice Tully Hall as a presentation by the Walter W. Naumburg Foundation.

Chronologically this piece follows Quintet for Groups and has several elements in common with its predecessor, String Quartet Number 2. The microtonality is still controlled by the prime numbers 2, 3, and 5 so the same pitch lattice and 53-toned scale are used. There are familiar abrupt emotional changes such as an expressive marking of "tender" suddenly followed by an "angry" passage, and some of the phrase shapes and modulating material are similar. This

Quartet No. 3

Benjamin Johnston

Example 13. Microtonal version of C in String Quartet Number 3. Copyright 1985 by Smith Publications. Used with permission.

is especially obvious in comparing the opening pages of each work. (Compare Example 1, page 77, with Example 13.)

However, there are some differences. String Quartet Number 3 is one short through-composed movement. It is slightly less difficult because the texture is thinner, and some parts are obviously melodic, such as an extended melody that sounds like something Sergei Prokofiev might have written. Also, the rhythmic patterns are not complicated because there are no polyrhythms. When the Cordier Quartet performed String Quartet Number 3 at 1982 New Music America held in Chicago, it only took two hours of rehearsal time for Johnston to work with the musicians in checking that tunings and so on were correct.

As in most of Johnston's music, pitch was controlled by means of an elaborate pre-compositional plan. At this time he tried to apply combinatorial serial procedures to his tuning system. He divided his 53-tone scale into the twelve pitch class areas and arranged these in a combinatorial row of C Eb D E C# F Bb G# A B F# G. This row structures the quartet. Within each of these chromatic areas he placed microtonal pitches, such as Dbb- C B# C+ C- (the five microtonal C's available in the 53-tone scale) and arranged them in patterns that he labeled as prime, inversion, retrograde, and retrograde inversion. The five C's are an inversion. Their prime order would be B# C- C C+ Dbb-. As a further complication Johnston designed individual 12-tone rows for each one of the fifty-three scale degrees, and these rows also follow a prime, inversion, retrograde, and retrograde inversion format. The majority are combinatorial, although at times some pitches are rearranged so that the combinatoriality is destroyed. Thus three layers of serialism are operative--the master row, the twelve rows attached to each pitch class of the master row, and then individual rows for his 53-tone scale. Figure 14 illustrates this tri-level relationship. (There are six C rows--one for each microtonal pitch and an additional diatonic C row. Some diatonic chromatic pitches have extra rows, like C, thus increasing the total number of microtonal rows from fifty-three to sixty).

Originally Johnston had an even more complicated plan, but he discovered that it would have generated an extremely long piece, so after fifty-six measures he abandoned plan one and began the master row with its first pitch--the "C" section. This noticeable change happens in measure 57. In Example 13 the first violin plays a melody that is one of the microtonal versions of C.

During measures 74-75 there are dramatic changes in dynamics, articulations, and tempo that announce the second section, the "Eb" of the master row,

chromatic row
C Eb D E C# F   Bb G# A B F# G

microtonal row
C+ Eb+ D+ E+ C#+ E#+   A#+ G#+ A+ B F#+ G

hyperchromatic row for the pitch "C"
B# G# B G C F Db- Bbb- Dbb- Bbb- Gb- Cb- Ab- C- G- D- A E B D F+ C+

Figure 14. Tri-level serial relationship in String Quartet Number 3.

which begins in measure 76. Each member of the row is associated with similar kinds of changes. The "D" is "Intense," "E" is "Tender" and melodic, "C" is "Sotto voce" and non vibrato, "F" is another melody that is "Tender" with normal vibrato that suddenly turns into an "Angry" mood, "B" is "Sharp, Playful," "G#" and "A" are merged together into a crescendo, "B" is "Slow; as if distant," "F#" is "Agitated," and "G" is "Slow, intimate."

Probably the most remarkable aspect of String Quartet Number 3 is that Johnston was able to take the vast quantity of serialized pitch material and shape it into a piece that does not rely on repetition or traditional formal patterns for its coherence. The listener is not aware of the serial pitch scheme because the process is so well hidden that Johnston himself could not remember or figure out how the serialism was working. Without the aid of the sketches it would be impossible to unravel the complex processes. What the listener does hear is an expressive piece that is unpredictably sectional while at the same time having familiar textures such as accompanied melodies and quasi-homophonic settings. Ideas and pitches are repeated and prolonged, and although the chromaticism is apparent, it is not as concentrated as the first movement of String Quartet Number 2 where each measure was a 12-tone row that ascended one degree of the 53-tone scale. In String Quartet Number 3 Johnston devoted an entire piece to this process, with each row appearing within a larger row. The process is more gradual, and one has time to hear the changing relationships.

This string quartet is usually paired with String Quartet Number 4 in a performance titled "Crossings." Johnston labeled String Quartet Number 3 as "Vergings" which is followed by a two-minute period of silence. String Quartet Number 4 is the "Ascent."

After completing the quartet Johnston wrote a short work, Prayer, for boys choir. Robert Smith, the director of a boys choir in the Champaign-Urbana area, was preparing Benjamin Britten's War Requiem with the choir and needed a composition that would drill the troublesome interval of the tritone that is featured in this work. As a result Johnston wrote Prayer, a three-voice canon at the unison that stresses tritones, but the choir never performed it. As a composer Johnston is comfortable with switching from the theoretical, as in String Quartet Number 3, to the practical need of a director's request.

Notes

1. Ben Johnston, "Scalar Order as a Compositional Resource," Perspectives of New Music, Spring-Summer 1964, pp. 56-76.

2. For more information about Stevens' work see S. S. Stevens, "Mathematics, Measurement, and Psychophysics" in Handbook of Experimental Psychology, S. S. Stevens, editor (New York: Wiley and Sons, 1951), pp. 1-49.

3. "The Corporealism of Harry Partch," Perspectives of New Music, xiii/2 (1975), pp. 93-94.

4. "Scalar Order," p. 74.

5. This recording also contains John Cage's and Lejaren Hiller's collaboration on HPSCHD, the famous multi-media piece using computer-generated sound tapes that was premièred at the University of Illinois. Teresa Sterne, a representative of Nonesuch Records, was present at several of the Festivals of Contemporary Arts and selected pieces for various records.

6. William Duckworth and Edward Brown briefly discuss String Quartet Number 2 in their book, The Theoretical Foundations of Music (Belmont, CA: Wadsworth, 1978), pp. 296-298.

7. For more information see J. G. Bennett, Enneagram Studies (York Beach, ME: Samuel Weiser, 1983).

8. P. D. Ouspensky explains the laws of triads and octaves in The Fourth Way (New York: Knopf, 1957), pp. 187-215.

8A. This quartet's second movement was the only occasion that Johnston remembers using the enneagram. How much this dynamic symbolic figure subtly influenced his music composed during the 1960's is difficult to determine. On several occasions I tried to trace the enneagram's number sequence in noticeable emotional changes, such as in the Sonata for Microtonal Piano/Grindlemusic, but found no evidence of the enneagram's influence.

9. Terry Southern and Mason Hoffenberg, Candy (New York: Putnam, 1958).

10. These notes are published both in the score which is available from Smith Publications and the recording "Sound Forms for Piano," NW203.

11. John Jeffrey Gibbens, a student at the University of Illinois, is preparing a detailed analysis of this piece for his doctoral dissertation.

11A. A tape recording of these concerts is available through the Tape Archive of the University of Illinois' School of Music. Richards performed the Grindlemusic version at the Festival of Contemporary Arts March 11, 1967. Other pianists who have performed the piece are Neely Bruce, Virginia Gaburo, Deborah Richards, and Robert Miller, who recorded the Sonata for New World Records, "Sound Forms for Piano," NW203.

12. This information is from the score and record liner notes.

13. It was at this time that Johnston met Joel Mandelbaum, a composer

also interested in tuning systems, who wrote his doctoral dissertation about the "Multiple Division of the Octave and the Tonal Resources of 19-tone Temperament," unpublished Ph.D. dissertation, Indiana University, 1961. Johnston met Mandelbaum at a conference on microtonality sponsored by the American Society of University Composers that was held in St. Louis in 1967. The conference papers are published in American Society of University Composers Proceedings, 1967. This issue has articles by Johnston, Mandelbaum, Carlton Gamer, and Peter Yates which address the question of microtonality.

14. There is an error in the score. The "S" version should be 5:4 and the "G" version should be 3:2. These two ratios are accidentally reversed. Gibbens has found many more errors in the published score.

15. Stockhausen experimented with these kinds of durational relationships in Zeitmasse (1955-1956), Gruppen (1955-1957), and Klavierstuck XI (1956). Messiaen organized time through a series that he called chromatic durations. See his Messe de la Pentecôte (1950) and Chronochromie (1960). Nancarrow has been experimenting with piano rolls and is able to achieve complicated rhythmic ratios. His music is available on 1750 Arch Records, and some of his scores are published in Soundings.

15A. There is another error in the score. The metric modulation should be $\eighthnote = \dotted{sixteenth}$ (5:4).

16. There were times when Johnston wrote compositions that he did not consider to be good pieces, such as Of Vanity (1964) for chorus and two percussionists which was not available for me to study.

17. Johnston wrote a review about the 1963 Festival in "Letter from Urbana," Perspectives of New Music, II/1 (1963), 137-141.

18. "Proportionality and Expanded Pitch Relations," Perspectives of New Music, V/1 (1966), 112-120.

19. "Scalar Order as a Compositional Resource," p. 120.

20. Yates discussed Johnston's music in Yates' book, Twentieth Century Music: Its Evolution from the End of the Harmonic Era to the Present Era of Sound (New York: Pantheon, 1968), pp. 229 and 323. In 1969 Yates even tried to interest Johnston in accepting a position at the State University of New York at Buffalo, but Johnston declined, feeling that he was content with his work at the University of Illinois.

21. Johnston describes some of these problems in Gagne and Caras' Soundpieces.

22. "Ben Johnston: Quintet for Groups," Perspectives of New Music, 1968, pp. 110-121.

23. "Ben Johnston: Quintet for Groups," pp. 115 and 117.

24. This information was obtained from sketches of the composition.

25. "Ben Johnston: Quintet for Groups," p. 121.

26. Johnston, "On Context," American Society of University Composers Proceedings, III (1968), 36.

27. "On Context," p. 36.

28. Johnston, "On Bridge-Building," an unpublished manuscript.

During the Contemporary Chamber Ensemble's 1966 Summer European tour John-ston visited his college friend Ward Swingle, who by this time had established an international reputation as the leader of the Swingle Singers. Swingle was in the process of commissioning music for his group, so he invited Johnston to compose a piece. This interested Johnston, and he completed the commission "Ci-Gît Satie et des autres" on Thanksgiving of 1966.

The title is a tombstone phrase meaning "here lies Satie." The piece is a pastiche of quotes, satire, and different jazz styles. It is scored for eight sing-ers, drums, and double bass, the ensemble that Swingle used. "Ci-Gît Satie" sounds like pop music. The text is scat syllables (a specialty of the Swingle Singers), and originally Johnston had intended that they choose the syllables. When Swingle received the piece he decided it was too difficult to program on a pop concert, and the group has never performed it; however he commissioned another piece from Johnston for the Swingle Singers II, which was premièred in 1981.

Naturally, Johnston was disappointed, but Kenneth Gaburo's New Music Choral Ensemble at the University of Illinois wanted to accept the challenge of learning "Ci-Gît Satie," and they premièred it on July 23, 1967. The same group also recorded the piece on Ars Nova Ars Antiqua Records (An-1005) and later performed it at the 1967 World's Fair in Montreal.

The piece is in just intonation, but Johnston only used the Pythagorean comma (the ratio of 80/81 which is twenty-two cents) plus the 4:5:6 ratios to produce a scale of thirty-one pitches that are almost equal. The score does not look microtonal because there are no pluses or minuses; instead the enharmonic differences are notated with double sharps and flats (see Example 1). The listener hears the music as being harmonically clear and precise.

Gaburo's group had some problems realizing the piece, which Johnston de-scribed in a letter to Swingle dated July 15, 1967.

> At first, I'm told, the harmonics merely sounded lush and flabby. There were two causes: 1) insufficient clarity in just intonation (ap-proximate equal temperament produces a blurring which "blends" only too much), 2) rhythmic sloppiness; insufficient <u>beat</u> (no loose, relaxed play), and insufficient precision of attack and release.

Example 1. Beginning measures of "Ci-Gît Satie" showing use of just intonation, scat syllables, and jazz style. Forthcoming from Smith Press. Used with permission.

Gaburo was concerned about projecting the piece's meaning, so Johnston prepared the following program notes:

> The piece involves wit, satire, even at times parody. It involves meta-morphosis of style, allusion to music outside the piece, to manners of performance, even to languages. A history and criticism of musical style (with references to Perdido, I'll Remember April, Satie's Gympno-pedies, Spanish flamenco, Lotte Lenya, American big-band vocal groups, Stravinsky's Symphony of Psalms, the Route 66 "theme song," Ibert's Escales, the shipwreck in Mallarmé's Un coup de dés, Tristan und Isolde), "Ci-Gît Satie" is about "innocence regained."[1]

Much of this meaning is either hidden or lost, especially since the piece is short, only fifty-six measures long. There is simply not enough time to register differences, so the audience misses these sophisticated nuances. Probably the listener hears "Ci-Gît Satie" as an attempt to imitate a jazz style but in a too controlled and restrained manner.

The score reveals the reference to Satie. Like Satie, Johnston wrote interpretive descriptions and inserted numerous stylistic directions, such as "Poco Flamenco," "Sempre flamenco ma poco Weimarisch," "Faites chaud," "Faites Escales," "Faites-le (ayez souvenance)," and "Faites Côte." The Tristan quote, which is not an obvious one, is even labeled "bonjour Tristan." But these directions were not sufficient for Gaburo and his group to interpret the music adequately, so Gaburo asked Johnston to give some of his associations about the piece to help them with the interpretation. One performer's score is marked: "nasal and angry," "nostalgic" (for the "Poco Flamenco"), "get more outrageous and put down jazz," "pop German," "cool jazz," "serious jazz," and "commercial jazz."

The Swingle Singers are well known for their performance of Luciano Berio's Sinfonia, a piece that has many musical quotations. Sinfonia was completed in 1968, after Johnston had written "Ci-Gît Satie," and it is interesting that both composers used quotations. Generally, Berio's quotations, such as Mahler's music, are obvious so the listener can follow the intended meaning. Johnston's quotations are hidden, so the meaning is private. This was also the case with the Sonata for Microtonal Piano/Grindlemusic. The quotations in Newcastle Troppo and Ivesberg Revisited are more overt. One questions why Johnston reverted to imitating jazz styles and using quotations, especially the reference to Satie. Johnston did not have strong aesthetic bonds to Satie's music, as Cage does, and the different jazz styles are difficult to write and perform convincingly. Part of the reason may be nostalgic--Swingle reminded Johnston of his college days when he was playing jazz and studying French. For him the piece was "innocence regained."

The year 1967 was a productive one. In the letter to Swingle, Johnston wrote:

> I have never had such a run of professional success as this year. In a way, it figures. I was awarded the year, to do just that; and I have been, with others, tending crops for a long time that now reach harvest. All along, cooperation and unifying seem to have been the secrets to whatever works--with one significant exception: the research in intonation and related theory, in which only this year have I made contact with others in the field and only after some years of solitary investigation. That, too, now seems to be ready to bear fruit, both in works (of mine) which I respect, and in recognition.[2]

In addition to this professional success, Johnston also enjoyed having John Cage as composer in residence at the University of Illinois during the years 1967-1969.[3] Cage arranged to have his suppers with the Johnstons, and then the family and Cage would spend the evening playing games, such as Scrabble, bridge, and solitaire.[4]

Cage's presence had some effect on Johnston's composing because Johnston tried using The I Ching,[5] Cage's technique for making compositional choices, for One Man, a piece for solo trombone that Johnston wrote in 1967. Before writing the piece Johnston threw coins to generate three hexagrams from The I Ching, one for each movement of the piece. The results were number 29--"The Abysmal (Water)," which Johnston renamed "Cross," number 52--"Keeping Still," and number 51--"The Arousal." Each hexagram consists of two identical trigrams. "Cross" ("Abysmal") is yin-yang-yin; "Keeping Still" is yin-yin-yang; and "The Arousal" is yang-yin-yin. Each trigram has the yang (male line) in a different position but there is only "one man" in each half of the hexagram.

The hexagrams do not structure the music as literally as in Cage's compositions because Johnston was also incorporating other elements, such as just intonation using the seventh partial. But it is possible to plot the pitch relationships on the 2,5,7 lattice used in some sections of "Cross" (the first movement of One Man) and "Keeping Still" (the second movement) and compare them to the numeral value of the yin or yang line of the hexagram. If the vertical move of one position north or south on the lattice is considered to be a value of three, and a horizontal move one position east or west is a value of two, then a yang line (which is 2+2+3 or a permutation of this progression) is realized by two moves east or west followed by one move north or south on the lattice, and a yin line (3+3+2) would be two moves north or south and one move east or west. A hexagram having changing lines (a condition when all three coins are either heads or tails) would be three consecutive moves in one direction. Although this information is not highly significant to One Man (Johnston says the hexagrams helped shape its emotional tone), it does show that at this time Johnston was trying to apply ratio scales to many different aspects of a composition. Theoretically choices from any two-dimensional lattice could be manipulated by hexagrams.

One Man was commissioned by Stuart Dempster, a trombonist who is known for his use of extended techniques.[6] Many composers have written for him, and Johnston had an opportunity to hear some of these experimental works by Barney Childs, John Cage, Robert Erickson, Luciano Berio, and Pauline Oliveros on Dempster's concert that was part of the 1967 Festival of Contemporary Arts.[7]

One Man is an important piece in Johnston's catalog, not on account of The I Ching, but because this is the first composition in which Johnston used the seventh partial.[8] The trombone seemed like the ideal instrument for the seventh since the natural seventh harmonic is available in each slide position except the "f" side of the tenor-bass trombone. In tempered tuning this pitch is usually avoided and replaced with substitutes found in other slide positions.

Johnston used this seventh partial to create scales that included several new intervals. The septimal minor third (7/6) and major third (9/7) are heard in "Cross" and "Arousal," and the septimal major second (8/7) is present in all three movements (see Example 2, page 114).

Johnston's notation for the ratios using the seventh partial is a 7 and *L*
(depending upon if the ratio is measured above or below), which raises or lowers
a pitch by 49 cents, almost a quarter-tone. This symbol is not new; Giuseppe
Tartini (1692-1770) used it to indicate a "semi-flat," a small amount of tuning;
Adriaan Fokker used a similar symbol for his 31-tone equally tempered scale; and
Alain Daniélou indicated the ratio of 16/15 (a major half-tone) with *L*.[9] The seven
symbol can be combined with sharps, flats, +'s, -'s, and other 7's, as evident in
Figure 1 and Example 2.[9A]

Example 2. Septimal seconds and thirds in "Cross" from <u>One Man</u>. Copyright
1972 by Media Press. Used with permission.

The addition of the seventh partial now made it possible for Johnston to
create new lattices. Using four partials (2,3,5,7) requires a three-dimensional
diagram (which will be shown later), while omitting one partial, such as 3 or 5,
still made it possible to diagram these relationships on a two-dimensional plane.
In <u>One Man</u> Johnston used the 2,3,7 and 2,5,7 lattices to create two different
scales. "Cross" and "Arousal" are based upon the 2,3,7 lattice. The 3 and
7 ratios do not create a just major third because the necessary fifth partial
is excluded. Instead, the third is lower, for example C to Eb7 is the ratio of
7/6 and sounds 49 cents lower than 6/5, about a 1/4 tone. The lattice for 2,3,7
is shown in Figure 1, which also includes a diagram for determining the 12-tone
septimal scale. This scale has several different sizes of chromatic half steps,
such as the 49/48 between C and Db7 and the 28/27 between G and Ab7.

"Keeping Still," the middle movement of <u>One Man</u>, uses the 2,5,7 lattice.
The perfect fifth is missing in this system (the third partial is not available) so
the lattice's columns are read as just major thirds (instead of perfect fifths as
would be the case in the 2,3,7 system). The rows are septimal sevenths. The
pitch Ab77+ is a 7/4 ratio to Bb7 and so on. Johnston made the properties of
this lattice clear in the beginning measures of "Keeping Still." The major third
of C to E (5/4) and the inverted septimal seventh of C to D*L*- (8/7) are heard
in the first measure. These ratios define the vertical and horizontal relationships
around the center pitch of C. Measure two explores one move west (D*L*- to E*LL*-,
see Example 3).

Another first for <u>One Man</u> is that the score contains an explanation of

G#L	F#+	E+	D7	C7#+		$\frac{81}{49}$	$\frac{81}{56}$	$\frac{81}{64}$	$\frac{567}{512}$	$\frac{3969}{2048}$
C#L	BL	A+	G7	F7#+		$\frac{54}{49}$	$\frac{27}{14}$	$\frac{27}{16}$	$\frac{189}{128}$	$\frac{1323}{1024}$
F#L	EL	D	C7+	B♭7+		$\frac{72}{49}$	$\frac{9}{7}$	$\frac{9}{8}$	$\frac{63}{32}$	$\frac{441}{256}$
BLL-	AL	G	F7	E♭7		$\frac{96}{49}$	$\frac{12}{7}$	$\frac{3}{2}$	$\frac{21}{16}$	$\frac{147}{128}$
ELL-	DL-	C	B♭	A♭7		$\frac{64}{49}$	$\frac{8}{7}$	$\frac{1}{1}$	$\frac{7}{4}$	$\frac{49}{32}$
ALL-	GL-	F	E♭	D♭7		$\frac{256}{147}$	$\frac{32}{21}$	$\frac{4}{3}$	$\frac{7}{6}$	$\frac{49}{48}$
DLL--	CL-	Bb-	A♭	G♭7		$\frac{512}{441}$	$\frac{64}{63}$	$\frac{16}{9}$	$\frac{14}{9}$	$\frac{49}{36}$
GLL--	FL-	Eb-	D♭-	C♭7		$\frac{2048}{1323}$	$\frac{256}{189}$	$\frac{32}{27}$	$\frac{28}{27}$	$\frac{49}{27}$
CLL--	B♭--	Ab-	G♭-	F♭7		$\frac{4096}{3969}$	$\frac{1024}{567}$	$\frac{128}{81}$	$\frac{112}{81}$	$\frac{98}{81}$

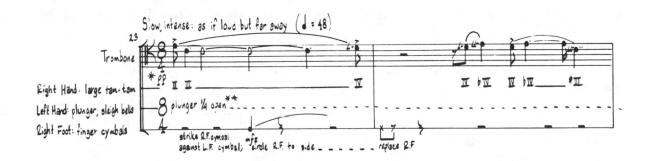

Figure 1. Lattices and septimal scales using the second, third, and seventh ratios. Property of the composer. Used with permission.

Example 3. Beginning measures of "Keeping Still" showing exposition of the 2,5,7 lattice. Copyright 1972 by Media Press. Used with permission.

Johnston's notational system and directions for realizing just intonation on the trombone. The uppercase Roman numerals under the pitches, as seen in Examples 2 and 3, indicate which slide position to use, and the accidentals show

Pitch names						Ratios				
D𝄪	C𝄪	B#	A#+	G#7+		250/196	125/112	125/64	875/512	6125/4096
B♭↓↓	A#↓	G#	F#+	E77+		50/49	25/14	25/16	175/128	1225/1024
G#↓↓	F#↓	E	D7	C77+		80/49	10/7	5/4	35/32	245/128
E♭↓	D♭↓	C	B♭	A♭7+		64/49	8/7	1/1	7/4	49/32
C♭↓↓	B♭↓	A♭	G♭	F♭7+		256/245	64/35	8/5	7/5	49/40
A♭↓	G♭↓	F♭	E♭♭	D♭♭		2048/1225	256/175	32/25	28/25	49/25
F♭↓↓	E♭♭↓	D♭♭↓	C♭♭	B♭♭♭		8192/6125	1024/875	128/125	224/125	196/125

$$\left[\ \ \frac{1}{1}\ \ \frac{35}{32}\ \frac{8}{7}\ \cdots\ \frac{5}{4}\ \cdots\ \frac{175}{128}\ \frac{10}{7}\ \cdots\ \frac{25}{16}\ \cdots\ \frac{8}{5}\ \cdots\ \frac{7}{4}\ \frac{64}{35}\ \cdots\ \frac{2}{1}\right.$$

C —35/32— D7 D♭↓ 250/245 —35/32— E —35/32— F#7↓ F#↓ —35/32— G# 128/125 A♭ —35/32— B♭ 256/245 B♭↓ —35/32— C

Figure 2. Lattices and septimal scales using the ratios of two, five, and seven. Property of the composer. Used with permission.

how much that position needs to be altered from the equal-tempered system. Also, there are instructions about the staging, equipment, and performance of One Man. Dempster prepared this material, and he even included advice about how to practice the tuning.[10] Such careful attention to detail is typical of him.

The circumstance that the trombone's construction includes the seventh partial does not make it any easier to learn the piece. Dempster states that the performer will need at least two hundred hours to prepare One Man, and then later he reported in his book, The Modern Trombone: A Definition of Its Idioms, that the piece is difficult to maintain in a repertoire because the tuning slips without regular practice.[11]

One Man was the first piece in which Johnston incorporated theatrical elements. Finger cymbals are strapped around the performer's lower ankles; a tambourine is strapped to the inside right leg just below the knee; and wind chimes are put over the head to surround the face, hair, and neck. A bass drum, tom-tom, and "sizzle" cymbal are played by the feet and at times hands. The piece is choreographed. For example, the movements notated in "Cross," which are carefully explained in the instructions, actually form a cross. Dempster must perform as if he were a dancer and a one-man band. This agility coupled with the difficulties of producing the exact pitch ratios of just intonation seem like an impossibility; however Dempster is a type of performer that invites such challenges. Physically he is supple due to intensive practice of Yoga, and since he has been able to develop circular breathing, he can play passages that would otherwise be impossible. Nevertheless, it was four years before he premièred the piece on May 1, 1971 at the University of Illinois. Such other trombonists as Jim Stahley, Jim Fulkerson, and Benny Sluchin have performed the piece, and Vinko Globokar has expressed interest in learning One Man.

During 1968 and 1969 Johnston worked with musique concrète and indeterminacy. For a while it seemed he had abandoned just intonation. Part of the reason for this unexpected change was a commission from the Smithsonian Institution to produce an electronic music tape to accompany an orientation exhibit for the Institute's museum. Jim Weaver, a former student at the University of Illinois and an employee at the Museum, recommended Johnston for the project. Johnston's idea was to prepare a four and one-half minute presentation that would feature a historical survey of the United States' technological history. Dates of important inventions, such as the telegraph, telephone, and automobile, would be used as a ratio durational scale that controlled the piece's timing and shape.

Johnston collaborated with Jaap Spek, an audio engineer, on this and several other projects. Spek had worked with Stockhausen on Kontakte (1959-1960) and Mikrophonie (1964) before coming to Urbana to be audio director of the Krannert Center for the Performing Arts. Technically, Museum Piece is well done, and the listener hears a progression of sounds and aural cues that are a time line to both the piece and its content. However Museum Piece is dated because other composers, such as Edgard Varèse, had done similar works ten years earlier.

But, the personnel at the Smithsonian liked Johnston's ideas and commissioned him to do another piece for an exhibit of old automobiles. Johnston and Spek went to great effort to collect suitable sounds. They visited the Indianapolis Speedway for the Hoosier Auto Show and Swap Meet Association, an Illiana Antique Automobile Club show in Danville, Illinois, and an Amish community near Urbana. The last-named would not cooperate, so Spek and Johnston were unable to collect the pre-automobile sounds that they wanted. Unfortunately the Smithsonian project was never completed because when President Nixon took office in 1968 the funds for the project were taken away.

During the late 1960's the University of Illinois was expanding. The School of Music received a new building, and a large performance arts complex was built with money donated by the Krannert family. Johnston's most outrageous composition, CASTA*, was performed on one of the dedicatory concerts.

CASTA* is part of a collection of indeterminate pieces titled Four Do-It-Yourself Pieces that were composed in 1969. The individual titles are: CASTA* for Norma Marder, RECIPE for a * for Katherine Litz, CONFERENCE: a telephone happening for John Cage, and KNOCKING PIECE II for Jack McKenzie. In an interview Johnston described these pieces as recipes and an opportunity to collaborate with performers.

> I've also written a lot of pieces where it's just a recipe, the performer is really doing most of it. The performer makes most of the conventional decisions, the ones you think of the composer as usually making. A lot of the others I've made--but that's the influence of Cage.... Chance has to operate on something, and when you select what it's going to operate on, there you have made the composition. And it can be just as signed and identifiable as anything else, because chance may not operate on anything you didn't give it to operate on, and you've given it these things. You can even have other people select those things, but you've biased it in a certain way, and what they select is sure to turn out within a certain ambience....
> It's operating at several removes from the material--a little bit like scientists using mechanical hands to manipulate radioactive materials. You can't handle these things yourself, but you do it. I've been interested in that process, the process of manipulating the thing at some remove. And, lately, even the audience--trying to write pieces that will involve the audience; set it up so that when the audience gets involved, they will do so in certain ways. That's been only partly successful. I'm interested in that problem, though.[12]

Johnston's use of chance is partly due to Cage's influence and partly to Johnston's own search of trying to build a bridge from chaos to order. He considered an ordinal scale (one that is rank-ordered in terms of some attribute) to be "a good theoretical basis for many indeterminate modes of organization."[13] In Quintet for Groups Johnston tried combining all four scalar orders in one composition, and finding that the indeterminate graphic sections caused such performance problems, it seemed logical that he should experiment with writing compositions that were based upon the indeterminate properties of the ordinal scale.

CASTA* is probably the best-known of Johnston's indeterminate pieces because it is available as CASTA Bertram on the Nonesuch recording (H-71237), "The Contemporary Contrabass: New American Music by John Cage, Pauline Oliveros, Ben Johnston" in a performance by Bertram Turetzky. CASTA Norma (the performer is to substitute his or her first name for the asterisk) was also performed by the singer Norma Marder on a gala concert celebrating the opening of the Great Hall of the Krannert Center for the Performing Arts.[14] The piece involves an elaborate set-up featuring a recording station, a place where the performer types and the sounds of the typewriter are recorded, a spotlighted performance area, and a technician's table where the recording and playback of tapes are controlled. The score contains a picture of the staging, and detailed flow charts explain the use of the tape recorders, mixers, microphones, and headphones.[15]

The performer has the following preparations to make for CASTA*: "Prepare four segments of 45 seconds each of noises of all kinds you make instrumentally and/or vocally. At least one third of the sounds should be vocal. A significant number should be scatological. Write down a list of these sounds such that from it you could identify each sound. Prepare a sequence of at least twenty-five excerpts ranging from very brief to a phrase or two in length, selected from standard repertory works you can perform. A significant number should be virtuosic."[16]

Norma Marder chose obvious excerpts for her realization--she sang parts of Vincenzo Bellini's Norma. This collecting and categorizing of sounds is the same working method that Johnston had used for Museum Piece and Auto Mobile, and the scat syllables are sounds he had used in "Ci-Gît Satie."

The performance consists of making three tape loops of these forty-five-second sound segments. The soloist then goes to the typewriter, inserts file cards, and types the scores for twenty-five of the sounds that have been made. Meanwhile the sounds of the typewriter are mixed with those of the tape loops, and as the loops are played, the soloist shuffles the file cards that have just been typed, and then performs the notated sounds one by one, throwing each card out into the audience as the sound is completed. The final cadence is throwing away the score.

The other compositions in Four Do-It-Yourself Pieces are as carefully described and controlled as CASTA*. Each one is imaginative and permits some kind of personal statement from the performer, such as the following direction in RECIPE for a *: "Design a stage set which is as much like your own bedroom as possible, unless your room is too cramped for practicing your performing. If it is, modify the design to permit such movement as is necessary. The room should be completely furnished with real objects."[17]

CONFERENCE: a telephone happening was written for John Cage. It was to be part of a Bell Telephone exhibit at the Chicago Museum of Contemporary Arts that did not take place. Claes Oldenburg was to have made a floppy telephone sculpture for the exhibit. Johnston's score for the happening shows how he used The I Ching as an ordinal scale to control the number of performers, content, and duration of his piece, and how he understood the philosophy of indeterminacy, something that is often confused by other composers. The score reads:

> Get the telephone numbers of a number of people who are reachable
> (wherever they may be) by telephone. The number of people shall be
> equal to the number of a hexagram of I CHING obtained by tossing coins.
> Assign to each a topic of conversation (e.g. politics, sex, religion, gossip, science, etc.). Toss coins again, once for each participant to
> determine from the text and commentaries of each hexagram his topic of

conversation. At an agreed upon time place a conference call to all of these people.

Each person shall prepare for the conference by collecting a number of quotations pertinent to his topic, each containing no less than 64 words. The number of quotations each participant has shall be equal to the number of a hexagram of I CHING obtained by tossing coins. Something of their overall character can be inferred from the text and commentaries of this hexagram. These quotations should be written down, each on a separate slip of paper, to be put into a hat and drawn out one by one to be read at the time of the conference.

On the occasion of the conference call, each participant, as he draws out a quotation to read, tosses coins successively to determine by I CHING the number of words of it he will read. The order in which participants speak is determined informally, conversationally, politely. When each participant has read all of his quotations, he says "Good-bye," but remains on the line until all are finished. When the initiator of the conference notices from the goodbyes that all participants have finished, he thanks them and says, "Good-bye," terminating the conference.[18]

At one time Johnston intended to include a fifth piece in his Do-It-Yourself series. This was a plan for a concert debate that would involve audience reaction to prepared statements by performers. Each person was assigned a particular political view about art and was to write an essay that he or she would read as part of the piece. The composition was titled Age of Surveillance and was premièred in November 1979 at De Paul University in Chicago for a regional meeting of the American Society of University Composers. The performance did not work because it was too staged and artificial, and what little audience participation did take place was humorous--one person put a paper bag over his head and tried to interact with the panelists. By 1979 the idea of audience participation was dated, and Johnston's strong personal feeling about the need for a catholic view of contemporary art was not as passionately expressed as he had intended.

For several years Johnston had been involved in a series of attacks against academicism in composition. Much of his concern was about a closed-mindedness that was often expressed as a strong adherence to European styles and traditions accompanied by a denial that John Cage's music was a significant aspect of contemporary American music. Some of Johnston's ideas appear in his lecture "On Context," which was published in Proceedings,[19] and in a letter to Perspectives of New Music in which Johnston admonished the editors for their biased academic views, particularly to the music of John Cage. Johnston wrote:

I take vehement exception to PERSPECTIVES' perennial one-sided treatment to John Cage, so consistent that it seems to amount to an editorial policy.... Like post-war American painting, American indeterminate music has become the vanguard of style.

How PERSPECTIVES can ignore a phenomenon of this importance is hard to understand. If I did not know personally many of the people involved, I would suspect prejudice. I must attribute short-sightedness to them, nevertheless, since this policy indicates at the very least a lack of the kind of "perspective" which purports to be the aim of the magazine.[20]

The years 1968 to 1970 were a hiatus in Johnston's theorizing about proportionality. He spent this time writing and lecturing about aesthetic matters. In his contribution to the IMC Panel "The Sounds of Things to Come, the Attitude of Youth, and the Composer, the Performer, and the Changing Audience,"[21] Johnston spoke out against the attitude of "the establishment" which ignored the music of young composers (Johnston was forty-two at the time) and defended the position of the composer-teacher, noting that the universities have generated their own musical life equipped with composers, performers, and audience, and that the music of these composers was frequently less "academic" than that performed at the typical contemporary concerts heard in large cities.

In his lecture "Art and Survival,"[22] which was the keynote address at the "Renaissance '69??" series at the Museum of Contemporary Art in Chicago, Johnston tried to answer the questions of what it means to be an artist, the meaning of art, and how art educates the emotions. When comparing this paper to his "A Semantic Examination of Music," written in the mid-1950's for a philosophy class, it is evident that during this fifteen-year period Johnston had discovered his own artistic identity. His short-term experimentation with indeterminacy was not so much an attempt to keep current with the fads but an inquiry into one level of artistic order. Johnston discovered that he was not comfortable with indeterminacy.

Before returning to just intonation Johnston had one more project to complete that, like his article "Art and Survival," was a summary of his development as a composer. Wilford Leach had performed Zodiac of Memphis Street at Sarah Lawrence College where he taught, and he programmed Gertrude when he became director of the New York City acting company, ETC of La Mama. It was such a success that he decided there should be another Leach-Johnston collaboration. Leach wanted to write a vampire story using a plot adapted from a novella by La Fanu. Leach's idea was to create a rock opera that was based upon the psychosexual fantasies of a young woman, Laura, who at the age of six years had a nightmare where she was confronted by a vampire figure, the dark-haired Carmilla. In the drama Laura is eighteen and falls in love with Carmilla, who has been her imaginary childhood companion. Unlike the classic vampire formula where in the end the vampire is killed, Laura is finally completely dominated by the vampire Carmilla.

When Leach proposed writing a rock opera, Johnston hesitated. He had had no experience with rock music but, remembering the successes they had writing and producing their college musical, Leach convinced Johnston that he could do it. Johnston was to write lead sheets from which the ensemble would make their own arrangements. Some of the score would even be improvised.

Johnston finally agreed to accept the challenge, and Leach seemed especially confident about the music.

Johnston had several difficulties. First, he did not have complete control over the music. Just providing lead sheets was a drastic change from the type of writing he had been doing. Then, he also distrusted improvisation. An added frustration was that Leach divided the opera into thirteen scenes but sent Johnston the script in segments that were out of order, so he never had an opportunity to read the script in its entirety.

During the opera the two women sit on a Victorian bench while slides and a film are projected behind them. Because there are only three characters (Laura, Carmilla, and a mountebank) and minimal stage action, the vocal lines are very important. Leach depended upon the music to convey the drama. Johnston chose to use modal melodies so lines would be accessible to the performer and listeners, and he was especially aware of writing melodies in which the words could be heard. Carmilla was recorded on Vanguard Records (VSD79322), and this vocal clarity is immediately apparent when listening to it. The story is easy to follow and adapted well to a recording.

Carmilla was a success, and ETC of La Mama took it on tour with performances in numerous festivals held in France, Germany, Holland, and Italy. The company also performed it in Los Angeles, Berkeley, Santa Barbara, and Detroit. Carmilla is still in their repertory. The opera department at the University of Illinois produced it under the direction of Peter Franklin-White, who added several mime scenes.

Although Johnston was distrustful of the improvised sections in Carmilla, in 1975 he had an opportunity to work closely with an improvisation group. Herbert and Norma Marder (who performed CASTA Norma) had a performance group they called the New Verbal Workshop. There were six members--three men and three women--and they asked Johnston to join the group when one of the members had to leave for an extended period of time. He was pleased with the invitation because it had been a long time since he had actually performed music, and the group asked Johnston to do a piece for them.

There were several intriguing aspects about this project. One was experiencing how an improvisation group works, and Johnston knew he was fortunate to be associated with the New Verbal Workshop whose members were excellent musicians and serious about vocal improvisation. Another aspect was discovering a theme and related texts that would act as creative catalysts, and, lastly, there was the challenge of suitably documenting the work.

The actual piece the group produced is Visions and Spels (1976), which was tape-recorded, and Johnston has played it on several concerts.[23] It is available on a recent release by Composers Recording Incorporated Ben Johnston (CRI SD 515). The score to the entire process is Vigil. It begins with an explanation of how to form an improvisation group and is an excellent compositional examination of how the improvisation process works.

> The preparation for this piece begins with the formation of an improvising speaking group, optimally six people with contrasting natural voice qualities and ranges. Meetings are arranged to provide three consecutive hours once a week at a regular time. Exercises are learned or devised to improve and develop (1) awareness and clear and agile articulation of phonemes; (2) development and control of a wide variety and clear differentiation of spoken, chanted, sung, hummed, whispered, shouted, screamed timbres (and many others, as needed and discovered); (3) gradual and sensible development of extreme, moderate, and very subtle ranges of loudness and range in vocal projection; (4) exploration of vocal and percussive body noises; (5) gradual but ultimately bold overcoming of voice and performing inhibitions and ingrained habits, trained or unconsciously acquired, not so as to abrogate all individual idiosyncrasies, but so as to render these both conscious and unselfconscious, and so as to open the mind and the body to new and unfamiliar ones; and (6) willingness and ultimately affirmative group determination to diversify and rearrange continually as growth indicates, the leadership, critical, arbitrative, serving, and other roles in the working groups.
>
> The group will be advised at first to develop short themes with a view to (1) clarity of intention; (2) awareness of and reaction to each other; (3) timing (especially: "How long is too long?", "When is an idea squelched rather than put aside?", "Is a sequence of events goal-directed or simply a fabric? And what duration of it is optimal?", "How much and what kind of musical metered time is appropriate?", etc., etc.); (4) roles and masks and the dropping and changing of these as an integral part of group performance; (5) solos, and the group reaction to these; and (6) balance between accepting spontaneous inspirations and adhering to the theme. Themes are abstract, very concrete, representational, obvious, secret, or in many other discoverable categories.
>
> With practice and confidence, longer themes and patterns of themes will grow, and eventually entire compositions.[24]

This was the process that Johnston used for Visions and Spels. Any group involved in improvisation would benefit from considering his procedural suggestions. Of particular importance is the question of "How long is too long?" Timing may be the most crucial aspect of improvisation.

Johnston added another dimension to preparing Visions and Spels--the leader is to spend an all-night vigil on behalf of an oppressed group of people who will be the subject of the piece. Johnston was the New Verbal Workshop's leader for this piece, and he chose the American Indians as the oppressed group. He selected John Cage and Robert Ashley (both are part Indian) and Pauline Oliveros as his three representatives. Part of this choice and the idea of the piece itself was influenced by Oliveros. At this time she was preparing her ceremonial opera, Crow II (1975), which was based upon Indian themes. During the spring of 1975 Johnston was in residence at the University of California at San Diego, where Oliveros taught, as a recipient of a research grant from the University's Center for Music Experiment and was interested in Oliveros' work, especially her Sonic Meditations[25] which she used with improvisation groups. A meditative vigil appealed to Johnston, especially since several years earlier he had spent a month-long retreat at a Benedictine monastery in South Dakota.

The third stage of preparation was selecting the texts. Johnston chose American Aborigine texts from Technicians of the Sacred edited by Jerome Rothenberg and American Indian Poetry edited by George Cronyn. One especially effective text is "Sounds," a Navaho poem with such lines as "HEYA HEYA HEYA.A YO.HO...."[26]

Johnston's work with indeterminacy and improvisation was limited, and although the jazz styles in "Ci-Gît Satie" and the vocal writing in Carmilla were idioms he had used during his early twenties, Johnston knew that his creative focus should be directed towards extended just intonation.

Notes

1. These notes were printed in the program for the July 23, 1967 performance. Johnston mentioned some of these ideas about "Ci-Gît Satie" in his letter to Ward Swingle dated July 15, 1967.

2. During this time Johnston frequently wrote long and detailed letters to his friends in which he expressed ideas about his music. He has kept drafts of many of these letters.

3. For more information about Cage's activities at the University of Illinois see Stephen Husarik, "John Cage and LeJaren Hiller: HPSCHD, 1969," American Music, volume 1, number 2, Summer 1983, 1-21.

4. Betty Johnston has described Cage as having a disciplined working schedule where he composed from 8:00 a.m. to 5:00 p.m. and then enjoyed the evening playing cards and other games.

5. For those not familiar with The I Ching, the edition edited by Richard Wilhelm and translated into English by Cary F. Baynes is recommended. It is part of the Bollingen Series published by the Princeton University Press.

6. For more information about extended techniques for trombone see Stuart Dempster, The Modern Trombone: A Definition of Its Idioms (Berkeley, CA: University of California Press, 1979).

7. Johnston's Grindlemusic was performed during the 1967 Festival of Contemporary Arts.

8. This partial can have various names, such as the natural seventh, pure seventh, or septimal seventh.

9. Adriaan D. Fokker. New Music with 31 Notes, translated by Leigh Gerdine (Bonn-Bad Godesberg: Verlag für systematische Musikwissenschaft GmbH, 1975). Fokker discusses the pure seventh on pages 39-42. Also see Alain Daniélou, Introduction to the Study of Musical Scales (London: The India Society, 1943), pp. 42-47.

9A. In Johnston's notation the sevens and later other symbols are attached to sharps and flats. They have been separated in this text for ease of reading and printing. Also, markings, such as the sevens, last for one measure.

10. This kind of preface is needed for many of Johnston's works.

11. Dempster, The Modern Trombone, p. 56.

12. Cole Gagne and Tracy Caras, Soundpieces: Interviews with American Composers (Metuchen, NJ: Scarecrow Press, 1982), p. 257.

13. This statement is from Johnston's unpublished article "On Bridge Building."

14. Other performances have been by Joseph Celli and Nora Post (oboists), David Gibson (cellist), Jon Deak (double bassist), and Paul Zonn (clarinetist).

15. These schematics were prepared by George Ritscher, the technician who was part of the Krannert performance.

16. Score copyrighted 1970 by MEDIA PRESS. Used by permission.

17. Score copyrighted 1970 by MEDIA PRESS. Used by permission.

18. Score copyrighted 1970 by MEDIA PRESS. Used by permission.

19. Ben Johnston, "On Context," American Society of University Composers Proceedings, III (1968), 32-36.

20. Ben Johnston, "Communications," Perspectives of New Music, Spring-Summer 1972, p. 176.

21. The proceedings of the panel were published in The Composer, vol. 2, #1 (June 1970), 6-8.

22. This lecture is published in <u>The Composer</u>, vol. 3, #1 (Fall/Winter 1971), 9-16.

23. Johnston used the Indian spelling of spels.

24. Copyrighted 1977 by Smith Publications. Used with permission.

25. For more information about Oliveros' work see Heidi Von Gunden, <u>The Music of Pauline Oliveros</u> (Metuchen, NJ: Scarecrow Press, 1983).

26. <u>Technicians of the Sacred</u>. Edited with commentaries by Jerome Rothenberg, (New York: Doubleday, 1968), p. 8.

After using the prime number seven in <u>One Man</u>, Johnston derived other scales incorporating higher prime numbers and more generating ratios, such as lattices of four numbers instead of three. The computer was the logical instrument for this study, so Johnston applied to the Research Board of the University of Illinois and received money to establish a computer program and an assistant to help him. His plan was to conduct the work in three phases--Phase 1 would be defining a system for deriving scales; Phase 2 would be designing a computer program that would assist in making compositional decisions about how to use these scales; and Phase 3 would be interfacing a small computer with a musical synthesizer so that there could be a real-time interaction between the computer and a performer.[1]

Edward Kobrin and later Peter Rumbold (both graduate students in composition at that time) worked as research assistants. The project was never completed, but Johnston and Kobrin were able to generate lattices using two prime numbers of 3, 5, 7, or 11 combined with the number 2 (the prime number needed so that the scales would repeat at the octave, a condition that Johnston always maintains). This material was published as "Phase 1a" in <u>Source</u>.[2] The program produced nine scales from the prime numbers 2 and 3. All the ratios between the scale steps were some exponent of the 2/3 ratio. In the scale of 17 tones (one of the nine possible scales) there were four pitches between C and D, their ratios being 1/1 (C), 256/243 (Db--), 2187/2048 (C#++), and 9/8 (D).

Although Johnston never composed music with the computer and only Phase 1a was completed, the research was valuable to him because it confirmed what he had already discovered intuitively. As a result, he was able to explain how to derive the major and minor diatonic scale, the chromatic scale (a mixture of parallel major and minor scales), and hyperchromatic scales (additional notes from all directions on the lattice added to the chromatic scale).[3] These scales could be generated from any combination of prime numbers, such as lattices of 2,3,7 or 2,11,13 and so on. Johnston determined that "An acceptable ratio scale must have as few different intervals between its adjacent notes as possible: no more than the quantity of prime numbers in use (including 2)."[4] In selecting chromatic and hyperchromatic scales the same condition of controlling the number of adjacent ratios applied.

Interestingly, Johnston derived all of these scales before using the computer program. His notes and sketch books are filled with computations for various possible scales. The notations are precise and orderly, showing his patience and concentration during such time-consuming work. In his unpublished paper "Algorithm for Generation of Ratio Scales" Johnston explained what he gained from the experience.

> It will be obvious that this process is easier to carry out with the assistance of a computer. Nonetheless, in the process of generating the program to facilitate finding these scales, it was necessary for me to derive all the scales which were to be made available by means of the program before it existed, in order to be sure of covering all eventualities. It may seem, therefore, that producing the program achieved nothing. This is assuredly not so, since it was the pressure of having to be so extremely specific and inclusive that made possible my solution to these theoretical problems. I needed the program not mainly for derivation, but in order to make possible the study of reasoning processes necessary to translate an intellectual process which is at least partly holistic in character entirely into a binary language.

What Johnston really discovered was that the acceptable scales were the ones where the scale steps were discrete but not equal. The adjacent intervals between scale steps needed to be large enough for the ear to distinguish the difference and frequent enough for the listener to sense a basic integrity. Also, the adjacent intervals had to be related harmonically so that the vertical constructions were heard as properties of the scale.

Ten years earlier Johnston had discovered a patterning between adjacent intervals and written about it in his first theoretical article "Scalar Order as a Compositional Resource."[5] He stated that his 53-tone just intonation scale derived from the three prime numbers of 2,3,5 used a three member patterning for the diatonic scale that also occurred in the hyperchromatic scale where the larger diatonic intervals were divided into smaller ratios. The patterning for the diatonic scale is ABCABAC where A = 9/8, B = 10/9, and C = 16/15 (the half steps, C, are the same size while A and B are two different whole steps). In the 53-tone just intonation scale the 9/8 interval was divided into nine pitches ([C] C+, Dbb-, C#, C#+, Db-, Db, Cx+, D-, D) and the adjacent ratios between these pitches formed a similar pattern of ABCABACBA where A = 81/80, B = 2048/2025, and C = 3125/3072. He even used this interval patterning to determine meter changes in the first movement of String Quartet Number 2. Recall that an 8/8 measure was used when the serial order of the music arrived at a diatonic interval in the scalar pattern.

Johnston began designing scales using three, four, and even five prime numbers. As the number of generating ratios increases, certain complications result. One is the inability to show the network of relationships on a two-dimensional plane, such as a piece of paper. A system using four generating ratios needs to be represented with a three-dimensional design. With the help of some graduate students Johnston was able to plot lattices that would show these four dimensions, such as the lattice for a system using prime numbers 2,3,5,7 as shown in Figure 1. Notice that this lattice maintains the 3/2 ratios on the vertical axes, the 5/4 ratios on the horizontal axes, and the 7/4 ratios are the third dimensions seen as axes behind (for the seventh above) and in front (for the seventh below) of the 3/2 axes. This lattice produces natural dominant seventh chords if one reads vertically one block north (for the 3/2 ratio), one block horizontally east (for the 5/4 ratio), and one block to the rear of the 1/1 ratio (for the 7/4 ratio).

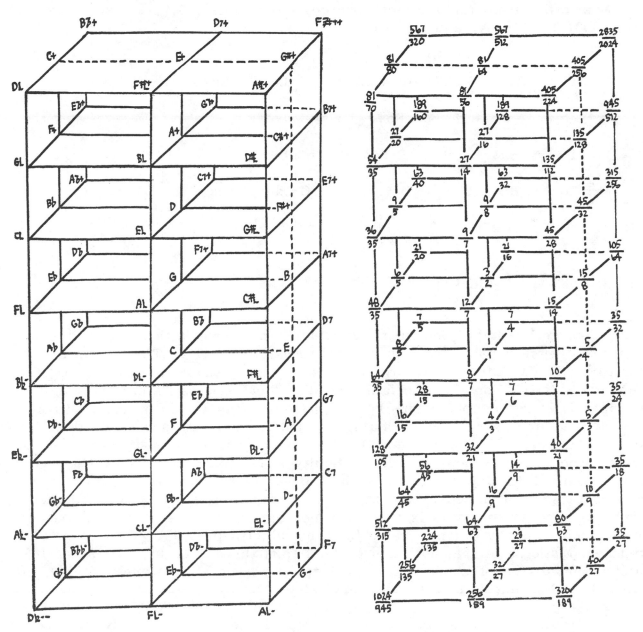

Figure 1. Lattice for the 2,3,5,7 system. Property of the composer. Used with permission.

Other possibilities for a three-dimensional system are ratios of 2,3,5,11 or 2,5,7,11, and so on. The characteristic intervals and acceptable ratio scales in each system are different. For instance a 2,5,7,11 system has no perfect fifths (or fourths) because the third partial is not present. Instead, several tritones are produced. The 7/5 ratio is a fairly consonant sounding diminished fifth, and an 11/8 augmented fourth is more dissonant when combined with lower ratios. A new second (11/10) is available, and it is slightly smaller than the just major second of 9/8, a second which is not possible with a 2,5,7,11 system. Other differences are present, and these can be observed in the scale shown in Figure 2. The four ratios used for adjacent scale degrees in this 2,5,7,11 system are 275/256, 3136/3125, 50/44, and 615/616.

C	C#↑	Eb7↑b7b	Db↑-	CxL	Eb7b
D#↓	Fb7↓b7+	Eb↓	E	DxLL-	Fb
F↑	ExL	Gb7	F#L	Ab7bb	G↓
G#	Bb7b7b	Ab	A↑	G#Lx	Bb7
A#L	Cb7b	B↓	B#	Db7b7	C

Figure 2. Scale using the 2,5,7,11 system.

Five generating ratios must use a four-dimensional lattice, and Johnston designed a system using the generating primes 2,3,5,7,11. The lattice in Figure 3 contains three structures that need to be visualized as fitting together. The middle lattice contains the familiar 3/2 vertical axis as its center pole. To its right is a dotted pole. This is the lattice showing the 11th partial, which Johnston notated as an arrow pointing upward for the 11th above and downward for the 11th below. The axis for the 7th partial is in the same position as the system mentioned previously. The difficulty is locating the 5/4 and 8/5 horizontal axes which are the lattices to the right and left of the central lattice. One must imagine these as attached to and projecting from the central figure. Another difficulty is reading the symbols which can be superimposed, such as the axes to the far left or right which combine the 7th and 11th partials. The acceptable hyperchromatic scale that Johnston derived from this lattice has a scale of 143 pitches and divides the 9/8 ratio into thirty-two scale steps while the 10/9 (between D to E using C as 1/1) has thirty steps.

It would seem that Johnston's music would become increasingly more complex as he explored new scales using more ratios, but this was not the case. Just the opposite happened--Johnston's music became simpler and tonal. Before beginning to write a composition he had to decide which scale and its related aural qualities

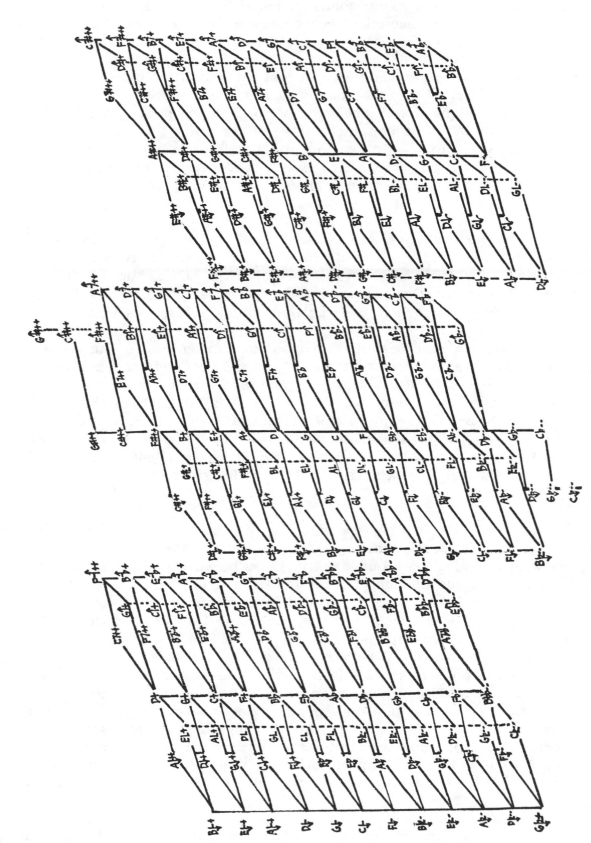

Figure 3. Lattices for the 2,3,5,7,11 system. Property of the composer. Used with permission.

he wanted to use. As a result Johnston began to compose tonal music that he could tune to the exact amount of consonance and dissonance that he needed.

Rose (1971) for SATB choir was the first piece where he tried to simplify his music while still experimenting with just intonation. There are several reasons for this. First, Rose was special because his daughter Sibyl, who was in high school, wrote the text. She gave her father the poem not mentioning that it was hers. Knowing his daughter (the two are quite close), Johnston sensed that the poem was Sibyl's and decided to set it for the high school choir at Champaign Central High, where Sibyl was a student. Because this would be for a young and inexperienced group Johnston had to keep the music relatively simple.[6]

His personal challenge was to use a 2,3,7 system (which can also be represented as partials 6:7:8), as he did in One Man, where there are no major or minor triads. The choir had to tune perfect fifths and septimal thirds (7/6), which are a just minor third lowered about 1/4 tone. These were harmonically tuned with common tones held over so that tuning references were available.

He chose a 15-tone scale based upon the fundamental A for a four-part setting of limited ranges and rhythms. The scale contains three dorian modes of A, D-, and E. This 6:7:8 tuning is effective for dorian because the interval between the leading tone and tonic is 7/4 which is larger than the whole step that would be heard in the just major second of 10/9. Also, the third and sixth scale degree steps use the seventh partial so that the mode's lower tetrachord sounds different from that of a natural minor. The smallest interval is 28/27 which occurs between the second and third and sixth and seventh scale degrees. See Figure 4.

Rose sounds like a Renaissance motet with open fifths and exact sevenths. The dorian mode is clearly heard, and the A center does not drop (as frequently happens with choral music) but stays in place because of the careful tuning. Areas where the mode changes from A to D- or A to E are heard because the pitches common to both modes are placed in different ambitus settings--they appear in a different tetrachord, such as the E F#+ G7 A7+ beginning tetrachord of E dorian being similar but not exactly the same as the E F#+ G7 A tetrachord of A dorian. The difference between A7+ and A is crucial. Also, notice that the D- dorian begins on a pitch that is not even available in A dorian, which has D7 as its fourth step. The D- is a fifth below A and a close relation, whereas D7 is a modal tone that identifies the tuning system. Johnston took the opportunity to use the subtleties of his tuning system to highlight certain words in his daughter's poem. Text painting occurs for the word "coloring" where he used utonality --F#↓ an 8/7 below E as a way of coloring the mode. The word "blood" has a G7 sounding with a G, a dissonant unison that is 49 cents flat (see Example 1, page 134).

Part of the reason Johnston's music became tonally centered was due to a

15-tone scale for <u>Rose</u>

A   B   C7   C#*L*-   C#+   D7   D-   E7   E   F#*L*-   F#+   G7

G   A7   A7+

3 dorian modes derived from above scale

A   B   C7   D7   E   F#+   G7   A

$$\frac{9}{8} \quad \frac{28}{27} \quad \frac{9}{8} \quad \frac{7}{4} \quad \frac{9}{8} \quad \frac{28}{27} \quad \frac{7}{4}$$

D-   E   F7   G7   A   B   C7   D-

$$\frac{9}{8} \quad \frac{28}{27} \quad \frac{9}{8} \quad \frac{7}{4} \quad \frac{9}{8} \quad \frac{28}{27} \quad \frac{7}{4}$$

E   F#+   G7   A7+   B   C#+   D7   E

$$\frac{9}{8} \quad \frac{28}{27} \quad \frac{9}{8} \quad \frac{7}{4} \quad \frac{9}{8} \quad \frac{28}{27} \quad \frac{7}{4}$$

Figure 4. 15-tone scale and three modes used in <u>Rose</u>.

spiritual commitment that affected his creative work. On the feast of Corpus Christi 1970 he celebrated his conversion to the Roman Catholic Church.[7] As a result he made a decision about his creative work. "I am trying very hard to let every work be a religious intention, not simply an 'expression' of my ego. It means taking on quite a lot (and not writing large numbers of works)."[8]

<u>Mass</u> (1972) for SATB choir, ten trombones (or organ), string bass, and drums was a result of this decision. Harold Decker, the director of choirs at the University of Illinois, asked Johnston to compose a piece for the Undergraduate Concert Choir. Decker specified that since this would be a less experienced choir, the music should be approachable while still being intellectually challenging. A Latin Mass was the ideal text to use for the choir and the ideas that Johnston wanted to express. <u>Mass</u> was scheduled as part of the activities of the Phoenix '73 Contemporary Music Series, a revival of the Festival of Contemporary Arts. It was premièred at St. John's Chapel on the campus of the University of Illinois on the last Sunday before Lent with Reverend Darrell Rupiper officiating; Harold Decker conducted the choir.

Like <u>Rose</u>, <u>Mass</u> is modal and uses the seventh partial. However, Johnston added several drone parts for tuning purposes. Ten trombones double on a five-part texture. Staggered breathing makes the drone continuous, and it sounds

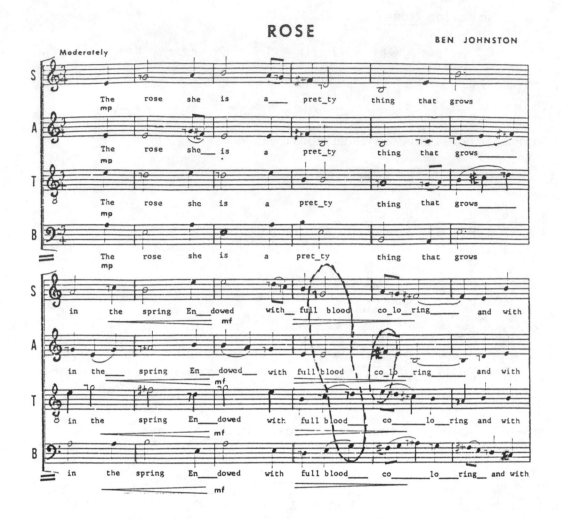

Example 1. Text painting in <u>Rose</u>. Copyright 1976 by Smith Publications. Used with permission.

like a pipe organ. (Using ten trombones at a large School of Music was not a problem, but Johnston indicated in the score that it would be possible to have only five trombones. If an organ is used, then certain notes that would be out of tune with just intonation are marked to be omitted.)

With <u>Rose</u> Johnston discovered that the seventh partial made modality sound both old and new and, for Johnston, this was a connecting link between tradition and experimentation. Incorporating higher ratios with 2,3,5 produced tonalities that were distinctive. Modal structure was clear to the listener because tunings were selected to emphasize those structural differences, such as the low dorian seventh scale degree in <u>Rose</u>.

The organ-like trombones were another old/new aspect, and Johnston added a string bass and drum set that gave the traditional Mass setting a contemporary jazz sound.[9] The jazz ensemble was also a personal expression of Johnston's own musical past, and parts of Mass, especially the Credo, sound like passages in Carmilla. Some of the rhythms and meter changes in the Mass are like those that Johnston used in Gambit (where there was also a drum set).

For "Kyrie Eleison" Johnston used a 6-tone mixolydian mode of F G Bb7 C D Eb7 from the 2,3,7 lattice. The pitches are tuned in perfect fifths (F C G D and Eb7 Bb7), and the trombones sustain an F and C drone to support the tuning. The septimal major second (F to Eb7 and C to Bb7) is featured in the tenors' and bass' ostinato patterning that begins the Mass. The ostinato is an organum of perfect fifths which is juxtaposed against the more contemporary patterns of the string bass and drum. The sopranos' and altos' canon, which is superimposed upon the ostinati, features step-wise movement that outlines the mode. The "Kyrie" cadences on G and D, common tones that Johnston used for a change of mode and tuning. See Example 2, page 136.

The "Christe" section is in a lydian mode (G A+ B C#+ D E+ F#+) based upon the previously sounding G. The mode uses the 2,3,5 lattice and interval patterning of 9/8, 10/9, 9/8, 15/8, 9/8, 10/9, and 15/8. There are no septimal intervals, and the lydian's half step between the seventh and eighth scale degrees is about 112 cents, slightly larger than an equal-tempered half step. These changes in space (rising from the "Kyrie's" F mode to the "Christe's" G mode), modality, and tuning lattices are noticeable. The listener may not be able to identify what they are, but there is a sense that the pitches are new.

The last "Kyrie" has a new mode, E dorian (E F#+ G7 A B C# D7), using a three-dimensional lattice of 2,3,5,7. The tuning sequence is a series of fifths, A E B F#+ and then G7 D7 (related as 7/4's to A and E). The C# is a 5/4 to the A. The resulting scalar interval patterning is 9/8, 28/27, 7/4, 9/8, 10/9, 21/20, 7/4. Johnston used F# and D- as two other pitches from the 2,3,5 lattice which add color to the second and seventh scale degrees and make it possible to write just major thirds as a harmonic interval that has not been heard in the "Kyrie" texts.

"Gloria" is marked with a "lively" tempo and has frequent changing meters caused by dance-like rhythmic groupings of two's and three's. The setting is syllabic, so this movement is energetic and one large gesture, rather than smaller sections which is often the case with choral settings of the text. The trombones sustain a G D F7+ drone the entire time, and the F7+ locks into the G as its natural seventh to create a mildly dissonant interval. "Gloria" begins with a 6-tone mixolydian mode of G A+ C7+ D E+ F7+, which is an exact transposition of the mixolydian mode used for the beginning "Kyrie." However, Johnston added a B. This new pitch mixes systems so that now the mode is from a 2,3,5,7 lattice, making it possible to have a just major triad which is introduced for the text "Domine Deus Rex coelestis." In the measures that follow Johnston built other tertian structures using septimal and major thirds. The differences are subtle, but they allow the composer to control dissonance. This is especially

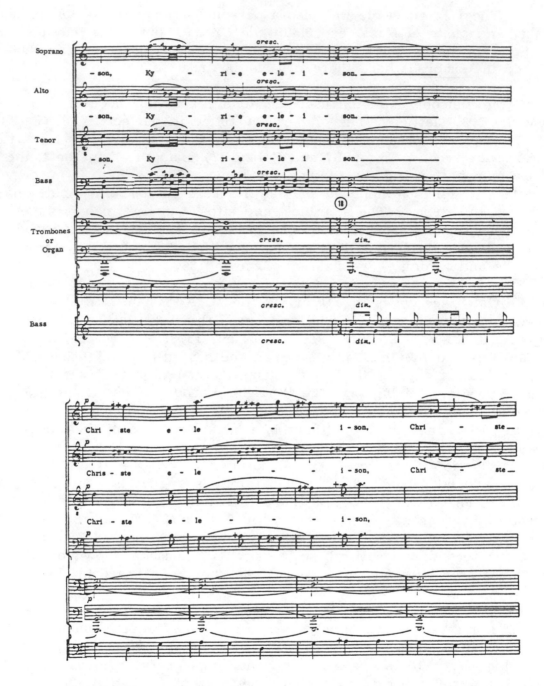

Example 2. End of "Kyrie" and beginning of "Christe" showing change of modes in Mass. Copyrighted 1974. Used by permission of Mark Foster Music Company, Champaign, Illinois.

noticeable for the text "Qui tollis peccata mundi" where an F+ in the soprano is against an F7+ in the tenors and basses (see the circled pitches in Example 3).

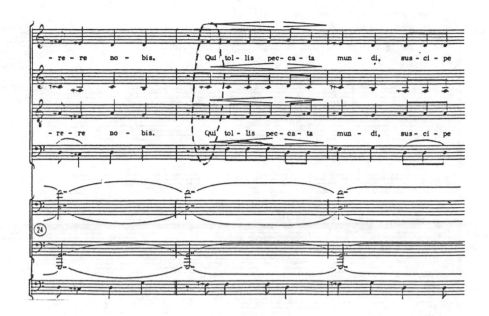

Example 3. "Qui tollis peccata mundi ..." from the "Gloria" of <u>Mass</u>. Copyrighted 1974. Used by permission of Mark Foster Music Company, Champaign, Illinois.

The "Credo" is in an aeolian mode of A B C7 D7 E F7 G7 with an alternate D- and F used for several tuning conveniences. The interval patterning is 9/8, 28/27, 9/8, 7/4, 28/27, 9/8 which features just major seconds, a septimal major second (D7 to E), and septimal minor seconds (B to C7 and E to F7). The contrast among these intervals is heard in a chant-like melody that is a canon at the octave and at the distance of two measures between the female and male voices. The "Credo's" long text is divided into three canons that are interrupted with homophonic sections.

"Sanctus" is a hypnotic nine beat ostinato sung by the women with the added support of a trombone drone and string bass ostinato of fourths and fifths. The male voices sing the remaining text as a duet to the ostinato with several measures of silence separating their phrases. The "Sanctus" is in a dorian on D E+ F7+ G A+ B C7+ using a 2,3,5,7 lattice. The intervals of the mode are 9/8, 28/27, 7/4, 9/8, 10/9, 21/20, 7/4. The small major second of 10/9 has only been previously heard in the "Kyrie," and the distance of B to A+ is featured in the top line of the vocal ostinato (see Example 4, page 138).

The "Agnus Dei" is an example of the beauty of economy. Its scale is pentatonic using a one-dimensional lattice of 2,3. The pitches are E F#+ G#+ B

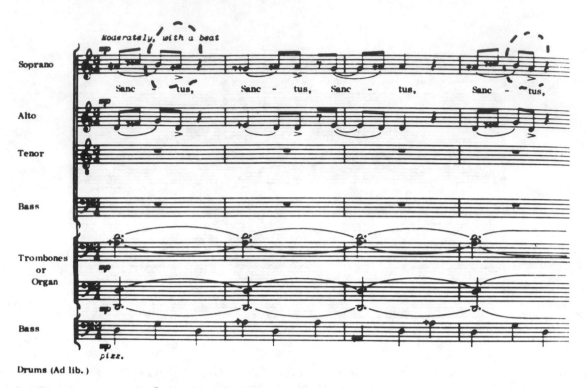

Example 4. "Sanctus" from <u>Mass</u>. Copyright 1974. Used by permission of Mark Foster Music Company, Champaign, Illinois.

C#+ derived from a stacking of fifths (E B F#+ C#+ G#+), which are heard in the trombone and string bass. The scale's intervals are 9/8, 9/8, 27/16, 9/8, 27/16, and the small minor third (27/16) is a prominent feature of the spiraling melodies that are a double canon between soprano and tenor and alto and bass. The scale's limited number of pitches was no handicap for Johnston. This movement is especially beautiful and is most appropriate for the text's message of peace.

After composing <u>Mass</u> Johnston began his <u>String Quartet Number 4</u> (1973), which has been his most popular piece. It is available on the Gasparo recording GS-205 "Fine Arts Quartet." Frequently the third and fourth quartets are performed on the same program in a version titled "Crossings." A period of silence separates the two compositions, and Johnston considers <u>String Quartet Number 3</u> as "Vergings," the silence as "The Silence," and <u>String Quartet Number 4</u> as the "Ascent." Thus the two quartets represent a symbolic crossing from serialism to tonality. By 1973 Johnston's organizational techniques had changed drastically since the serial <u>String Quartet Number 3</u>. He had extended just intonation to include the seventh partial and experimented with the new tonal and modal possibilities available with the enlarged tuning system.

"Crossings" is also a symbol of mental and spiritual changes that were happening to Johnston. The mid-1960's was a difficult time when his mental health was fluctuating. Some of this turmoil was due to his experiences with the Gurdjieff Foundation which are reflected in Sonata for Microtonal Piano/Grindlemusic. Catholicism provided him with the kind of religious support that he felt he needed, and the differences between Mass or String Quartet Number 4 and the Sonata are obvious. But Johnston does suffer from states of depression that are caused by a chemical imbalance. It took many years before doctors adequately understood his condition and were able to treat it properly. The periods that surrounded these depressed states and their resolutions were especially creative times for Johnston.

String Quartet Number 4 reflects these changes in his life. The most striking compositional change was Johnston's abandonment of serialism and his use of tonality, as evident in his article "Tonality Regained." Johnston felt secure as a composer. His music was receiving recognition and respect because of its just intonation and not necessarily for the complex serialism. For a while he thought that it was necessary to be conversant with serialism because it was the contemporary interest of many composers, particularly those in academia. The tonality of Mass influenced other compositions, and he began to write in neoclassic forms, particularly theme and variations that he had so often used in his earlier works.

String Quartet Number 4 is a set of variations on the hymn tune "Amazing Grace." The tune appealed to him for symbolic and musical reasons. Randall Shinn, a former student of Johnston, thoroughly examined String Quartet Number 4 as part of his doctoral dissertation and wrote about it in his article "Ben Johnston's Fourth String Quartet," which was published in Perspectives of New Music.[10] Shinn described Johnston's use of tonality as centric which implies "systems with definite pitch hierarchies, of which functional harmony is but one example."[11]

He compared Johnston's use of the "Amazing Grace" to Ives' use of pre-existing melodies saying:

> A connection with Ives seems particularly apt in that the texture of this quartet appears simultaneously to stem from the hymn and to transcend it--this transcendental atmosphere ultimately transforming our perception of the hymn itself and making distinction among the original substance, the transformation, and the transformed imagery difficult.[12]

If the quartet is reminiscent of Ives' music, there is another aspect to Johnston's music that differentiates it from that of Ives. Every aspect of String Quartet Number 4 is proportional. Like the Sonata for Microtonal Piano/Grindlemusic, rhythm and tempi are governed by the same ratios that control pitch. This is the organic unity that Johnston tried to achieve in some of his previous works, such as the Sonata and Knocking Piece. String Quartet Number 4 is the first time he was able to exert this precision without the burden of serialism.

The result is a beautiful piece that can be appreciated and understood on many levels. Frequently listeners react emotionally, knowing that somehow this music moved them but not quite certain why it did. Hearing the quartet is an experience that is not easily forgotten. John Rockwell in his <u>New York Times</u> review of a performance of "Crossings" by the Concord String Quartet at Alice Tully Hall wrote: "The Fourth Quartet (or 'Ascent') is a set of rhythmically complex variations on the old hymn 'Amazing Grace,' the harmonic context flowing and shifting as the intonation changes hues. It's almost corny, but manages to stop short of that and be simply beautiful instead."[13] Pandit Pran Nath, the renowned Indian musician, later heard a taping of the quartet, and afterwards in a conversation with Johnston said that he understood the tuning and used the phrase that the music was like the "voices of angels."[14]

But this beauty is the result of many complexities, such as the seventh partial, polyrhythms, and metric modulations. Some of these are evident in Example 5. Frequently quartets have commissioned works from Johnston and then delayed learning them because of difficult passages; however, the music is possible to perform as the Fine Arts and Concord String Quartets have demonstrated.[15]

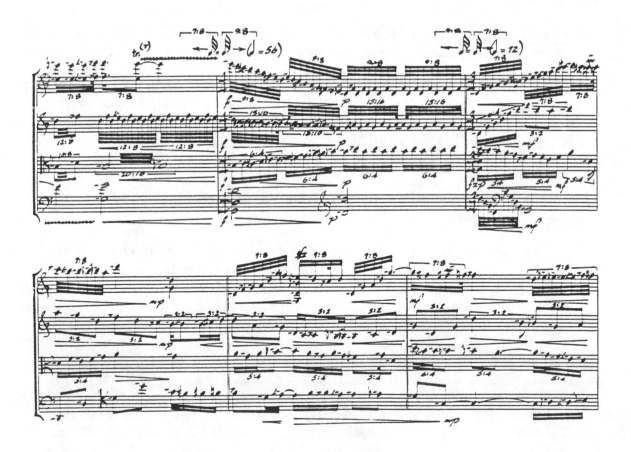

Example 5. Complexities in <u>String Quartet Number 4</u>, first system on page 15 of the score. Copyright 1985 by Smith Publications. Used with permission.

The complexity of String Quartet Number 4 gradually develops. It begins with the two violins and viola playing a simple harmonization of "Amazing Grace." Because the melody is pentatonic, Johnston could use a Pythagorean scale which is derived by tuning two consecutive perfect fifths upward and downward from the pitch A forming the scale G- A B D- E G-. The hymn sounds resonant due to the perfect fifths and fourths, which provide a clarity and simplicity that suggest evolving complexities. The Pythagorean scale is maintained for the first two variations (Johnston did not number the variations in the score, but the divisions are obvious). By the second variation the listener is introduced to rhythmic changes. Shinn discovered that the variation is a set of nested 3/2 ratios. The cello's cycle of four dotted eighth notes performed as a double stop of fifths establishes the pulse against which the cello also adds an eighth-note pattern, so the 3/2 ratio is actually established as a 4/6 (see Example 6). The viola is notated in a 6/8 meter forming a 3/2 relationship to the cello's upper eighth notes. The second violin's part is in a 9/16 meter creating a 3/2 pattern with the viola, while the first violin is notated as a 27/32 meter which theoretically forms a 3/2 ratio with 9/16. However, this is not audibly noticeable since the violin has the hymn tune and does not articulate a steady stream of twenty-seven thirty-second notes.

Example 6. Nested 3/2 rhythmic relationships in the second variation of String Quartet Number 4. Copyright 1985 by Smith Publications. Used with permission.

The third variation has a different scale. The G tonality is maintained, but Johnston used a G- major scale in just intonation rather than the G- Pythagorean pentatonic. The new scale introduces more pitch ratios, and these are reflected in the subdivisions of the beat into 5/4, 4/3, and so on. A more dramatic presentation of the new intervals and pitches (such as F# and B-) is heard in the violin's material, which is an ornamented version of the hymn tune that sounds as if it is independent of the surrounding material. There are frequent meter changes in the first violin's part, and Shinn showed how these correspond to the ratios between scale steps.[16] A further complication is that the intervals of the chordal accompaniment, which forms the basis of the other three instruments' parts, are expressed by the rhythmic figures of that measure. Thus a tonic triad is set to rhythmic figures of 1/1, 3/2, and 5/4 corresponding to the root, fifth, and third of the triad (see Example 7). This is true throughout the entire variation.

Example 7. Beginning measures of the third variation of String Quartet Number 4 showing rhythmic and harmonic unity. Copyright 1985 by Smith Publications. Used with permission.

Johnston introduced the prime number seven for the fourth variation, and this new partial causes a change in scalar material creating a collection that Shinn titled a 12-tone "major" scale. The new generating number affects the second, fourth, sixth, eighth, and eleventh scale degrees; many of these are modal degrees which color the scale. Shinn described this scale as being similar to "blues" scales, and these "blue" notes are characteristics that Johnston featured in this variation.

Rhythmic and pitch complexities increase for the fifth variation in which Johnston used the rhythmic ratio of 36/35 between the cello and viola parts to correspond to the 36/35 ratio of the notational accidental he employs.[17] Added to this dense texture are multiple-stop chords that mark the proportions of the 12-tone scale so that the duration of the entire variation is a reflection of the scalar structure in which the progression from one degree to the next is signaled by this added density.[18]

All of the variations maintain a G- tonal center, and in the sixth variation Johnston followed the classic tradition of changing from one mode to the other by inverting the "Amazing Grace" tune, causing his 12-tone scale to also invert and produce a new form, a 12-tone "minor" scale whose pitches are G- Ab- A𝐿- Bb- B𝐿- C C# D- Eb- E𝐿- F F# G-. Just intonation affords the possibility of inverting relationships, a property that fascinated Harry Partch and that he called utonality.[19] This inversion drastically changes the harmonic relationships, and Johnston set this variation in a simple uncomplicated texture so that one can hear the inversion.

The seventh variation is a combination of both 12-tone scales (the previously used major and minor scales), and originally Johnston wanted the rhythmic activity to reflect scalar structure; however, he modified his plan due to the unmanageable length an exact mirroring would have produced. Instead, he used a method of measuring the scale in terms of cents and then divided the number of cents by 6 or 7, thus producing such numbers as 7, 9, 10 and so on that became the numerator of sixty-fourth note meters. The distance between the first two notes of the scale, G- and Ab7-, is 63 cents, so the first violin has seven measures of a 9/64 meter totaling sixty-three articulations representing the sixty-three cents (see Example 8).[20]

Shinn aptly described the eighth variation as "A somewhat frenzied rhapsody."[21] Johnston maintained his 22-tone scale in places in which the first violinist

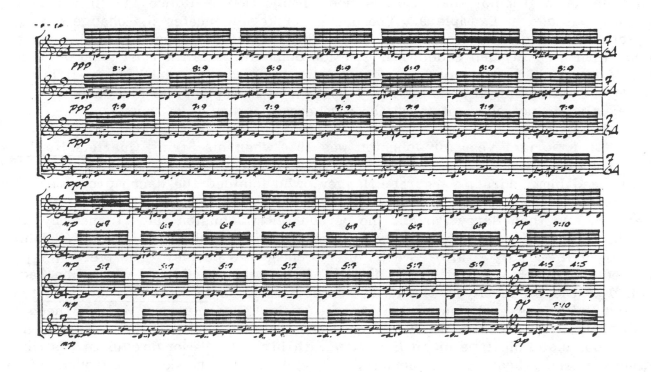

Example 8. 22-tone scale and its rhythmic representation in the seventh variation of String Quartet Number 4. Copyright 1985 by Smith Publications. Used with permission.

and cellist have fast linear scale passages requiring them to measure the intervals melodically rather than harmonically (see Example 5, page 140). The rhythmic figurations of 5/4, 3/2, and 7/8 represent the tonic seventh chord possessing those same ratios.

The last variation is a gradual return to the hymn tune's simplicity at the beginning of String Quartet Number 4. Johnston used the 12-tone major scale, and, then, during the final measures of the piece, the 7-tone major is heard. The variations end with an open fifth built upon G-.

Having experimented with "Amazing Grace" Johnston harmonized "I'm Goin' Away," an Appalachian folk tune, for SATB chorus, although he had no specific choir in mind. Johnston used a 19-tone scale from the 2,3,5,7 lattice but concentrated on writing triads formed by the ratios of 6:7:8. The result is a harmonically rich seventh chord with a missing third.

Since each composition is an opportunity for Johnston to discover more properties of just intonation, in "I'm Goin' Away" he tried modulating to the relative minor. The text tells of a mother losing her son, and in the first stanza the son speaks about going away. This stanza is in F, as the tune suggests, but an F that fluctuates between F major and F mixolydian. The second stanza is the same melody (see Example 9), but the speaker is the mother waiting for the return of her loved one. Instead of using an F tonal center, Johnston harmonized this stanza in D minor that also has modal implications. Notice the circled C# C natural passage in Example 9. The change of key delineates the change of perspective, showing the second person's feelings about the departure. The song ends with a mixolydian cadence in F. "I'm Goin' Away" is the most tonal of Johnston's pieces in just intonation. The relative minor is unusual because it is a 5/3 ratio and requires a modulation (the C#'s in Example 9) to a section of the lattice that is not adjacent to all the members of the relative major.

An important year for Johnston was 1974 when his String Quartets Numbers 3 and 4 were premièred. The year also marked the deaths of two people who had influenced him. First, Margaret Erlanger, who founded the dance program at the University of Illinois and with whom he worked during his early years at the University, and then Harry Partch, the person whom Johnston said "turned my music in the direction that most strongly characterizes it,"[22] also passed away. Johnston composed In Memory (1975) as a tribute to these two people. The piece was premièred October 5, 1975 at the dedication of the Erlanger House, which she had willed to the University. The piece was performed as In Memory, Harry Partch at the National Association of Schools of Music's 1975 Convention in San Diego, California, on November 24.[23] This version includes slides of Harry Partch and an almost inaudible tape of an interview with him. In Memory requires a string quartet, string bass, percussionists, and singer. The music is controlled by the overtones of 10 Hertz that generate an Eb eleventh chord spanning six octaves. The score is sixty-three bars long (63 being a duration of 5 minutes and 45.6 seconds that can be repeated any number of times). The chord acts as a drone

1st stanza

I'm goin' a-way for to stay a lit-tle while, But I'm

I'm goin' a-way____ for to stay__ a lit-tle while_____, But I'm

I'm goin' a-way for to stay__ a lit-tle while_____, But I'm

I'm goin' a-way____ for to stay a lit-tle while, But I'm

2nd stanza

Yan-dro. He's gone a-way for to stay a lit-tle while, But he's

Yan-dro. He's gone a-way for to stay__ a lit-tle while_____, But he's

Yan-dro____. He's gone a-way__ for to stay a lit-tle__ while, But he's

Yan-dro. He's gone a-way for to stay__ a lit-tle while, But he's

Example 9. Beginning measures of stanzas 1 and 2 of "I'm Goin' Away." Copyright 1977 by Smith Publications. Used with permission.

to the sequence of changing slides and to a sung passage that occurs directly in the middle of the sixty-three measures.

Notes

1. Johnston described this project in "Tonality Regained," American Society of University Composers Proceedings, 1973, pp. 113-119.

2. Source, volume 7 (Summer 1970), 27-42.

3. See "Tonality Regained."

4. This information is from Johnston's unpublished paper "Algorithm for the Generation of Ratio Scales."

5. "Scalar Order as a Compositional Resource," Perspectives of New Music, ii/2 (1964), 56-76.

6. There was one disappointment with Rose--it was too difficult for the choir at Champaign Central High School to perform. Johnston had to wait until the University of Illinois' Summer Chorus could perform it under the direction of Neely Bruce before the piece received a good performance.

7. He took instruction from Reverend Darrell Rupiper.

8. This is from a letter to the author dated April 3, 1976.

9. It was during the early 1970's, not long after Vatican II, that many composers and congregations were experimenting with folk and jazz settings of the Mass. Many of these were not successful and the deplorable state of contemporary church music was something that Johnston could not ignore.

10. Perspectives of New Music, Spring-Summer 1977, pp. 145-175.

11. Shinn, "Ben Johnston's Fourth String Quartet," footnote 4 on p. 147.

12. Shinn, p. 149.

13. The New York Times, Wednesday, March 17, 1976.

14. This information is from a conversation with Johnston on March 13, 1983.

15. Other string quartets that have played Johnston's music are: the Kronos Quartet (String Quartet Number 4), Tremont Quartet (String Quartets Numbers 4 and 5), the Composers Quartet (String Quartet Number 2), the Walden Quartet (Nine Variations), the La Salle Quartet (Nine Variations), the Manhattan Quartet (String Quartet Number 3), the Cordier Quartet (String Quartet Number 3), and the New World Quartet (String Quartet Number 6).

16. See example 4 on p. 154 of Shinn's article.

17. See page 154 of Shinn's article for an explanation of the relationship.

18. See Shinn's charts and calculations on pp. 154-155 of the article.

19. See Harry Partch, Genesis of a Music, second edition (New York: Da Capo Press, 1974), pp. 88-90, 110, and 455.

20. There are only twenty-one meter changes in this variation. There are two adjacent scale intervals of the same size (D- and Eb7-) requiring a 9/64 meter so that a change between them is not required. This explains why one meter change is lacking.

21. Shinn, p. 158.

22. This information is from Johnston's program notes to In Memory,
Harry Partch (1975).

23. Partch had died in San Diego on September 3, 1974. The New Grove's
Dictionary of Music has the year of Partch's death as 1976. That is incorrect.

Having completed his scalar research, Johnston began to extend just intonation to include the upper partials of the 11th, 13th, 15th, 17th, 19th, 21st, and 27th. This gave him the opportunity to tune eleventh and thirteenth chords and to write modulations. Extended just intonation can make old musical styles sound new; jazz styles are more interesting; and even contemporary music has a special enhancement when written in extended just intonation. Interestingly, Johnston returned to the piano, the instrument that had propagated the lie of equal temperament, to begin his experiments with these upper partials and found that he could easily mix modality, tonality, and serialism.

However, extended just intonation causes added notational complexities. One pitch might have a chain of ratio symbols. Commas (such as a # or b or a + or -) and chromas (such as the 7 or 𝘓 showing the seventh partial, the ↑ and ↓ showing the 11th partial, or the 13 and ƐⱢ showing the 13th partial) can be combined so that one pitch is affected by two or more adjustments. Frequently performers find it necessary to make their own realization of Johnston's notation, often indicating exact frequencies. But when parts are fitted together, and the correct tempi and musical nuances are observed, the harmonic basis of the notation is clearer, and what at first seemed impossible, is realized.

As Johnston became more familiar with extended just intonation, he transposed lattices to specify exactly which pitch frequency he wanted. "The Songs of Innocence" (1975) use a 2,3,5 lattice that is tuned to octaves of a 60 cycle B. With A 440 cycles per second as the pitch standard, then B 480 cps (an eight octave transposition of B 60 cps) is the ratio of 12/11, which in Johnston's notation, is B↓ (see Figure and Example 1). "The Songs of Innocence" were not commissioned, so, as had been his custom, he wrote for musicians who would be willing to perform his music. Barbara Dalheim, a local soprano, who was part of the ensemble that premièred "Ci-Gît Satie," was soloist with Paul and Wilma Zonn, (clarinetist and oboist), Thomas Fredrickson (bassist), John Fonville (flutist), and John Garvey (violist).

Johnston chose three poems by William Blake, "Night," "The Divine Image," and "A Cradle Song," that form a grouping of nativity songs. Again, Johnston's conversion to Catholicism influenced his choice and, like his other recent works, they are tonal and modal. Each one has a distinctive stylistic characteristic. "Night" sounds like a Renaissance madrigal; "The Divine Image" is Romantic with a jazz-like accompaniment; and "A Cradle Song" is almost a crooning style tune

Ab+↓	C+↓	E+↓	G#+↓	B#+↓	Dx+↓
Db↓	F+↓	A+↓	C#+↓	E#+↓	Gx+↓
Gb↓	Bb↓	D↓	F#+↓	A#+↓	Cx+↓
Cb↓	Eb↓	G↓	B↓	D#↓	Fx+↓
Fb↓	Ab↓	C↓	E↓	G#↓	B#↓
Bbb-↓	Db-↓	F↓	A↓	C#↓	E#↓
Ebb-↓	Gb↓	Bb-↓	D-↓	F#↓	A#↓

Figure 1. Lattice showing B as 60 cps in a 2,3,5 system.

Example 1. Beginning measures of "Night" from "The Songs of Innocence."
Forthcoming from Smith Publications.

but laced with an intricate contrapuntal accompaniment. Some of these styles are
reminiscent of his early pieces, such as the jazz-like "somewhere i have never
traveled" or the Renaissance madrigals of Gertrude. Johnston considered these
stylistic references in just intonation to be an explanation of what would have
happened if equal temperament had not been adopted. For him just intonation
is like restoring an old painting so that the colors are correct.[1] He achieved
this restoration in "The Songs of Innocence." The changes in modes and tonal
centers are distinct; modulations support the emotional tone and poetic structure. Each song uses several scales and modes, such as dorian, lydian, minor,
and major. Often a section is polymodal.

After writing "The Songs of Innocence" Johnston was involved with his improvisation project, <u>Visions and Spels</u> (see Chapter 7). There was a period of time when he did not write much. He was busy with guest lectureships at Yale University and Dartmouth and also traveled to Yugoslavia, West Germany, Scotland, and England where he spoke about his own music and the work of Harry Partch. Since Partch's death there has been a growing international interest in Partch's music. Johnston's lecture included a taped performance of <u>In Memory</u>. Later in the year he participated in the International Conference on Microtonal Music at Webster College, St. Louis, Missouri.

Johnston did find time to write several simple hymns, "Since Adam" (1977) and "12 Psalms" (1977). "Since Adam" is a three-part setting of a hymn that Johnston intended to use with the première of his <u>Mass</u>, but then he decided not to have congregational singing. "12 Psalms" is a collection of four-part hymns that he harmonized in just intonation while spending a month at the Blue Cloud Abbey in South Dakota.

The following year, 1978, was productive with several commissions. One was from pianist Roger Shields, a former student at the University of Illinois.[2] It had been thirteen years since Johnston had composed <u>Sonata for Microtonal Piano/Grindlemusic</u>, and he decided to write a suite that incorporated several different styles and also introduced partials of the 13th, 17th, and 19th.

Johnston retuned the piano for his <u>Suite for Microtonal Piano</u> but used a tuning different from his earlier <u>Sonata</u>. The entire piano is tuned to the partials of its lowest C with the fifth register featuring the 16th, 17th, 18th, 19th, 20th, 21st, 22nd, 24th, 27th, 28th, 30th, and 32nd partials of that C. This produces a chromatic scale of C C#17 D Eb19 E F7+ F↑ G Ab13 A+ Bb7 B that he used tonally, modally, and serially. The tuning gave Johnston an opportunity to check his inner hearing and to discover the acoustical properties of these upper partials. No music that Johnston knew had ever used them. He found that the tuning made the piano more resonant, and that chords and harmonies were much clearer than in equal-tempered tuning. Linearly the difference between some pitches is almost negligible, but the vertical relationship is what makes the difference.

<u>Suite for Microtonal Piano</u> (1978) resembles a baroque keyboard suite. Its five movements follow the sequence of fast, slow, fast, slow, and fast, yet the listener knows that the work is not merely an imitation of a past style, but a contemporary composition that is an important addition to piano literature.

The <u>Suite</u> begins with an "Alarum," which is a Shakespearian stage direction indicating a grand entrance. It is an appropriate title since the movement is a fanfare introducing partials number 7, 11, 13, 17, and 19. As the monophonic line rises, new partials are presented. Melismatic gestures make it possible to hear the tuning and scalar relations (see Example 2). This simple movement was a clever choice because it provides a setting for the rest of the suite.

Suite for Microtonal Piano
for Roger Shields

1.   Ben Johnston

Alarum

Example 2. Beginning measures of "Alarum" from Suite for Microtonal Piano.
Copyright 1979 by Smith Publications. Used with permission.

The second movement is "Blues," and stylistically it would seem that a
Renaissance "Alarum" followed by the twentieth-century "Blues" would be in-
compatible. But the two movements complement each other because "Alarum" is
introductory, and "Blues" is such a distinctive style that the movement is like
a character in a play. Its modal melody is in D dorian (although the accompaniment always uses the lowered sixth degree). Johnston took advantage of his
tuning to use two different mediant and dominant scale degrees, F+7, F↑ and A+,
Ab13. These differences contribute to the "blues" spirit so that the melody
sounds vocal, something that is impossible to do with equal-tempered tuning,
and the listener senses that this is how the "blues" should really sound (see

Example 3.   Section of "Blues" from Suite for Microtonal Piano showing different mediant and dominant scale degrees.   Copyright 1979 by Smith Publications. Used with permission.

Example 3).   The movement is in a modified ABA form with the middle section being faster and thicker; however, the D tonal center is kept throughout.

"Etude," the third movement, is another stylistic change.   Its quickly moving figures sound like Xenakis's stochastic writing, although Johnston was able to achieve this sense of randomness by using serialism.   The row is F7+ E Eb19 Bb7 A+ C D C#17 Ab13 B F↑ G with one member of each pitch class represented. "Etude" is physically difficult to play because of its "As fast as possible" tempo and rhythmic patterning of 5:4 and 6:4.   As the figuration expands and contracts the listener hears the entire range of the piano.   Johnston used various forms of the row often combining a prime for one hand with an inversion for the other. This "Etude" is reminiscent of his first serial piece, the Etude that he composed in 1949.   (See Example 2 of Chapter 2 and compare it to Example 4.)

The fourth movement is a simple song in E phrygian.   The scale of E F7+ G A+ B C D features a whole tone of 10/9 for the leading tone and a small half-step of 21/20 for the distance between the first and second scale degrees.   These intervals accentuate the phrygian modal qualities.   Later, in the middle section of this ABA song, a modulation to D dorian occurs and, again, the change in modes is more noticeable than in equal temperament.   Like "Blues," the melody has a vocal characteristic unheard in keyboard music.   The intervallic variety plus the enhanced resonance add a prolonging quality that disguises the piano's normally fast decay.

3.

Etude

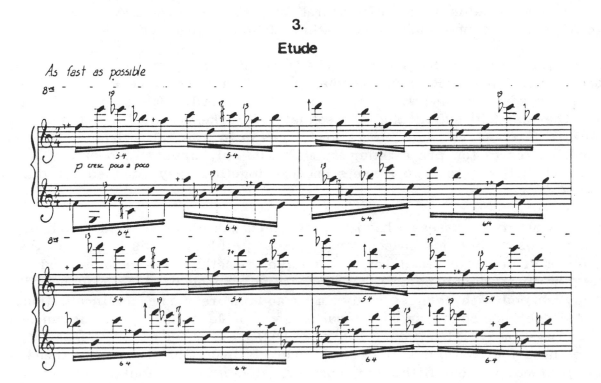

Example 4. "Etude" from Suite for Microtonal Piano. Copyrighted 1979 by Smith Publications. Used with permission.

The last movement, "Toccata," is a virtuosic piece in the style of the French toccata so popular in the organ literature from the early part of the twentieth century. It is in an ABA form with repeating motives and frequently changing meters that produce a strong rhythmic drive. The piece remains clearly in C, and its frequent triads show the harmonic orientation of the tuning first presented in the "Alarum."

The sectional nature of the Suite and juxtaposition of different styles work well. Previously this had been a flaw in Johnston's writing, such as St. Joan and Gambit, but his sense of style is what makes this piece so interesting. It programs well on a concert of contemporary or traditional music.

Johnston's next commission was for the Contemporary Chamber Ensemble at the University of Illinois, which, at this time, had an extensive touring schedule. The commission has several unusual twists. At first Johnston wrote just for the ensemble (flute, oboe, clarinet, trumpet, trombone, tuba, viola, and double bass), but then decided he didn't like the piece because the music sounded like an accompaniment that needed a solo line as a foreground. Gordon Brock, a baritone with an extremely wide range, was touring with the Ensemble, and this gave Johnston the idea of superimposing a vocal part derived from the instrumental lines. The voice adds a dramatic timbral dimension because Brock had a wide range of three and one-half octaves, which Johnston featured.

Another twist is that Johnston tried two different texts. First he used Wallace Stevens' poem "Evening Without Angels," and the piece was premièred, but the words seemed awkward and could not be heard. Johnston decided to change the text and substituted two sonnets of Shakespeare, "What potions have I drunk of Siren tears" and "Sweet love, renew thy force," without making any drastic changes to the pre-existing music. The only unusual aspect is that there is no break between the two sonnets because together they equalled the duration of Stevens' poem.

This ability to assess what is wrong and make changes is the mark of a mature composer, but one reason for the vocal problem in this piece was that Johnston reverted to a strict serial technique, something he had not used since 1966. The instrumental parts are Webernesque, especially since each note is carefully shaped with changes in dynamics and timbre nuances. In addition, the piece does not sound as microtonal as some of Johnston's previous music because he used a 2,3,11 lattice. The row, G D C↑ G↑ A+ F↑ C F Bb↑- Eb↑- Bb- Eb-, features fourths and fifths rather than his usual thirds because the 2,3,11 lattice produces perfect fifths and fourths, half-augmented fourths (F↑ to C 11/8) and neutral thirds (D to F↑ 11/9). The row contains a second (D to C↑ and G↑ to A+, both 11/6's) which is 151 cents, halfway between an equal-tempered major and minor second. Also, the row generates aggregates of Viennese fourth chords (a perfect fourth and an augmented fourth), another Webernesque trait. Structurally, the row divides into two pentachords and a dyad. The first five members are adjacent relations on the lattice; the second five are an inversion or utonality; and the last two are fifths (see Figure 2). Johnston also used all forty-eight versions of the row, something he had not done with his other serial music.

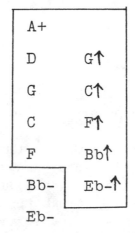

Figure 2. Lattice of 2,3,11.

Two Sonnets of Shakespeare has a rhythmic plan that is unique to Johnston's music and is an idea that he had used previously. He designed a metric pattern based upon the 35-tone scale generated by his set matrix (see Figure 3).[3] The scale is characterized by two intervals: 53 cents (33/32, the distance between C and C↑) and 8 cents (243/128, the distance between C↑ and C#↓++). Various combinations of other scale degrees equal 53 cents, such as 29 cents + 24 cents (C#↓++ to C#++) or 16 cents + 37 cents (Eb↑- to Eb-).

G	D	C↑	G↑	A+	F↑	C	F	Bb↑-	Eb↑-	Bb-	Eb-
C	G	F↑	C↑	D	Bb↑-	F	Bb-	Eb↑-	Ab↑-	Eb-	Ab-
D↓	A↓+	G	D	E↓+	C	G↓	C↓	F	Bb-	F↓	Bb↓-
G↓	D↓	C	G	A↓+	F	C↓	F↓	Bb-	Eb-	Bb↓-	Eb↓-
F	C	Bb↑-	F↑	G	Eb↑-	Bb-	Eb-	Ab↑-	Db↑--	Ab-	Db--
A↓-	E↓-	D	A+	B↓+	G	D↓	G↓	C	F	C↓	F↓
D	A+	G↑	D↑	E+	C↑	G	C	F↑	Bb↑-	F	Bb-
A+	E+	D↑	A↑+	B+	G↑	D	G	C↑	F↑	C	F
E↓+	B↓+	A+	E+	F#↓++	D	A↓+	D↓	G	C	G↓	C↓
B↓+	F#↓++	E+	B+	C#↓++	A+	E↓+	A↓+	D	G	D↓	G↓
E+	B+	A↑+	E↑+	F#++	D↑	A+	D	G↑	C↑	G	C
B+	F#++	E↑+	B↑+	C#++	A↑+	E+	A+	D↑	G↑	D	G

Scale:
C C↑ C#↓++ Db-- C#++ Db↑-- D↓ D Eb↓- D↑ Eb- Eb↑- E↓+ E+ F↓ E↑+ F F↑ F#↓++ F#++ G↓ G
cents: 53 8 29 24 29 8 53 37 16 37 53 8 53 37 16 37 53 8 53 37 53

(G) G↑ Ab- Ab↑- A↓+ A+ Bb↓- A↑+ Bb- Bb↑- B↓+ B+ C↓ B↑+ C
53 37 53 8 53 37 16 37 53 8 53 37 16 37

Figure 3. Matrix and resulting scale for Two Sonnets of Shakespeare. Property of the composer. Used with permission.

Johnston developed an isorhythm for the 53 cents. The pattern is (3+3+2) + (2+3+3) + (3+3+2) + (3+2+3) + (2+3+3) + (3+2+3) + (2+3) = 53 which encompasses six measures of an 8/8 meter plus one measure of 5/8. The small 8-cent interval

is always represented with two bars of 8/16 and has a pattern of 2+2+2+2.
The 29 cents is three bars of 8/8 and one bar of 5/8, and the 37 cents is four
bars of 8/8 and one bar of 5/8. See Example 5 where the piece begins its metric
scheme with C (53 cents), C↑ (8 cents), and part of C#↓++ (29 cents).

The entire scale is represented and governs the duration of Two Sonnets
of Shakespeare. A small coda of twenty-four beats is added at the end. This
organic relationship between time and pitch is an idea that Johnston had used in
String Quartet Numbers 2 and 4, but the isorhythmic aspect is new. This regular rhythmic grouping in twos and threes, another trait of Webern, may be an additional reason why Johnston did not like the piece at first. His previous modal
and tonal compositions had asymmetrical rhythmic qualities that are more characteristic of his music. It is interesting that this less distinctive tuning with the
eleventh partial replacing the fifth partial in a two-dimensional lattice produced
a conservative rhythmic plan.

The piece was performed as Two Sonnets of Shakespeare in February 1979
at a National Convention of the American Society of University Composers with
Philip Larson as soloist and Bernard Rands conducting the Sonor Ensemble. Larson has an amazing vocal range of over three octaves including a reliable falsetto.
He is the ideal singer for the piece. Johnston plans to have a computer realization of the instrumental parts so that Larson can perform the Two Sonnets of
Shakespeare as a solo with tape accompaniment.

During 1978 Johnston was invited to the Warsaw Autumn Festival as Guest
Composer, and he planned a project to be realized in the Studio Eksperymentalne
of Radio Polskie. Johnston was to produce an electronic tape piece that reflected
the partial series from eight to sixteen in both pitch and rhythm. The composition, Strata (1978), was to be a layered mixture of recordings from a retuned piano
that featured 142 tones in various 12-tone patterns. Johnston composed the piano
part, and then Bohdan Mazurek, a composer at the studio, realized the tape so
that layers were recorded at different speeds. Johnston agrees that his plan was
not successful. The piece is too thick and sounds muddy. A low rumble, which
is the fundamental speed, masks the clarity of the other parts so that the listener
does not have a chance to hear any of the relationships. Johnston calls it an ugly
piece. Perhaps if Strata could be heard as sixteen channels, it would be more
interesting.

The fourth commission during 1978 was from the husband-wife violin duo in
the Netherlands, Jeanne Vos and Bouw Lemkes. They frequently perform microtonal music, especially repertoire associated with Fokker's 31-tone temperament.
Johnston chose to write a neoclassic piece, Duo for two violins (1978), which is
in three movements--"Fuga," "Aria," and "Toccata." Like Rose, the piece has
both old and new ideas. "Fuga," the first movement, is a four-voice fugue
(there are double stop passages). Johnston had composed a fugal movement in
Sonata for Two for violin and cello (1961), but "Fuga" is a much stricter fugue.
The string writing is typical of some other pieces. During "Aria" the second

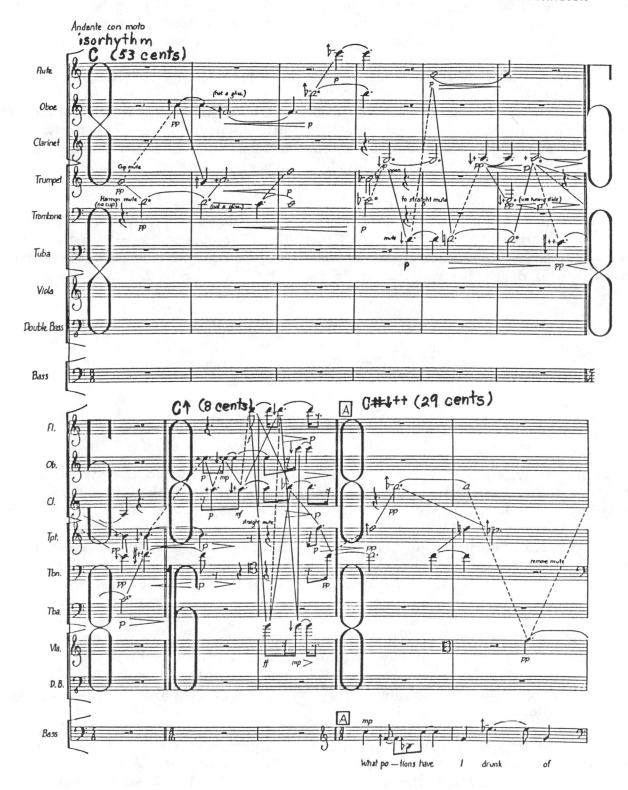

Example 5. Beginning measures of <u>Two Sonnets of Shakespeare</u>. Copyright 1979 by Smith Publications. Used with permission.

violin accompanies with high tremolo passages somewhat similar to passages in "Taking Leave of a Friend" from Three Chinese Lyrics, and the Duo's "Toccata" is a shared composite texture of keyboard-like figuration similar, again, to the duo string writing in Three Chinese Lyrics.

The newer aspects of Duo are its scale and long spun-out melody. The piece is tuned to a new lattice, a 2,3,5,7,11,13 system, and no representation of this lattice is available because of the difficulties of diagramming a five-dimensional figure. Duo is the first time that Johnston wrote all partials up to the 13th for stringed instruments. The Suite for Microtonal Piano was tuned to higher partials, but the performer did not have to actually produce the pitches.

Johnston used this complete partial spectrum to clarify several aspects of tonality. "Fuga" is based upon an A aeolian mode shown in Figure 4. The eleventh and thirteenth partials make it possible to emphasize the dominant and leading tone scale degrees by approaching them with intervals not usually heard, such as D↑- to E (33/32) and F13 to G# (195/128).

$$A \quad B \quad C13 \quad D\!\uparrow\!- \quad E \quad F13 \quad G\#$$
$$\frac{9}{8} \quad \frac{39}{32} \quad \frac{143}{128} \quad \frac{33}{32} \quad \frac{39}{32} \quad \frac{195}{128}$$

Figure 4. Aeolian mode and interval distance in "Fuga" of Duo for two violins.

Johnston took advantage of this tuning when he composed the subject for "Fuga." The head consists of a descending fourth, a conventional procedure, followed by an upward leap of a seventh, another common occurrence, but the seventh is the interval of 11/6 which is larger than the 16/9 interval that would occur in a 2,3,5 system. This 11/6 interval has an even stronger tendency to resolve to the dominant, which Johnston deliberately delayed. Instead the dominant is decorated with F13, a small second of 13/12 that wants to resolve downwards. The result is an active tonal subject that has subtle harmonic implications. Notice that the answer in measure 3 of Example 6 has an ascending leap of 33/32, an augmented octave, rather than a stretched seventh. This helps the listener identify the answer because it has definite tonal differences. "Fuga" has a standard four-voice exposition, episodes, stretti, and even inverted subject and answer entrances. It is a classic example of eighteenth-century counterpoint, as can be seen in Example 6.

"Aria" is in a G- minor that begins to change mode due to various tuning possibilities. Before long the continuously winding melody of the first violin rises in a gradual ascent through the 47-tone scale, much like the first movement of String Quartet Number 2 used every member of its 53-tone scale, although "Aria" is not serial. A high tremolo figure in the second violin is a harmonic foundation upon which the first violin measures its various interval sizes.

DUO for two violins

Ben Johnston

Example 6. Subject and answer used in "Fuga" from Duo for two violins. Copyright 1979 by Smith Publications. Used with permission.

The "Toccata" is an ABA form with frequent repetitions and reversals of lines. The A sections have an E drone against which various scalar patterns are measured. The title is especially appropriate since the texture sounds like a "touch" piece. The second violin plays pizzicato the entire time, and the first violin changes from arco to pizzicato for A'.

Duo was premièred by Lawrence Shapiro and Paul Primus at the Chicago Public Library at a New Music Circle Concert in November 1979. The audience, which consisted of composers, musicians interested in contemporary music, library patrons, and residents of the area, gave Johnston an instant standing ovation. Many people responded to the tonal clarity and familiar forms, while others were fascinated by the pitch subtleties of extended just intonation.

By this point in his career Johnston was receiving more commissions than he was able to complete. One was a request for a new string quartet from the Concord Quartet. Johnston did not finish the commission on time for its scheduled première in 1976, and there were even plans for the Kronos Quartet to première String Quartet Number 5 at the 1982 New Music America held in Chicago, but these arrangements were not successful. However, the work was premièred by the Tremont Quartet on December 16, 1983, on a concert of Johnston's music at the Arts Club in Chicago.[3A] In his program notes for this occasion Johnston wrote:

String Quartet Number 5 was composed at the suggestion of the Concord Quartet, but they have not yet played the piece. It is in one-movement form, and makes use of the Appalachian tune, Lonesome Valley. The tuning is based on an elaborate system involving all the overtone relationships through the 16th partial, and is thus one step more complex than the musical language of Harry Partch, though like his music it involves "extended just intonation" and complementary "otonality (overtone)" and "utonality (undertone)" harmonic aggregates. Unlike Partch, the music is modulatory. I have no idea as to how many different pitches

it used per octave. The form is organized in successive "evocations,"
like Debussy's L'apres midi d'un Faune. Each has several thematic
units and each treats these elements uniquely.

While writing String Quartet Number 4 Johnston found that he enjoyed folk
tunes and chose "Lonesome Valley" as the subject of his next quartet. The tune
gave him an opportunity to work with melody, one of his strongest compositional
assets, and the implied text helped to guide the emotional and expressive aspects
of the composition.

"Lonesome Valley" is pentatonic, and Johnston took advantage of its simplicity to show different kinds of tuning systems available in extended just intonation. Having experimented with various lattices, he used six different tunings to color the third and sixth modal degrees of the tune (see Figure 5).

    m.1   F- G- A↓ C- D↓-
             (partials 2,3,11)

    m.76   G- A- B- D- E-
             (partials 2,3)

    m.97   C- D- Eb7- G- Ab7-
             (partials 2,3,7)

    m.128   F- G↓- Ab- C- D∠--
             (partials 2,3,5,7,11)

    m.135   F- G↑b- Ab- C- Db--
             (partials 2,3,5,11)

    m.168   F↑- G- Ab13- C- D-
             (partials 2,3,11,13)

Figure 5. Six different tunings for "Lonesome Valley."

These pitch relationships are shown on the 2,3,5,7,11 lattice in Figure 3
of Chapter 8. (The thirteenth partial is not represented because it is not used
as extensively as the other partials in this quartet and, again, it would add
further difficulties to an already complex diagram.) String Quartet Number 5
is based upon an F- fundamental in order to accommodate the quartet's open
strings which in Johnston's system are notated as C- G- D- A for the cello and
viola and G- D- A E for the violins.

The beginning measures of the quartet are an example of how this tuning system works. The cellist performs an ostinato of just fifths (3/2) in an analogous rhythmic figuration of 3:2, showing the quartet's central tuning system. The violist and second violinist have an ostinato that indicates the additional partials used (the 5,7,11) and the utonal (minor) tuning based on G- with Eb- (8/5), A⌐- (8/7) and D↓- (12/11).

Example 7. Beginning measures of String Quartet Number 5. Copyright 1985 by Smith Publications. Used with permission.

From this point on String Quartet Number 5 becomes complex. The form is not a series of variations, as in String Quartet Number 4, but statements of the theme followed by freer sections called evocations. The evocations present three ideas. One idea is melodic in which conjunct lines feature the many different seconds available in the hyperchromatic scale, or wide leaps illustrate the differences among intervals measured by the 7th, 11th, or 13th partials. Another idea is scalar. These evocations are dense hyperchromatic ascending and descending passages supported by rearticulated drones, as in the "Toccata" of Duo for two violins. Occasionally an evocation is a modulating homophonic passage.

The modulations were important theoretical experiments for Johnston. Partch never used modulations, and Johnston was anxious to discover what effects modulation would have in extended just intonation. He had used modal modulations in earlier vocal works, such as Mass, but this larger lattice made tonal modulations possible. Several modulations take place before the theme is repeated in m.32. The first modulation is heard in m.8 in which vibrato begins to replace the opening non vibrato. A complex E⌐- as a thirteenth chord representing an utonal aggregate based upon the seventh partial (E⌐- G#⌐- B⌐- C⌐13- A⌐↑-) upsets the previous tuning. A temporary F# emerges in m.16, and by

Example 8. Utonality in String Quartet Number 5. Copyright 1985 by Smith Publications. Used with permission.

m.21 C- becomes a clear tonal area supported by its 11th chord. At times utonality is prominent, such as the undertones of C- in m.106 in Example 8.

The many modulations and modal changes between otonality and utonality cause scale formations to constantly change. One example is an evocation where a canonic section beginning in m.61 creates tension between C- as a fundamental or unity and C↑- as the eleventh partial to G-. Other lines are also in canon and reflect a similar uncertainty (see Example 9). The tension is released in m.77 where the tune returns in a simple tuning of fifths and major thirds (G- A- B- D- E-).

The tune's next appearance is in a C septimal minor with its third and sixth scale degrees from the septimal lattice. Following this is a statement of "Lonesome Valley" in Db7--, which acts as a Neapolitan to the previous C-.

Metric modulations elaborate the pitch action. The first modulation in m.23 is a tempo increase of 5/4 or a major third (150/60 = 5/2 which, when reduced to within the range of one octave, is 5/4). The passage that follows is an elaboration of the tune's anacrusis figure of a major third. Other metric modulations form ratios using the factors 2,3,5,7 (again, similar to pitch ratios), and later in the quartet there are superimposed tempi of 120, 135, 150 and 160 which form a harmonic series of 8:9:10:11.

The formal aspect of String Quartet Number 5 is difficult to follow making this piece more complex than any of Johnston's other compositions from the 1970's. It is never predictable when the theme will appear, and sometimes the evocations are a linking of two or three sections. They gave Johnston an opportunity to try harmonic, melodic, and contrapuntal textures using extended just intonation.

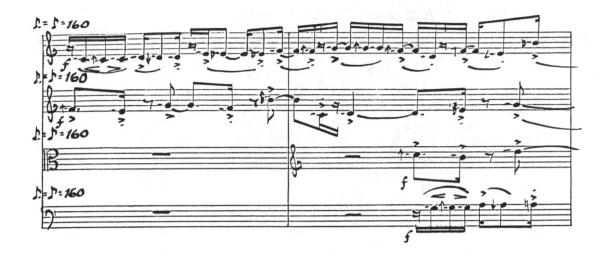

Example 9. Tonal uncertainty in a canonic section of String Quartet Number 5. Copyright 1985 by Smith Publications. Used with permission.

Johnston continued to experiment with extended just intonation with Diversion (1979) for eleven instruments. Leo Kraft, the composer and faculty member at Queens College in New York, asked Johnston to write a piece for the New Repertory Ensemble of New York, which is a combination of performing faculty members from New York University and Queens College. The ensemble had one of every instrument, except tuba. Johnston used the occasion to write a piece where serialism is governed by theories of extended just intonation. The row is combinatorial, C B7b G D F↑ E A+ G#↓+ B F#+ D#𝐿 C#+, with the second hexachord being a retrograde inversion of the first hexachord. The intervals are also inverted--D#𝐿 and G#↓+ are utonal versions of Bb7 and F↑. The row is from a 2,3,5,7,11 lattice, and its otonal and utonal structure is shown in Figure 6, page 164. The fundamental of the utonal hexachord is B, which is bracketed in the figure because it is actually a member of the fifth partial column. The transposition was made to preserve the same configuration.

Johnston used the row in many different ways. There are pairings, solos, accompaniments, duets, canons, and fused ensemble chords. The entire piece sounds serial, and two intervals (7/4 for C to Bb7 and 11/9 for D to F↑ and their inversions of 8/7 and 12/11) signal how the row is working. This is important in later sections in which the tetrachords are reordered. Often tetrachord 1 is paired with or followed by tetrachord 3, and the remaining tetrachords are presented as a retrograde. This happens in the canons and duets in the middle sections of Diversion. In Example 10, page 164, the duet between the flute and oboe has this rearrangement of the row, as labeled.

Diversion is a dance-like piece with rhythmic patterns of 2, 3, and 5 and predominant meters of 5/8 and 7/8. Johnston considered Diversion a divertimento, something he had not written since the late 1950's; Septet (1959) is its predecessor.

Otonal hexachord using C as the fundamental

```
                        D
                        G    [B]
                        C      E      Bb7    F↑
Partial Numbers         3      5      7      11
```

Utonal hexachord using B as the fundamental

```
   G#↓+    D#↳    A+      C#+
                          F#+
                          B
   11       7      5       3      Partial Numbers
```

Figure 6. Diagram of otonality and utonality of the 12-tone row used in <u>Diversion</u>.

Example 10. Duet with reordering of the row and new rhythmic grouping from <u>Diversion</u>. Used by permission of the composer.

<u>Diversion</u>'s tempo moves quickly, and careful articulations and dynamic markings emphasize the rhythmic qualities. Sections are caused by meter changes, new rhythmic groups (such as 4 + 3 and so on), and changes in articulation. Notice the new rhythmic patterning of 3+2+2+3+2 in Example 10.

Because of Diversion's varied instrumentation Johnston tried several timbral changes, such as fused chords of three instruments playing at the same time, often in extremely high or low registers. The results are a composite timbre in which the components are difficult to identify. Frequent dynamic changes make these fused chords (which are trichords) sound like a klangfarbenmelodie (see [B] in Example 11). Later, Johnston exaggerated dynamic envelopes in an extended passage of sustained notes.

Example 11. Fused chords in Diversion. Used by permission of the composer.

For several years Johnston had been working on his String Quartet Number 6, but it was not finished until January 1980. Originally, he planned to write it for the Concord Quartet as a commission from the Naumburg Foundation; however, he was unable to complete the piece in time for their scheduled première and lost the commission. The New World String Quartet also won a Naumburg Award, and upon the recommendation of Robert Mann (the first violinist with the Juilliard String Quartet), the New World String Quartet asked Johnston for a new piece.[4] He sent them his String Quartet Number 6.

The quartet was to première it in the spring of 1980 but found that they needed more practice time. They began seriously working on the piece several years later and were discouraged with their progress until Johnston carefully showed them how to listen and tune in extended just intonation. He had the group prolong harmonic structures, such as dominant seventh chords, carefully adjusting each pitch until it was in tune, and the quartet began to hear the results of just intonation which they described "as gossamer having a buzzing and shimmering glow" that they had never heard before.[5] The tuning made the quartet sound like more than just four instruments.[6] This experience gave them new incentive to work on String Quartet Number 6. Having met Johnston, they realized that extended just intonation was not just a theory--it was something Johnston heard, and now they heard it too.[7]

Plate 3. Johnston and the New World String Quartet standing left to right, Robert Dan (violist), Ben Johnston, Curtis Macomber (violinist), Vahn Armstrong (violinist), and Ross Harbaugh (cellist).

String Quartet Number 6 is one movement that lasts about twenty-two minutes. It is a series of long solo lines supported by accompanying harmonic drones; each instrument has its solo. The melodic emphasis characterizes String Quartet Number 6 as a romantic piece, especially since the melodies are continuous; there are no cadences or breaks, and the ends and beginnings of solos are elided (see Example 12 which is the first fifteen measures of the quartet).

Johnston used a palindrome to create an arch-like structure. Because the melodies are continuous and have many rising and falling gestures, they work

Example 12. Beginning fifteen measures of <u>String Quartet Number 6</u>. Copyright 1985 by Smith Publications. Used with permission.

equally well forwards and backwards. Like the last movement of String Quartet Number 2, which is also a palindrome, there is a chordal section that signals the midpoint, and the reversal is easy to detect because the second violinist, who was the last soloist, begins the retrograde.

The pitch scheme is serial. The first hexachord of this semi-combinatorial row is two major triads, and the second is two minor triads showing the otonal and utonal properties of extended just intonation. The row is D- A F# G↑- C7 E B G# D# A#↓+ E#ↆ C# and is from a 2,3,5,7,11 lattice (see Figure 7). The bracketed pitches belong to the second hexachord but are included in the first part of the figure to show their structural relationship on the lattice. However, to illustrate utonality, D# G# and C# are transposed to the column of third partials for the second hexachord.

First hexachord of major triads

	[B]	[D#]		
	E	[G#]		
	A	[C#]		
	D-	F#	C7	G↑-

Partial numbers	3	5	7	11

Second hexachord of minor triads

A#↓+	E#ↆ	B	D#
			G#
			C#

11	7	5	3	Partial numbers

Figure 7. Otonal and utonal structure of the row for String Quartet Number 6.

Johnston used all forty-eight forms of the row having common tones link one version to another, but he did not write in any set patterning. The melodies are composed for their expressiveness, with notes repeated out of their serial order when necessary to support the tuning. His triadic emphasis is somewhat similar to the way Alban Berg constructed his 12-tone rows. As has been the case in Johnston's later works, he used serialism as a convenient device to organize pitch--the serialism is subservient to the extended just intonation.

When hearing the quartet the listener has the sensation of spinning and turning in space. This is partly due to the rising and falling character of the solo lines and to the palindrome which is an exact pitch retrograde (all forty-eight row forms are used in the forward presentation of the palindrome). The listener also notices that many different pitches are used. Johnston's lattice constructions are more audible in this piece than in any other he has written.

A series of metric modulations is also part of the palindrome. Each solo has its own tempo caused by metric modulations that use ratios from a 2,3,5,11 lattice (see Figure 8). One wonders why Johnston did not include a ratio of 7 in his tempi to match the pitch ratios he was using. The fundamental and beginning tempo is ♪ = 180. The 180 is stated again at the turning point of the palindrome, but the duration is 180 = 11/32 (notated as ♩♪), and not the eighth note duration it originally had. Tempi increase as the piece progresses so that the ending coda is ♪ = 360, twice the original speed.

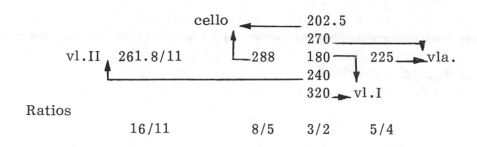

Figure 8. Tempi ratios in String Quartet Number 6.

The New World String Quartet first performed String Quartet Number 6 in February 1983 at Harvard as an open rehearsal and later played it at Hope College and Calvin College in Michigan. The quartet sent Johnston a tape of the Harvard performance, and he realized there were problems that should be fixed. The piece sounded monochromatic, and some passages were too low. Since String Quartet Number 6 is a palindrome with the tempo of the retrograde two thirds faster than its original, the midpoint's climax occurs at about two thirds of the tonal duration--the golden mean. Because of this ratio Johnston decided that the Fibonacci series would be an appropriate scheme for adding the dynamics and articulations that would give the needed color. Each solo plus the mid-turning point section is divided into the proportions of this series, and Johnston placed changes in dynamics and/or articulations to mark the proportions.

This revision was successful, and the New World String Quartet was able to perform the new version at the New York première in Alice Tully Hall in a Naumburg Foundation Concert on April 26, 1983. In his program notes for their performance Johnston acknowledged the group's efforts.

It [String Quartet Number 6] has required not only more than usual care and creative partnership from within the quartet but also, during the rehearsal period, from me. Without a spirit of true collaborative participation in realizing and projecting the artistic aims of the work, a convincing performance would not have been possible. I am permanently grateful to these four men for their understanding, dedication and hard work.[8]

Some members of the quartet were afraid that the audience might leave in the middle of the performance because of their nonacceptance or lack of understanding, however just the opposite happened--the audience was mesmerized. Not long after this performance the New World String Quartet made a recording of the quartet which is available on "Naumburg Prize Winners Perform Naumburg Commissions" (CRI SD 497).

Johnston did not experiment with any new aspects of extended intonation in String Quartet Number 6. He had used a 2,3,5,7,11 lattice before and even included up to the 32nd partial in Suite for Microtonal Piano. Metric modulation was not new, and the Fibonacci series is found in Quintet for Groups. One aspect, though, was becoming clear. Johnston had often used the term "bridge" to explain his theories, and by 1983 he acknowledged that his work had outstripped Partch's explorations of extended just intonation. In program notes Johnston stated:

> In fact, once Partch's ingenious and revolutionary system of intonation had been made by him the basis of his own instrument designs in case after admirable case as he built up his large ensemble over his whole life, his compositional procedures increasingly reflected the instrument designs themselves rather than the acoustic implications of his own theories.
>
> I recognized early that Partch had not explored the compositional implications of his own monumental creative book.... It [the continuity of musical excellence] needed someone without Partch's outsider's resentment/rejection of occidental music ... and equally it required someone without Schoenberg's counter-prejudices. One could compare it to the design and building of a bridge.

Johnston has been the bridge-maker, and this is clearly heard in his string quartets. Nine Variations, the first string quartet, is equal tempered and a mixture of neoclassic and serial ideas. String Quartet Number 2 is radically different, like the music of a contemporary Gesualdo (a comparison Johnston has made), and its simple lattice structure of 2,3,5 illustrates the emotional and intellectual complexities available in this basic use of just intonation. String Quartet Number 3 is less intense and is an example of how well just intonation can adapt to serialism. String Quartets Numbers 4 and 5 are an Ivesian mixture of familiar tunes embedded in more complex structures, and Number 6 is a romantic web of continuous melody.

Although the string quartets have been the trusses in Johnston's bridge, songs or some association of music with text have been important towers in his catalog because many of his songs began new phases in his use of extended just intonation. This is true with <u>Sonnets of Desolation</u> (1980), the piece he completed after writing <u>String Quartet Number 6</u>.

Johnston's second occasion to write for his friend Ward Swingle produced the <u>Sonnets of Desolation</u>. Swingle applied to the Fromm Foundation for money to commission Johnston to write a piece for The New Swingle Singers. For the text Johnston chose four sonnets by Gerard Manley Hopkins, "Carrion Comfort," "I wake and feel the fell of dark, not day," "Patience, hard thing!," and "That Nature is a Heraclitean Fire and of the Comfort of the Resurrection." The New Swingle Singers premièred the piece in November 1981 at their concert in the Krannert Center for the Performing Arts at the University of Illinois. Johnston's songs were the highlight of the concert, and Swingle had designed a program featuring a mixture of popular and classical music that best illustrated The New Swingle Singers' repertoire. Many people attended the concert, not just those interested in new music. It was even broadcast live over the local Public Radio Station, and the tape of this performance was used for the Composers Recordings Incorporated <u>Ben Johnston</u> (CRI SD 516).

While listening to the <u>Sonnets</u> one senses that the poetry and the music are an ideal match. This may be due to some similarities between Hopkins and Johnston. Both were converts to Catholicism and often reflected this spirituality in their artistic medium, and both men were simultaneously revolutionists and traditionalists in the way they used their artistic material.

Hopkins wrote the sonnets in 1885, and all four express the determination to resist succumbing to spiritual despair. A Jesuit priest, Hopkins was sensitive to this condition which St. John of the Cross called the "dark night of the soul." As a poet he was a revolutionist with language, often forming unusual compounds and even new words to describe his observations of nature which he termed "inscapes." "Wring-world" and "lionlimb" are two examples of inscapes from "Carrion Comfort." He created "sprung rhythms" as an innovative way of altering periodic metrical stress, such as this line from the above sonnet: "Cheer whom though? the hero whose heaven-handling flung me, fóot tród Me?" Hopkins was also a traditionalist in his frequent use of such Old English and Anglo-Saxon words as bonfire, beacon, comb, coil, and peel.[9]

Johnston has experienced similar spiritual trials and often used spiritual texts and themes in his music, such as these <u>Sonnets</u>, the liturgy for <u>Mass</u>, and "Amazing Grace" for his <u>String Quartet Number 4</u>. He is a revolutionist in the way he uses pitch; perhaps microtones are musical inscapes. Yet Johnston is a traditionalist in that he stays within the confines of the European musical heritage, often using familiar forms and textures.

As has always been his custom, each piece explores some new aspect of just intonation. The <u>Sonnets of Desolation</u> presented an opportunity to try the higher regions of the 15th, 21st, and 27th partials. The New Swingle Singers are an octet of SSAATTBB, so the luxury of having an eight-voice group of professional singers made it possible for Johnston to write large tertian structures based upon the overtone and undertone series. The 15th partial is the ratio of 15/8, the fifth above the third. The 21st partial is the 7th partial of a 3/2 ($3/2 \times 7/4 = 21/8$ or the octave reduction of 21/16). The 27th partial is the third fifth above the fundamental ($3/2 \times 3/2 \times 3/2 = 27/16$; see Figure 9).

27 = A+

9 = D

3 = G   15 = B   21 = F7+

1 = C   5 = E   7 = B7   11 = F↑   13 = Ab13

Figure 9. Odd-numbered partials using C as the fundamental.

The first sonnet, "Carrion Comfort," uses all of the above partials. By the third measure there is an A13th chord for the word "feast" using partials 1(A), 5(C#), 7(G7), 9(B), 11(D-↑), 13(F13), 15(G#), and 27(F#+). Almost immediately following this chord there is a modulation to C. The word "thee" is a C11th chord using partials 1(C), 3(G), 7(Bb7), 9(D), 11(F↑), 21(F7+), and 27(A+). The C is preceded by A, F, and G in the lowest bass voice, and these are root movements that are clearly heard (see Example 13).

"Carrion Comfort" is homophonic, and frequent modulations define the sonnet's structural design. Each line of the quatrains has a different tonal center, as shown in Figure 10.

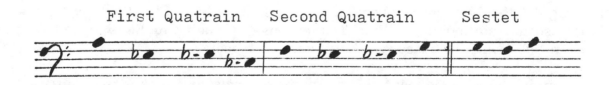

First Quatrain   Second Quatrain   Sestet

Figure 10. Tonal areas in "Carrion Comfort."

Notice that there are no obvious tonic-dominant relations, and although some pitches may look closely related, such as E and Eb-, they are actually remote relations five just fifths and a just major third away. The sestet (the last six lines of the sonnet) is much simpler, having fewer and more closely related tonal areas.

Example 13. Beginning measures of "Carrion Comfort" from Sonnets of Desolation. Used with permission of Lingua Press Publishers, P.O. Box 481, Ramona, California 92065.

The quatrains expose the more complicated properties of extended just intonation, while the sestet contains unison sounds or single lines, and a return to small number ratios of 5/6, 4/3, and 3/2 sounds fresh and new. During "Carrion Comfort" one first hears dissonance, then mildly consonant sounds, and finally clear consonances.

Johnston has always tried to preserve the clarity of the text, and he achieved this aim by carefully following Hopkins' rhythm. This did not require complicated rhythmic patterns, but sensitivity to the words and placement of accents. The sprung rhythms fall in the right places. Most of the text is syllabic so that the natural rhythms are not disturbed.

The second sonnet, "I wake and feel the fell of dark, not day," is a recitative which the first soprano and first alto sing in unison. The other six members sustain two open fifths. The pitches are doubled so that the singers can stagger their breathing to maintain a constant drone. The tight conjunct melody almost sounds like intoned speech, and it uses a mixed otonal and utonal version of partials 27 to 1. Theoretically A (the top member of the drone) is the center, just as it was for the previous sonnet, but G- (the bass member of the drone) is perceived as the fundamental. The first quatrain sounds like modal coloring of a G- center (see Example 14). There is a modulation to B- for the second quatrain, and the sestet is an otonal structure based upon G- that then returns to the opening tonality for the ending.

"Patience, hard thing!," the third sonnet, is the most complex tonally. It moves from A to G-, Eb-, Gb-, G, finally ending with an A major triad. Johnston experimented with pairing and contrasting different voices, as if The New Swingle Singers were a string quartet. This kind of texture is especially effective for the subject matter of the sonnet since the tonal ambiguity and the constant shifting among vocal registers requires patience and is a hard thing! The sestet begins with all eight voices, a noticeable contrast compared to the previous duo plus drone texture. The chord for the word "our" in Example 15, page 176, is C13 using odd-numbered partials 1-13, and the next word, "heart," is a G13 using the same structure. "Grate," the following word, is an inversion, a utonal 13 measured down from G.

"That Nature Is a Heraclitean Fire and of the Comfort of the Resurrection," the last sonnet, is a marked emotional change from the other three. Johnston captured the joyful spirit of Hopkins' text by having an ostinato of scat singing accompany the text. It was a marvelous idea and identifies the Sonnets of Desolation as belonging to the Swingle Singers, since scat singing has been their trademark. (Recall that "Ci-Gît Satie," the other piece Johnston wrote for the Swingle Singers, was also set as scat singing.) The beginning lines of the sonnet are: "Cloud-Puffball, torn tufts, tossed pillows flaunt forth, then chevy on an air-/ built thoroughfare: heaven-roysterers, in gay-gangs they throng; they glitter in marches," appropriate words for the light and airy sounds of scat singing (see Example 16, page 177).

The sonnet is long, and Johnston used a new modulatory technique. The tonality shifts to a new axis, the utonal seventh. In doing this he specified an

Example 14. Beginning of "I wake and feel the fell of dark, not day" from
Sonnets of Desolation. Used with permission of Lingua Press Publishers, P.O.
Box 481, Ramona, California 92065.

exact pitch frequency, as he had done for "The Songs of Innocence." E↓- the
32/21 to A is 729.2 cents; E the 3/2 to A is 702 cents. The next section is G-
but then it rises to C-↓, a shift of 551.3 cents rather than 498 cents of a 4/3.
These modulations color both the scat singing and the text because of the

Example 15. Beginning measures of sestet from "Patience, hard thing!" showing otonal and utonal 13th chords in Sonnets of Desolation. Used with permission of Lingua Press Publishers, P.O. Box 481, Ramona, California 92065.

differences between the fundamentals. Using the eleventh partial as the fundamental is like viewing a set of relationships from a different angle.

Later sections of this sonnet are recapitulations of the preceding sonnets. Homophonic textures are like the first sonnet; a recitative resembles the second; and there is a pairing and grouping that matches the third sonnet. Finally the texture returns to the original scat singing.

Example 16. Beginning measures of "That Nature Is a Heraclitean Fire and of the Comfort of the Resurrection" from Sonnets of Desolation. Used with permission of Lingua Press Publishers, P.O. Box 481, Ramona, California 92065.

The Sonnets of Desolation are among the finest of Johnston's compositions. His use of extended just intonation allowed him to choose the precise harmonic ratios and natural resonance that suited the sonic interpretation of Hopkins' text.

Theoretically, these upper partials push the limits of extended just intonation much further than Partch ever imagined, and this is done vocally with no supporting instruments of fixed pitch. While the songs are difficult and demand specialized performers, the results are outstanding. The audience responded enthusiastically to the première of Sonnets of Desolation, but, unfortunately The New Swingle Singers have not scheduled other performances of it. Too often the membership of a group changes, and the piece is not performed again. This is a risk that Johnston has taken, and in 1983 he wrote: "If the future of music is to be more global and less regional, as I believe it will be, I hope that this innovation [use of extended just intonation] may be a worthy contribution to that process."[10]

Johnston continued combining serialism and extended just intonation in Twelve Partials (1980) for flute and microtonal piano. It was written for Ruben Lopez-Perez, a Puerto Rican flutist who wanted a piece that he and his pianist wife could play together. The piano uses the same tuning as Suite for Microtonal Piano with the fifth register being partials 16 through 32 (C C#17 D Eb19 E F7+ F↑ G Ab13 A+ Bb7 B C). These pitches are arranged in an all combinatorial row of C E Eb19 C#17 D F7+ F↑ A+ Bb7 Ab13 G B. The matrix is especially important because the performers decide the order in which to play the Twelve Partials by choosing a row form from the matrix. The sequence of movements can be any one of forty-eight possibilities (see Figure 11).[11] The original matrix is represented in Roman numerals to match the numbering style on each movement, however Arabic numbers are used here for convenience. Also, notice that the matrix is a 1 through 12 system, not the usual 0 through 11.

1	5	4	2	3	6	7	10	11	9	8	12
9	1	12	10	11	2	3	6	7	5	4	8
10	2	1	11	12	3	4	7	8	6	5	9
12	4	3	1	2	5	6	9	10	8	7	11
11	3	2	12	1	4	5	8	9	7	6	10
8	12	11	9	10	1	2	5	6	4	3	7
7	11	10	8	9	12	1	4	5	3	2	6
4	8	7	5	6	9	10	1	2	12	11	3
3	7	6	4	5	8	9	12	1	11	10	2
5	9	8	6	7	10	11	2	3	1	12	4
6	10	9	7	8	11	12	3	4	2	1	5
2	6	5	3	4	7	8	11	12	10	9	1

Figure 11. Matrix for Twelve Partials.

All Twelve Partials use the same matrix and most begin with the original row and end on the beginning pitch of C. This creates a tonal center which is especially noticeable because the original and its inversion are the upper partials of C making these row forms more resonant and consonant than the others. Frequently rows overlap because the 11th and 12th pitches can begin a new row transposed up a fifth. The serial patterning is strict, but beginnings and endings of rows do not necessarily correspond with the phrasing. In some movements three rows are sounding simultaneously but moving at different rates of speeds.

Johnston even used a serialized dynamic row for Partial XI. The solo flute begins with an inversion, I5 using the above matrix. The dynamic row has eight members (fff mf pp ff mp f ppp p) and an inversion in which every gradation of loudness is replaced by an equal gradation of softness (ppp mp ff pp mf p fff f). Thus four versions of the dynamic row are possible: original, retrograde, inversion, and retrograde inversion (see Example 17).

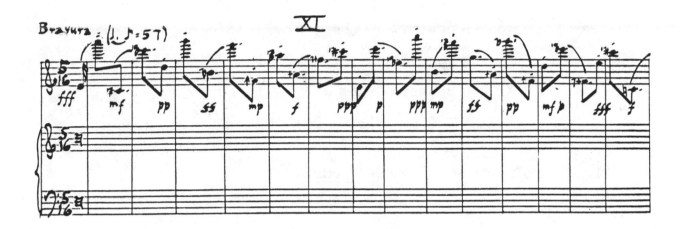

Example 17. Dynamic and pitch rows used in the eleventh movement of Twelve Partials. Forthcoming from Smith Publications.

Johnston used meters of 5/4, 11/16, 9/8, and 5/16 that reflected pitch ratios in Twelve Partials. He also designed the tempo of each movement as an odd-numbered partial of the fundamental tempo of ♩ = 60 in a series of 5 through 19. Thus when the movements are rearranged, the tempi are still complementary because they are all related (see Figure 12, page 180).

Each movement is short and compact making the entire collection seem like a series of vignettes, brief pictures of familiar materials in different settings. There are preludes, etudes, a fughetta, melodies, dances, meditations, and toccata-like partials. Johnston thought of the entire collection as allusions to the mid-European artistic ethos. These are not quotations, as in his earlier music, but reminders. Some of the vignettes suggest music by Stockhausen, Ligeti, Xenakis, and Messiaen. Partial III, marked "meditative (♩ = 75)" resembles bird song like Messiaen has used, especially the flute trill between the 7th and 11th partials (see Example 18, page 180). Messiaen claims that he hears

I.   Bold   ($\quad$ = 60)   4/4

II.   Sinuous   ($\quad$ = 180)   8/4

III.   Meditative ($\quad$ = 75)   5/4

IV.   Introspective ($\quad$ = 60)   4/4

V.   Dance-like ($\quad$ = 105)   7/4

VI.   Sweeping ($\quad$ = 135)   9/4

VII.   Sprightly ($\quad$ = 165)   11/4

VIII.   Brilliant ($\quad$ = 195)   13/8

IX.   Scurrying ($\quad$ = 225)   15/8

X.   Wind-like ($\quad$ = 255)   17/16

XI.   Bravura ($\quad$ = 57)   19/20

XII.   Solemn ($\quad$ = 60)   4/4

Figure 12.   Tempo relations in Twelve Partials.

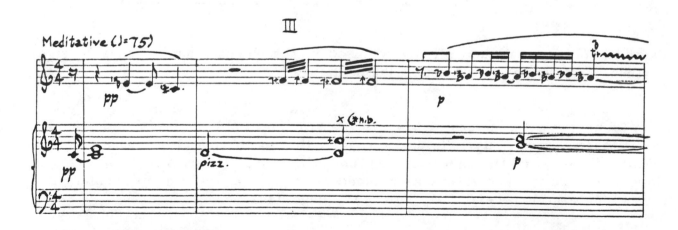

Example 18.   Bird song in Partial III of Twelve Partials.   Forthcoming from Smith Publications.   Used with permission.

the 11th partial as consonant to the fundamental, and augmented fourths are a characteristic interval in his music, although he has never used extended just intonation or any other kind of microtones.

The wit and allusion that Johnston used in Twelve Partials show that his hearing and tonal memory are sensitive and accurate. He hears what he writes. Pitches are not manipulated in a system just for the system's sake, but chosen for their expressive and musical significance. Writing in extended just intonation has meant learning to hear each lattice and knowing the sound of the individual partials and their related intervals.

As Johnston's reputation has grown, he continues to receive commissions and often writes shorter pieces that are not terribly difficult but yet use partials up to at least the thirteen limit. Frequently these compositions are neoclassic, such as Trio for violin, clarinet, and cello (1981) composed for the Omega Ensemble. The piece is in two movements both using rondo form. Johnston's intention was to write something that sounded like Mozart's music but in just intonation.

Another neoclassic piece is Toccata for cello (1984) which is also a rondo but only uses up to the eleventh partial. It was commissioned by Laurien Laufman at the University of Illinois, and she premièred it on January 30, 1985, at the Krannert Center for the Performing Arts.

The most recent large work is his String Quartet Number 7 (1984) commissioned by the Concord Quartet. It has not been performed as of this writing, but the quartet is a further step in Johnston's quest for organic unity. Its three movements--"Prelude," "Palindromes," and "Variations"--have a chromatic scale generated by a 2,3,5,7,11,13 system. "Prelude" is a short, freely composed movement that Johnston described as "Scurrying up to the 13th and 16th partials."[12] "Palindromes" features serialism similar to String Quartet Number 6, but this time each soloist performs the forty-eight row forms. "Variations" uses the above scale having the duration of each measure represent the number of cents between adjacent scale intervals while also participating in a rising pitch patterning that moves one note per measure. Since Johnston had discovered that acceptable ratio scales had a limited number of adjacent intervals, then, with this movement, he began to realize that his systematic presentation of pitch and duration also generates a limited number of harmonic, melodic, and rhythmic patterns so that the movement is a variation upon itself. Thus, a composition's tuning system can also be allowed to create the piece's form.

Johnston's output spans many different styles and performance mediums. His music has evolved from his beginning work with jazz bands to theater and dance collaborations. Then his first use of just intonation was limited to the second, third, and fifth partials, and gradually he has developed a theory encompassing the higher ratios of extended just intonation that can also be represented temporally.

Johnston knows his craft; he is equally comfortable writing a mass or a complicated string quartet. Yet, each composition is a quest for the truth about pitch. His artistic, spiritual, and expressive stance continues to deepen with each new composition. As a young man at the age of seventeen he realized that his musical path would not be easy, and this has proven to be true. Yet the integrity he has established between pitch and rhythm and the broad emotional palette made possible by extended just intonation have made Johnston one of America's outstanding composers. He has shown that he has the acoustical understanding of Harry Partch, the compositional courage of John Cage, and the spiritualism of Charles Ives. Johnston's resolve to build a bridge between chaos and order has given listeners and performers a broad spectrum of music that combines both old and new. For many it is an entrance into a beautiful new world of sound.

Notes

1. Jeff Markarian, a graduate student at the University of Illinois who is studying just intonation, suggested this image.

2. Shields has not performed the work due to tendonitis in his wrists, but John Rinehart premiered it in March 1980 at the Krannert Center for the Performing Arts at the University of Illinois.

3. The original matrix has some incorrect index numberings.

3A. The concert was sponsored by the American Conservatory of Music and arranged by Peter Gena. Kevin Johnson wrote an article, "Music Notes: Ben Johnston's pitch for perfection" for the Reader: Chicago's Free Weekly December 16, 1983 that appeared the same day as the concert and acquainted readers with some of Johnston's music.

4. The second violinist of the New World String Quartet who performed String Quartet Number 6 was William Patterson, but he is no longer with the quartet.

5. Ross Harbaugh made this analogy in an interview with the author on September 14, 1984.

6. Robert Dan made this statement during the above interview.

7. Johnston had shown them how to hear intervals using the seventh and eleventh partials, but during their own practice sessions they also added cent values for each pitch. This helped them to learn their parts, and eventually they memorized the piece.

8. From stagebill, April 1983, p. 18, the published program notes for events at Lincoln Center.

9. Siobhan Drummond Granner pointed out this aspect of Hopkins' work in her unpublished paper "The Sonnets of Desolation: Ben Johnston and Gerard Manley Hopkins."

10. From stagebill, April 1983, p. 20.

11. There is an error in the matrix in the manuscript version of the score. Johnston has corrected the matrix for the published version.

12. This information is from a conversation with the author on January 17, 1985.

• CHRONOLOGY •

1926   Ben Johnston born in Macon, Georgia, March 15.
1932   Studies piano with Mrs. A. E. Reese.
1939   Attends Thomas Jefferson High School in Richmond, Virginia.
1942   Editor-in-chief of The Jeffersonian. Performance of his Theme and
        Variations for piano and violin at the Musicians Club of Richmond.
1943   Wins first and second prizes in contest sponsored by Scholastic Maga-
        zine for "Homeward" and Fugue in D Minor. Awarded scholarship
        to attend William and Mary College.
1944   William and Mary College sponsors concert of his compositions. Enlists
        in the United States Navy.
1946   Wins second prize in the National Federation of Music Clubs' Composi-
        tion Contest for Young Composers. Discharged from the Navy and
        performs in dance bands.
1947   Returns to William and Mary. Meets Wilford Leach and wins Broadcast
        Music Incorporated prize for student musical.
1949   Completes bachelor's degree in fine arts at William and Mary. Becomes
        member of Phi Beta Kappa and Omicron Delta.
1950   Attends Cincinnati Conservatory of Music and awarded assistantship in
        theory. Meets Ward Swingle. Performances of "somewhere i have
        never traveled" and "Le Gout de Néant." Marries Betty Ruth Hall.
        Works with Harry Partch at Gualala, California. Enrolls in the
        University of California at Berkeley.
1951   Studies with Darius Milhaud at Mills College in Oakland, California.
        Performances of "A Nocturnall Upon Saint Lucie's Day Being the
        Shortest Day," and Concerto for Brass at Mills College. Receives
        appointment at the University of Illinois at Urbana-Champaign,
        Illinois. Wooden Bird is performed at Charlottesville, Virginia.
1952   Completes thesis piece Concerto for Percussion and receives Master of
        Fine Arts degree in absentia from Mills. Has several compositions
        performed at the Festival of Contemporary Arts and meets John Cage.
        Accompanist and composer for the dance department at the U. of I.
1954   Collaborates with Leach for The Zodiac of Memphis Street.
1955   Night performed at the Festival of Contemporary Arts. Collaborates
        with Sybil Shearer on St. Joan. Composes Three Chinese Lyrics.
1956   Collaborates with Leach for Gertrude, or Would She be Pleased to
        Receive It? Attends American Dance Festival held at Hartford,
        Connecticut.
1957   Arranges for Partch's The Bewitched to be performed at the Festival
        of Contemporary Arts.

1958   Awarded University of Illinois Research Board Summer Fellowship. Awarded summer residency at the Yaddo Art Colony.

1959   Cunningham Dance Troupe performs Gambit. Awarded Guggenheim Fellowship in musical composition to study at Princeton and with Cage. Begins tuning and compositional plans for Sonata for Microtonal Piano/Grindlemusic.

1960   Participates in the Second Princeton Seminar in Advanced Musical studies. Writes Five Fragments, first piece using just intonation.

1962-65   Chairman of the Festival of Contemporary Arts.

1962   Awarded summer residency at the Yaddo Art Colony. Completes Sonata for Microtonal Piano/Grindlemusic.

1964   Article "Scalar Order as a Compositional Resource" is published in Perspectives of New Music. Presents lecture "Proportionality and Expanded Pitch Resources" at Illinois Wesleyan University. Receives commission from the La Salle String Quartet for String Quartet Number 2 but premièred by the Composers Quartet.

1965   Receives a University of Illinois Research Board Grant for a summer workshop in analysis and performance of contemporary music. Commissioned by the St. Louis Symphony for Quintet for Groups.

1966   Participates in a European tour with the Contemporary Chamber Ensemble. Receives a commission to write a piece for the Swingle Singers. Article "Proportionality and Expanded Pitch Relations" published by Perspectives of New Music. Becomes associate member of the University of Illinois Center for Advanced Study and founding member of the American Society of University Composers.

1967   Receives a Sabbatical Leave Grant from the National Foundation on the Arts and the Humanities. Participates in an American Society of University Composers conference about microtonality. Begins using the seventh partial as generating material. Première of Quintet for Groups by the St. Louis Symphony.

1968   Participates in the panel discussion "The Sound of Things to Come: The Attitude of Youth: Composer, Performer, and the Changing Audience" at the International Music Council, New York City.

1969   Receives a Research Grant from the Graduate College Research Board of the University of Illinois to study computer applications of just intonation. Delivers the keynote address: "Art and Survival," at the "Renaissance '69?" series at the Museum of Contemporary Art, Chicago, Illinois.

1970   Collaborates with Wilford Leach for Carmilla which plays in New York City's Off-Broadway.

1971   Presented "Tonality Regained" at the American Society of University Composers Conference.

1973   Guest Composer at State University of New York, Buffalo, New York. Receives a grant from the University of Illinois Research Board to purchase the Scalatron.

1974   Première of String Quartet Number 4. Composer in Residence at the American University, Washington, D.C. and The University of Wisconsin in Milwaukee.

1975   Receives a research grant from the graduate College Research Board of the University of Illinois for the collection of biographical data and materials about Harry Partch and a research grant from the Center for Music Experiment at the University of California at San Diego.

1976   Guest Composer at the Naumburg 50th Anniversary Concert held in Alice Tully Hall, Lincoln Center, New York. Première of String Quartet Number 3.

1977   Guest Composer-Lecturer at Yale University, New Haven, Connecticut and Dartmouth University, Hanover, New Hampshire. Participates in International Conference on Microtonal Music at Webster College, St. Louis, Missouri. Lectures about Harry Partch in Yugoslavia, West Germany, Scotland, and England.

1978   Presents "Rational Structure in Music" at the National Meeting of the American Society of University Composers at the University of Illinois. Guest Composer and winner at the ISCM American Music Festival in New York City and Guest Composer at the Warsaw Autumn Festival, Warsaw, Poland. Begins using extended just intonation up to the 32nd partial.

1979   Diversion for eleven instruments premières in New York City by the New York Contemporary Repertory Ensemble.

1980   Receives a Naumburg Foundation Commission for String Quartet Number 6 for the New World Quartet and a Fromm Foundation Commission for Sonnets of Desolation for the Swingle Singers. Becomes member of the Executive Board of the American Music Center.

1981   Lectures in Europe.

1982   Sonnets of Desolation premières by The New Swingle Singers.

1983   The New World String Quartet premières String Quartet Number 6 and the Tremont Quartet premières String Quartet Number 5. Receives grant from the Illinois State Arts Council for a recording of his music. Retires as Professor Emeritus from the University of Illinois.

1984   Receives commission from the Concord Quartet for String Quartet Number 7. Becomes member of the Review Board for the Fromm Foundation. Guest Professor at Northwestern University at Chicago, Illinois.

• CATALOG OF COMPOSITIONS •

Compositions for piano

1949 Etude. Piano solo. Manuscript.

1953 Satires. Piano solo. Manuscript (lost).

Celebration. Piano solo. Published by Orchesis Publications, Inc., 1960.

Portrait. Piano solo. Manuscript (lost).

1954 Variations. Piano solo. Manuscript (lost).

1958 St. Joan. Arrangement as piano solo. Manuscript. Commissioned by Sybil Shearer.
Premièred February 27, 1958 by Claire Richards.

1959 Aubade. Piano solo. Manuscript (lost).

1962 Sonata for Microtonal Piano/Grindlemusic. Piano solo. Published by Smith Publications, 1976. Commissioned by Claire Richards.
Premièred 1965 by Claire Richards at Round House Concert, Urbana, Illinois.

1978 Suite for Microtonal Piano. Piano solo. (Written for Roger Shields.) Published by Smith Publications, 1979.
Premièred March 1980 by John Rinehart at the University of Illinois.

Vocal compositions

1949 "somewhere i have never traveled." Text by e. e. cummings. Tenor and piano. Manuscript.
Premièred May 7, 1950 at the Cincinnati Conservatory of Music.

1950 "Le Gout de Néant." Text by Charles Baudelaire. Baritone and piano. Manuscript.
Premièred May 7, 1950 at the Cincinnati Conservatory of Music.

1951 "A Nocturnall upon St. Lucie's Day." Text by John Donne. Baritone and piano. Manuscript.
Premièred Spring 1951 at Mills College, Oakland, California.

1955 Three Chinese Lyrics. Text by Li Po with translation by Ezra Pound. Soprano and two violins. Manuscript.
Premièred November 28, 1959 by Marianne Weltmann at Donnell Library, New York City.
Reviewed by Bain Murray, "Composers Exchange," Musical America, January 1962, p. 133.

<u>Night</u>. Text by Robinson Jeffers. Baritone, women's chorus, and chamber ensemble. Manuscript.

Premièred March 14, 1955, conducted by Bernard Goodman, Bruce Foote, soloist at the Festival of Contemporary Arts, University of Illinois.

1960   <u>Five Fragments</u>. Text by Henry Thoreau. Alto, oboe, cello, and bassoon. Published by Smith Publications, 1975.

1962   <u>A Sea Dirge</u>. Text by William Shakespeare. Mezzo-soprano, flute, violin, and oboe. Published by Smith Publications, 1974.

Premièred December 14, 1963 by Helen Hamm (soprano) at the Round House Concert, Urbana, Illinois.

1964   <u>Of Vanity</u>. Text by Ecclesiastes. Chorus. Manuscript (incomplete sketch).

1966   <u>Prayer</u>. Text, "Now I lay me down to sleep." Boys choir (SSA). (Requested by Robert Smith.) Published by Smith Publications, 1975.

1967   "Ci-Gît Satie." Text of scat syllables. Chorus (SSAATTBB), double bass, drums. Commissioned by Ward Swingle for the Swingle Singers. Forthcoming from Smith Publications.

Premièred July 23, 1967 by Kenneth Gaburo and the New Music Ensemble.

1971   <u>Rose</u>. Text by Sibyl Johnston. Chorus (SATB). Published by Smith Publications, 1976.

Premièred August 8, 1972 by the University of Illinois Summer Contemporary Chorus conducted by Neely Bruce.

1972   <u>Mass</u>. Liturgical text. Chorus (SATB), eight trombones, and percussion. Commissioned by Harold Decker. Published by Mark Foster Music Company, 1974.

Premièred May 13, 1973 by the University of Illinois Concert Choir conducted by Harold Decker.

Reviewed by Mark Behm, "ASUC: Region V Conference," <u>Perspectives of New Music</u>, 20, 1982-1983, 607.

1973   "I'm Goin' Away." Text is an Appalachian folk song. Chorus (SATB). Published by Smith Publications, 1977.

Premièred November 1981 by the Contemporary Choir conducted by Emily Brink.

1975   "Songs of Innocence." Text by William Blake. Soprano and ensemble. Forthcoming from Smith Publications.

Premièred June 29, 1979 by Barbara Dalheim.

1976   <u>Visions and Spels</u> (also known as <u>Vigil</u>). Texts from American Indian poetry. Improvisational vocal ensemble. Published by Smith Publications, 1977.

Premièred 1976 by the New Verbal Workshop.

1977   "Since Adam." Chorus (STB/SAB). Manuscript (lost).

"Twelve Psalms." Biblical texts. Chorus (SAB and STB). Manuscript (incomplete).

1978   <u>Two Sonnets of Shakespeare</u>. Texts by William Shakespeare. Bass-baritone/counter tenor. Published by Smith Publications, 1979.

Premièred July 21, 1978 by Gordon Brock and the Contemporary Chamber Players.

1980   Sonnets of Desolation. Texts by Gerard Manley Hopkins. Chorus (SSAATTBB). Commissioned by Ward Swingle for The New Swingle Singers with aid from the Fromm Foundation. Forthcoming from Lingua Press.

Premièred November 14, 1982 by Ward Swingle and The New Swingle Singers at the Krannert Center, University of Illinois.

String Quartets

1959   Nine Variations. Published by Smith Publications, 1985.

Premièred November 28, 1959 by the Walden String Quartet at the Donnell Library, New York City.

1964   String Quartet Number 2. Commissioned by the La Salle Quartet. Published by Smith Publications, 1985.

Premièred July 14, 1966 by the Composers Quartet at the University of Illinois.

Reviewed by Jennifer Standage, "New York," Musical Times, April 1968, p. 357.

1966   String Quartet Number 3 (revised in 1973). Published by Smith Publications, 1985.

Premièred March 15, 1976 by the Concord String Quartet at Alice Tully Hall, New York City.

Reviewed by Mark Blechner, "Concord String Quartet: 3 Premières," High Fidelity/Musical America, July 1976, MA 30-31; and John Rockwell, The New York Times, March 17, 1976.

1973   String Quartet Number 4. Commissioned by the Fine Arts Quartet. Published by Smith Publications, 1985.

Premièred by the Fine Arts Quartet, April 21, 1974 at Carnegie Recital Hall.

Reviewed by Andrew De Rhen, "Fine Arts Quartet: Johnston Première," High Fidelity/Musical America, August 1974, MA 31-32; John Rockwell, The New York Times, March 17, 1976; Mark Blechner, "Concord String Quartet: 3 Premières," High Fidelity/Musical America, July 1976, MA 30-31; and Steven Swartz, "Report from Buffalo--the North American New Music Festival 1983," Perspectives of New Music, vol. 21, 393.

1979   String Quartet Number 5. Commissioned by the Concord Quartet. Published by Smith Publications, 1985.

Premièred by the Tremont Quartet, December 16, 1983, Fine Arts Club, Chicago, Illinois.

Reviewed by A. Porter, "Musical Events," New Yorker, vol. 60, 137, May 14, 1984.

1980   String Quartet Number 6. Commissioned by the Naumburg Foundation for the New World Quartet. Published by Smith Publications, 1985.

Premièred April 1983 by the New World Quartet in Lincoln Center, New York City.

Reviewed by Kyle Gann, "Records," Chicago Reader, August 10, 1984, p. 18.

1984   String Quartet Number 7. Commissioned by the Concord Quartet. Forthcoming from Smith Publications.

Compositions for small chamber ensembles

1958   Septet. Woodwind quintet, cello, and bass. Manuscript.

Premièred February 23, 1972 by the Contemporary Chamber Players at the University of Illinois.

Ludes for Twelve Instruments. Chamber ensemble version of Gambit.

Premièred July 25, 1965 by the Summer Workshop at the University of Illinois.

1961   Sonata for Two. Violin and cello. Published by Smith Publications, 1984.

1963   Duo for Flute and String Bass. Written for Bertram and Nancy Turetzky. Published by Josef Marx, 1976.

Premièred December 21, 1965 by Bertram and Nancy Turetzky.

1966   Lament. Flute, trumpet, trombone, viola, cello, and double bass. Manuscript (transcription of the third movement of String Quartet Number 2).

1967   One Man (Revised 1972). Trombone and percussion. Written for Stuart Dempster. Published by MEDIA Press, 1972.

Premièred May 1, 1971 by Stuart Dempster at the University of Illinois.

Reviewed by H. J. Buss, "Trombone Theatre Pieces," Journal of the International Trombone Association, 1978, p. 7.

1969   Two Oboes and Two Tablas and Two Banyas. Manuscript.

1975   In Memory. Strings, eight percussionists, tape, and slides. Written in memory of Margaret Erlanger and Harry Partch. Manuscript.

Premièred October 5, 1975 at the dedication of the Erlanger House, Urbana, Illinois.

1978   Duo. Two violins. Written for Bouw Lemkes and Jeanne Vos. Published by Smith Publications, 1985.

Premièred November 1979 by Lawrence Shapiro and Paul Primus at the Chicago Public Library.

1979   Diversion. Eleven instruments. Forthcoming from Smith Publications.

Premièred 1981 by the New York Contemporary Repertory Ensemble conducted by Leo Kraft, New York City.

1980   Twelve Partials. Flute and microtonal piano. Forthcoming from Smith Publications.

Premièred 1981 by John Fonville and David Liptak at the University of Illinois.

1981   Trio. Violin, clarinet, and cello. Commissioned by Richard Rood for the Omega Ensemble. Manuscript.

Premièred February 1983 by the Omega Ensemble.

1984   Toccata. Solo cello. Commissioned by Laurien Laufman. Manuscript.
Premièred January 27, 1985 by Laurien Laufman at the Krannert Center of the University of Illinois.

Music for Theater and Dance

1951   The Wooden Bird. Text by Wilford Leach. Incidental music written in collaboration with Harry Partch. Manuscript.
Premièred January 11, 1951 at the University of Virginia.
Fire. Play by Arthur Gregor. Manuscript.
Premièred April 2, 1952 at the Festival of Contemporary Arts at the University of Illinois.

1954   The Zodiac of Memphis Street (Trapdoors of the Moon). Revised 1958. Text by Wilford Leach. Incidental music. Manuscript.
Ring Round the Moon. Play by Jean Anouilh. Incidental music for "Mexican Tango." Manuscript.
Premièred April 30, 1954.

1955   St. Joan. Ballet for Sybil Shearer. Piano score. Manuscript.
Ballet never performed.

1956   Gertrude, or Would She Be Pleased to Receive It? Play by Wilford Leach. Music for the dance-opera. Manuscript.
Premièred 1956 at the University of Illinois.
Of Burden, Of Mercy. Music for piano and two dancers. Written for Margret Dietz. Manuscript.
Premièred July 1956 at the American Dance Festival, Hartford, Connecticut.

1959   Gambit. Music for dancers and orchestra. Choreography by Merce Cunningham. Commissioned by the Cunningham Dance Company. Manuscript.
Premièred March 14, 1959 by the Merce Cunningham Dance Company at the Festival of Contemporary Arts.

1961   The Taming of the Shrew. Incidental music for the University of Illinois production of Shakespeare drama.
Premièred November 1961 by the University of Illinois Theater.

1970   Carmilla. Music for chamber opera. Text by Sheridan Le Fanu. Production by Wilford Leach and La Mama. Manuscript.
Reviewed by J. Kasow, "Holland Festival," Opera, Autumn 1972, pp. 105-108.

Miscellaneous compositions

1951   Concerto for Brass. Brass ensemble and tympani. Manuscript.
Premièred as four-hand piano version February 1951 at Mills College, Oakland, California and performed March 25, 1964 by Robert Gray and the University of Illinois Brass Ensemble.

1952   Concerto for Percussion. Manuscript.
            Premièred March 5, 1953 by Paul Price and the University of Illinois
                Percussion Ensemble.

1960   Ivesberg Revisited. Music for jazz band. Manuscript.
            Premièred March 10, 1963 by John Garvey and the University of
                Illinois Jazz Band.

            Newcastle Troppo. Music for jazz band. Manuscript.
            Premièred March 10, 1963 by John Garvey and the University of Illinois
                Jazz Band.

            Passacaglia and Epilogue from St. Joan. Orchestra piece. Manuscript.

1962   Knocking Piece. Two percussionists and a grand piano. Published by
                Smith Publications, 1978.
            Premièred by Jack McKenzie and Thomas Siwe December 14, 1963 at the
                Round House Concert, Urbana, Illinois.
            Reviewed by W. E. von Lewinski, "Where Do We Go From Here? A
                European View," The Musical Quarterly, vol. 55, 1969, 200-201.

1966   Quintet for Groups. Orchestra. Commissioned by the St. Louis Sym-
                phony. Manuscript.
            Premièred March 24, 1967 at the Kiel Auditorium in St. Louis, Missouri.

1968   Museum Piece. Sound track for a Smithsonian Institution orientation
                film done in collaboration with Jaap Spek.
            Auto Mobile. Sound environment on tape for an automobile exhibit at
                the Smithsonian Institution done in collaboration with Jaap Spek.

1969   Four Do-It-Yourself Pieces. Recipes for indeterminate pieces. Pub-
                lished by Media Press, 1970.
            Première of CASTA* (one of the Four Do-It-Yourself Pieces) on May 9,
                1969 by Norma Marder (soprano) and George Ritscher (electronics)
                commemorating the opening of the Krannert Center for the Perform-
                ing Arts.
            Knocking Piece Collage. Tape.
            Premièred February 1970 at an Electronic Music Concert at the Univer-
                sity of Illinois.

1978   Strata. Electronic tape for the Studio Eksperymentalne Radio Polskie
                done in collaboration with Bohdan Mazurek.

CARMILLA. Original cast recording of the Off-Broadway Musical performed by the ETC Company of La Mama/New York. Directed by Wilford Leach and John Braswell. Musical direction by Zizi Mueller and orchestrations by ETC Company. Vanguard Records, VSD79322.

CASTA BERTRAM. The Contemporary Contrabass: New American Music by John Cage, Pauline Oliveros, Ben Johnston. Performances by Bertram Turetzky, string bass, Nancy Turetzky, flute, and Ronald George, percussion. Nonesuch H-71237.

CI-GÎT SATIE. Performed by the New Music Choral Ensemble. Ars Nova Ars Antigua records, An-1005.

DIRGE, for percussion and piano. University of Illinois Percussion Ensemble. Conducted by Jack McKenzie. University of Illinois School of Music Custom Recording Series #6.

DUO, for flute and string bass. Performed by Nancy Turetzky, flute, and Bertram Turetzky, string bass. Advance Recordings, FGR-1.

DUO, for flute and string bass. American Contemporary Music from the University of Illinois. Performed by John Fonville, flute, and Thomas Fredrickson, string bass. Composers Recordings Inc., CRI 405.

SONATA FOR MICROTONAL PIANO. Sound Forms for Piano. Performed by Robert Miller, piano. New World Records NW203.

SONNETS OF DESOLATION, for SS AA TT BB choir. Ben Johnston. Performed by The New Swingle Singers. Composers Recordings Inc., SD 515.

STRING QUARTET NO. 2. Performed by the Composers Quartet. Nonesuch H-71224.

STRING QUARTET NO. 4. Performed by the Fine Arts Quartet. Gasparo - 205.

STRING QUARTET NO. 6. Naumburg Prize Winners Perform Naumburg Commissions. Performed by the New World String Quartet (Curtis J. Macomber,

William Patterson, Robert Dan, and Ross T. Harbaugh). Composers Recordings Inc., CRI SD 497.

VISIONS AND SPELS. Ben Johnston. Performed by The New Verbal Workshop directed by Herbert Marder. Composers Recordings Inc., CRI SD 515.

• BIBLIOGRAPHY •

Material by Ben Johnston

"Art and Survival." The Composer, Fall-Winter 1971, pp. 9-16.

"Beyond Harry Partch." Perspectives of New Music, xxii, 223-232.

"Communications." Perspectives of New Music, Fall-Winter 1970, pp. 155-156.

"Communications." Perspectives of New Music, Spring-Summer 1972, pp. 175-177.

"Contribution to the IMC Panel." The Composer, June 1970, pp. 6-8.

"The Corporealism of Harry Partch." Perspectives of New Music, xiii/2 (1975), 85-97.

"The Genesis of Knocking Piece." Percussive Notes, Research Edition, March 1983, pp. 25-31.

"Harry Partch." Dictionary of Contemporary Music, edited by John Vinton. New York: Dutton, 1974.

"How to Cook an Albatross." Source IV, 1, 1970, 63-65. Also in Arts in Society, VII (1970), 34-38.

"Letter from Urbana." Perspectives of New Music, II, 1 (1963), 137-141.

"Microtonality." Dictionary of Contemporary Music, edited by John Vinton. New York: Dutton, 1974.

"New Music Festival at U. of Illinois: Bigger but Not Better." High Fidelity/ Musical America, August 1971, MA28-29.

"On Context." American Society of University Composers Proceedings, III (1968), 32-36.

"Phase 1a." This article was written with Ed Kobrin. Source, VII (Summer 1970), 27-42.

"Proportionality and Expanded Pitch Relations." Perspectives of New Music, V, 1 (1966), 112-120.

"Rational Structure in Music." American Society of University Composers Proceedings, I/II, (1976-1977), 102-118.

"Scalar Order as a Compositional Resource." Perspectives of New Music, Spring-Summer 1964, pp. 56-76.

"Three Attacks on a Problem." American Society of University Composers Proceedings, 1967, pp. 89-98.

"Tonality Regained." American Society of University Composers Proceedings, 1973, pp. 113-119.

Material about Ben Johnston

Cage, John. Notations. West Glover, VT: Something Else Press, 1969.

Childs, Barney. "Quintet for Groups," Perspectives of New Music, vii/2, 110-121.

Cope, David. New Directions in Music. Fourth edition. Dubuque, IA: Brown, 1964, pp. 76-77, 83, 85, 103, 135, 138, 237, 338, 352, 366.

_____. New Music Composition. New York: Schirmer Books, 1977, pp. 90, 101, 340, 443.

Dempster, Stuart. The Modern Trombone: A Definition of Its Idioms. Berkeley, CA: University of California Press, 1979, pp. 25-26, 56-57, 78, and 96.

Dictionary of Contemporary Music. Edited by John Vinton. New York: Dutton, 1974.

Duckworth, William and Edward Brown. Theoretical Foundations of Music. Belmont, CA: Wadsworth, 1978, pp. 12, 294-298.

Gagne, Cole and Tracy Caras. Soundpieces: Interviews with American Composers. Metuchen, NJ: Scarecrow Press, 1982, pp. 249-267.

Johnson, Roger. Scores: An Anthology of New Music. New York: Schirmer Books, 1981, pp. 213, 330.

New Grove Dictionary of Music and Musicians. London: Macmillan, 1980.

Reynolds, Roger. Mind Models. New York: Praeger, 1975, pp. 195, 215-220, 215ff.

Shinn, Randall. "Ben Johnston's Fourth String Quartet." Perspectives of New Music, Spring-Summer 1977, pp. 145-173.

Von Gunden, Heidi. The Music of Pauline Oliveros. Metuchen, NJ: Scarecrow Press, 1983, pp. 34, 104.

Yates, Peter. Twentieth Century Music: Its Evolution from the End of the Harmonic Era to the Present Era of Sound. New York: Pantheon, 1968, pp. 229, 323.

Zimmermann, Walter, ed. Desert Plants: Conversations with 23 American Musicians. Vancouver: Aesthetic Research Centre, 1976, pp. 347-371.

• INDEX •